# Empire: The House That John H. Johnson Built

## The Life & Legacy of Pioneering Publishing Magnate

MARGENA A. CHRISTIAN

Chicago

First edition
Published by Doc.M.A.C. Write
Chicago, Illinois



ISBN-13: 978-0-692-13754-3

ISBN-10: 0-692-13754-8

Cover design by Raymond A. Thomas

This book is dedicated to my parents,
Edward Christian Sr.
and
Marion Teresa Christian

While conducting research for my doctorate, my primary advisor told me to locate a picture of Mr. John H. Johnson that brought me to tears but moved me to strength. She told me I was being called to "guard his honor and legacy."

Dr. Margena A. Christian

Courtesy Johnson Publishing Company, LLC. 

# FOREWORD

*JET* was our frame of reference to connect with black America. *EBONY* was the feature part. I looked forward to meeting John Johnson. When I came to Chicago for seminary, my wife and I ran out of money. I was looking for a summer job. North Carolina Governor Terry Sanford gave me a letter for me to meet with Chicago Mayor Richard J. Daley. That was a huge deal to meet with Daley. I didn't realize how big a deal it was with blacks in Chicago. I went to see him. He accepted the recommendation from Sanford and Daley offered me a job to be a toll collector. I was excited. That Sunday I came to church where Johnson's mother, Mrs. Gertrude, was a matron. She said, "Do you need a job for the summer? I can get you one with Johnny." I said to her, "Do you think you have that much pull with him?" She laughed and said, "I bet you."

I went to see him at eighteenth and Michigan. I told him I'd be glad to work in the mailroom and do some physical work where I can stay in shape at the same time. He said, "No. You communicate with the public too well. You should not be working in the mailroom." He gave me a car and told me, "I want you to go to different stops to sell magazines." Most of the newsstands were located on the South Side so I got to really know Chicago. I also found out we could not get *JET* and *EBONY* at the grocery store.

Daley saw me as a toll collector but he saw me as a communicator. He became my counselor and my guide. I wrote my first article for Negro Digest that summer. When Dr. King got to the city, they were looking for someone to work with him. I put them together. Johnson was one of a small group of guys who raised money for Dr. King.

What was amazing to me was how he had to borrow money from Mrs. Gertrude to get the business started because he couldn't get a loan from the bank. Later, I learned advertising. He wanted to get ads with General Motors. Once I started Operation Breadbasket, I started leveraging companies to force them to advertise with black magazines. That's really how black magazines got advertising from the automotive industry for the first time.

When he wanted to build the new building on Michigan Avenue, he couldn't borrow the money even though he was on board of directors and renowned. He used crazy things like the *EBONY* Fashion Fair as his way of promoting where they went from city to city and the sorority and fraternity crowd would come to the shows and also subscribe to *EBONY* and *JET*. He was a genius with creative advertising because he couldn't get it. Eventually, record companies saw a way to make their records hot was to get on the *JET* play list, so they started advertising after automotive companies did this. Then the magazine shifted and kept growing. Then he bought Supreme Life, the company he once worked for. That was his dream.

He also had a sense of black consciousness. His attorney was African American. His accountant was black. He went to conventions. He was around black people and at black events. He was authentic in his quest. Black America knew him. *JET* had positive stories because he said there was enough criticism about our people. For much of the South, *EBONY* became a teaching manual. You could count on *JET* and *EBONY* to keep up with civil rights and they became our manual. I was introduced to the public through *JET* and *EBONY*.

Maybe he couldn't envision going from print to digital but he would have made an adjustment. He would have held on to *JET* and *EBONY* in the ninety-ninth hour. The fact is some magazines are still standing. I was convinced that if anything could stand it would be *EBONY* and *JET*. But this is no reflection upon his legacy. The market changed and hundreds of magazines went out of business like *Life* and *Look*.

Every morning he was in the lobby at 8:00 a.m. He knew every janitor, writer and cook. He had high standards and was tough on them. He did not accept any excuses for the magazine not being out on time. He was a real pursuer of excellence. He had the only downtown building in America built by African-American people and it all started with a $500 loan from his mother.

REVEREND JESSE L. JACKSON, SR.
Chicago
October 6, 2018

# Contents

# ACKNOWLEDGMENTS

I want to thank my Chicago and St. Louis families and friends for offering the encouragement I needed to help me win this race. This includes my sisters, Cheryl and Rachel; my brothers, Dana and Eddie, and my nieces, Amenta and Alauna. Thanks for your unconditional love. I would also like to send a special thank you to those who provided personal and spiritual support: Dr. Scipio A.J. Colin III, Clarence Waldron, Rema Smith, Rev. Marrice Coverson, Dr. Ginnie Love Thompson, the Third Friday Crew (Eric, Randall, Reggie, Darren, Senalda and Nicolle), Sisters Coming Together (Tecela, Nicolle, Natasha, Jennifer, Valerie, Tracie, Deb and Ericka), Dr. Renee Matthews, James Young II, Dr. Adam Banks, the men of Alpha Phi Alpha Fraternity, Inc. (Xi Lambda) and my Johnson Publishing Company (JPC) family. And, where would I be without Norrisa Pearson and Dr. Reginald C. Jackson? They walked this entire journey with me, providing insight, offering guidance, listening ears and willing shoulders to cry on when I needed comfort most. People say that I'm strong, but this is only because I surround myself with those even stronger. To my big brother, Ajuma Muhammad, words can't express how I feel about you. In good times and in bad times, you've been there for me. Thank you for always showing and telling me what it means to be loved. You are family. Thank you to the mighty word slayer and my former City College of Chicago colleague, copy editor Corey Hall. Thanks also to my former JPC colleagues who assisted me in completing the production of this book, including longtime former *EBONY* art director Raymond A. Thomas, the artist who designed this cover, and former *JET* associate editor Katara Washington Patton, my developmental editor. You made crossing the finish line easy. Finally, thank you to my attorney, John S. Kendall, Esq.

# PREFACE

I was first hired as an editor at Johnson Publishing Company (JPC) in August 1995. Unlike my colleagues, who were interviewed by a team of editors before being offered a position, I was interviewed by only John H. Johnson and his daughter, Linda Johnson Rice, who was president and chief operating officer of JPC.

I was flown to Chicago for a day trip from my hometown, St. Louis, where I was a seventh grade language arts teacher at a Catholic elementary school and an entertainment columnist for a newsmagazine called *Take Five*. Two days after my interview, I received the message from LaDoris J. Foster, vice president and director of human resources, that I was hired as an assistant editor for *JET*, a weekly news publication. Mr. Johnson, as every employee called him, knew of my initial interest in writing for *JET* magazine's monthly sister publication *EBONY*. But because of my background with celebrity stories, he told me I would be able to do more of the kinds of articles I enjoyed at *JET*.

He was right because I wrote about everything. I penned cover stories about entertainers and major articles on news, education, relationships, and health. I was also in charge of handling hard copy images for JPC services with the Associated Press. After a few months, I would also freelance for *EBONY* Man, a magazine geared toward black men, writing entertainment and education articles. In 1997, I was promoted to an associate editor for *JET*.

Being an editor was more than a job to me. My fellow employees and I considered ourselves to be part of the JPC family. Under the watchful leadership and careful guidance of its iconic founder, Mr. Johnson, we did more than learn to write stories about African-American people, moments, and events. Mr. Johnson taught us the importance of being gatekeepers by writing history and shaping it through a lens framed from people who looked like its audience. This was rare and we knew it.

He impressed upon us how the story was the star and not us; therefore, we weren't seeking to promote ourselves because we were too busy promoting our race, promoting the magazines of record, *EBONY* and *JET*. Most of us who studied under the tutelage of Mr.

Johnson took our work seriously while making footprints in the sand. Being the editors and writers behind this iconic brand with a man of Mr. Johnson's stature was more than enough for us.

For a great majority of us employed at JPC, there was a sense of pride in being at a company founded by a man of color with magazines, products, and services catering to those who looked like us. Everyone at JPC was generally known on a first-name basis with the exception of Mr. Johnson and his wife, Eunice W. Johnson, called Mrs. Johnson by employees. We knew this was some place special and learned from its fearless founder that the movement came through the message. We learned to say it loud. We were black and proud.

*JET* and *EBONY* editors were gatekeepers of African-American culture. Our longstanding history allowed us to build coveted relationships that our subjects trusted. They came to us with exclusives about their professional and personal lives. During my time at JPC, the editorial team never had to go out of its way to find titillating stories. The stories always made their way to us.

After joining the *JET* editorial team, I was immediately assigned to cover stories for *EBONY* Fashion Fair, the pioneering traveling fashion show. I worked closely with Mrs. Johnson, the company's treasurer-secretary, who was also the founder-director of *EBONY* Fashion Fair. I can recall how the models strutted on and off the runway. They were trained on how to properly walk and pose off the runway on the seventh floor, which housed *JET* editorial, the library, theater room, and Mrs. Johnson's dainty cream-colored office. What made this stand out was that people were conducting interviews, doing research, and writing stories to the beats of loud music while they modeled. There was a lot of traffic on this floor and so much activity happening that it was difficult to concentrate. Still, *JET* editors never missed a beat or a deadline.

Mr. and Mrs. Johnson would sit on the couch and have the models do a private run-thru, changing any aspects of the show they disliked. Once Mrs. Johnson, barely balancing herself in her heels, told a model that she wasn't walking properly so Mrs. Johnson decided to show her how. Let's just say I still chuckle when I recall seeing the classy fashion pioneer, by then well into her seventies, give a modeling lesson on the animal-print carpet. Attractive male and female models, usually eleven ladies and two gentlemen—one dark and one with a lighter complexion—practiced moving up and down the long hallways. One year a beautiful female model's image was immediately removed before an article about the show in *JET* had gone to print. I later learned it was discovered that this model was actually a man. Another interesting story included a commentator telling me about the models' visit to Minneapolis where they met Prince, who invited them to hang out with him, but he barely spoke. She said the 5'2" music icon simply took delight in being in their presence and admiring their beauty all evening.

In 2001, I interviewed Mrs. Johnson and wrote the history of *EBONY* Fashion Fair, which was celebrating its fiftieth anniversary.[1] I dug deep through research and interviews with central figures to learn about the evolution of the world's largest traveling fashion show. I had been assigned to cover the show for *JET* since I started at the company and did so until its last tour in 2008 before being formally suspended in 2009 during its fifty-first annual season, The Runway Report.[2 3] When Mrs. Johnson died in January 2010, I wrote her obituary for *EBONY* that was ultimately sent to media outlets.

By May 2014, I was the only one who personally knew Mr. Johnson or worked under his leadership remaining in the editorial department of either magazine at JPC. I left on May 30, that same year, along with four other employees, when my position as *EBONY*'s senior editor was eliminated. That week was not only historic for me, signaling the end of my tenure as the last editor who worked under the direct tutelage of its founder but it was also the same week that *JET*, founded in 1951, was ended its print publication and became strictly digital.

My time at JPC had ended and I realized I had touched a dream. I recalled looking at a November 1980 issue of *EBONY* in which the company was celebrating thirty-five years of existence. Employees at the Chicago office alone, totaling 1,400, posed in front of the historic JPC headquarters. It was beautiful to see the sea of black faces, all shades and hues. The issue placed the spotlight on employees who had been at the company for twenty years or more. Mr. Johnson called them "family" and acknowledged that family extended beyond the walls at JPC.[4] Family included the loyal readers, many of whom had been subscribers since the beginning who had begun the tradition of passing down the magazines to family members. A legacy of reading, understanding, and learning about self was being inherited.

In that anniversary issue, Mr. Johnson recounted the story of a seventy-three-year-old named Mrs. Florence Taylor of Wilmington, Delaware, who saved her social security money and bought a train ticket to Chicago. She traveled all night on Amtrak just to visit JPC to meet "the beginner," as she referenced Mr. Johnson, and to get a tour of his building. She said she was moved to visit by an "unseen force." She wanted to meet Mr. Johnson in person to thank him for telling positive, inspirational, and educational stories about her people. She had been a subscriber to *EBONY* since before September 1948 when the magazine cost a quarter. Finally, she assured Mr. Johnson that he was doing a wonderful job and that by the company's very existence he had "kept the faith." Mr. Johnson reimbursed Mrs. Taylor for the cost of her train ticket and never forgot her story. When he died, *EBONY* magazine's former longtime Executive Editor Lerone Bennett Jr. recounted the story of "the beginner" at the 2005 funeral.[5]

Through his magazines, Mr. Johnson wanted to reach people of all ages. It didn't matter if a person was sitting in the barbershop or chatting it up with girlfriends in a beauty shop, his mission was to educate, inform, uplift, motivate, and inspire. He wanted to reach people in ways and in places that others did not dare to go by showing the beauty of being black and being able to do anything. He especially wanted to touch those who were poor, ignored, and looked down upon, as he once was as a kid growing up in Arkansas City, Arkansas.

At some point, in 2010, the same year I started graduate school to earn a doctorate in adult education, I decided to find a way to make certain that Johnson would never be forgotten. The best measure to remember a person, I reasoned, is by keeping his legacy alive, so I set out to conduct research on how JPC's founder used his magazines as textbooks to educate readers. JPC was a university of sort in that there were many classrooms (magazines, cosmetic line, TV show, fashion show, radio station, etc.) and modes of teaching people about African-American consumers.

My dissertation was ultimately titled John H. Johnson: A Historical Study on the Re-Education of African Americans in Adult Education Through the Selfethnic Liberatory Nature of Magazines. The same year I started graduate school, I provided *EBONY* with the motto, "It's more than a magazine. It's a movement." This came to me while writing the Legend section article about Mr. Johnson in the November issue, which commemorated the magazine's sixty fifth anniversary.[6] After reading his autobiography, I immediately thought of the slogan that was placed on *EBONY*'s spine.

Many have written stories about *EBONY* and *JET,* but only Mr. Johnson had written about himself in the 1989 memoir, *Succeeding Against the Odds.* Although he was in a high-profile position, he led a rather low-key life peppered with accolades and historic moments.

It is important that the world never forget that this giant of a man once walked this earth. Being able to say that I worked at his company, and alongside him for a decade, was an honor. Mr. Johnson once said it best:

> We do have a family-owned business but we also have the Johnson Publishing Family—a group of some of the best, most loyal people you'll find anywhere. It has been that Family of people and the millions of black readers who have supported all of us, who are responsible for *EBONY*'s survival and growth while so many other magazines failed.[7]

FIGURE 1: Pictured from left to right, the late *EBONY-JET* Art Director Herbert Temple, *EBONY* Executive Editor-author-historian Lerone Bennett Jr. and Photo Editor Basil O. Phillips shown, circa 1990, in Phillips' eighth-floor JPC office. The men were amongst the longest-serving employees. Phillips was the gatekeeper of the company's million-plus historic African-American photographs for more than 50 years.

# PROLOGUE

By the 1970s, most black households had *JET* and *EBONY* on the coffee table thanks to momma and grandma. For that reason, children would pick them up and leaf through pages, gazing at the images; eventually they would grow into readers of the iconic magazines as well. No barbershop or beauty shop was without several copies of *EBONY* or *JET*.

But I can honestly say that for as much as *JET* was considered the "Negro Bible,"[1] it was common knowledge within the *JET* fold and others who worked under Mr. Johnson's leadership that the newsmagazine was never a bonafide money maker. There were a few times when the issues sold out, but that was a rare occurrence. The fifty-two issues, along with the small size of 5 ¾" by 4" coupled with it being a weekly, often was a deficit for the company due to production costs.[2]

*JET* was truly a passion project and a labor of love on Mr. Johnson's part. It was the little engine that could—and did—while *EBONY* was considered to be the cash cow. The monthly was considered the company's engine. But few people could have ever imagined that it was often Fashion Fair Cosmetics that quietly pulled either magazine out of a financial bind, sometimes single-handedly keeping the company afloat, when Mr. Johnson was alive. This simply proved the fact that no matter how tough the economic climate became, women wanted to look good at any expense. Mr. Johnson knew business and he enjoyed making money. He became a legendary publisher because he was a shrewd businessman.

In Mr. Johnson's autobiography, he says in his Fiftieth Anniversary statement, "I believe today, as I believed in the beginning, that it is better to light a candle than to curse the night."[3] That message stayed with me, and I thought about it as I observed the changes at his company after his death. Instead of cursing the dark, I decided to light a candle.

Chronicling Mr. Johnson's legacy became a necessity and further solidified the importance of my research. I am a primary source who viewed and studied Johnson on a daily basis for a decade. Unlike with *EBONY* editorial, Mr. Johnson personally oversaw each of the *JET* daily meetings that included the editorial team.

In this book, I take a look at the groundbreaking journey of Mr. Johnson's life from his 1918 birth year to his death. He was once hailed as the Greatest Minority Entrepreneur in History. Mr. Johnson built a publishing empire, becoming a mighty symbol of black pride and minority ownership. Efforts extended beyond areas other than his publishing but also business endeavors such as the *EBONY* Fashion Fair, Fashion Fair Cosmetics, WJPC radio, the Black Achievement Awards and *EBONY/JET* Showcase. JPC's flagship magazine, *EBONY*, maintained the highest global circulation of any African-American focused publication. Under the leadership of Mr. Johnson, *EBONY* sustained its top position as the most subscribed to black lifestyle magazine in America.

The Arkansas native made history in 1976 when he became the first African American named to the board of Twentieth Century Fox, and in 1982 he became the first African American named to Forbes magazine's list of 400 wealthiest Americans.[4] The crowning achievement for Mr. Johnson took place in 1972 when an eleven-story headquarters was built at 820 S. Michigan Avenue, making it the first building owned by an African-American in the prestigious business center known as The Loop and the first major downtown Chicago building designed by an African American.[5]

In 1996, former President Bill Clinton bestowed upon Johnson the Presidential Medal of Freedom, the highest civilian honor of the United States. Since his death, a stretch of Michigan Avenue now has his name, the U.S. Postal Service issued a Forever Stamp in his honor, and a Chicago school has been named after him. In a day and age when many question the viability of the black press, Mr. Johnson's story is one that should never be forgotten.

Growing up a poor kid, "barefooted" and "walking in the Mississippi River mud" in Arkansas City, Mr. Johnson recalled in 1990 how his best Christmas was the one he spent in the dream headquarters he built in downtown Chicago. He said it "was more than a mere building, more than a toy. It was, in fact, the first building constructed in downtown Chicago by a Black American, and it reflected the tears and dreams of a lifetime."[6] Spending his first Christmas in the building in 1971, which was nearly derailed due to construction delays, was a memory he cherished the most and was indicative of Mr. Johnson's life and legacy—the JPC empire. He said:

> We moved on Monday, December 6, 1971 and celebrated Christmas in the tenth-floor assembly area. My mother, who always made a major spiritual statement at these pre-Christmas get-togethers, was at her best on that day, giving a prayer of joy and blessing that brought tears to our eyes. And looking back on that holiday, I remember not so much the building but the burning pride in her eyes and the fact that my whole family—my wife, Eunice, and my daughter, Linda, and my son, John Harold—was there to share the triumph of the dream. Six years later, my mother died. Ten years later, my son died.[7]

I consider myself one of Mr. Johnson's students, because I worked closely with him on the staff of *JET* and I considered him to be an educator. For as complex as he was simple, Mr. Johnson was always at work by 8:00 a.m. and usually enjoying a cup of coffee or hot tea with Lerone Bennett, Jr. at one of the tables in the tenth floor cafeteria. He read "about twenty newspapers a day, taking them home in shopping bags" where he pulled out clips and story ideas that might foster an article or help the publications get an ad.[8]

Each day he guided our daily editorial meetings, I learned something new. I observed his eye for news and how it affected African Americans. I watched how he studied magazine sales as a businessman to determine what our readers liked and disliked. I listened to the many stories he shared about his encounters with the likes of everyone from Ray Charles to Nat King Cole, with whom he attended high school. Countless times I heard him recount his decision to run the Emmett Till story with the battered images of the fourteen-year-old Chicago boy's face after being murdered in Mississippi. He shared how readers went to purchase that issue of *JET*. Almost acting it out, Johnson said, "They would cover their eyes, turn their head, and say, 'Oooh! That's terrible. Give me three issues of that magazine.'" Each time he told that particular story, the number of issues requested would progressively get higher. A man never at a loss for words, Mr. Johnson was a storyteller who enjoyed talking and teaching to whomever was willing to listen.

Just as he recalled the momentous occasion of celebrating Christmas for the first time in JPC in 1971, I, too, remember Mr. Johnson's last Christmas party with his family and extended JPC family in his empire. It was December 23, 2003. In all the years we enjoyed the glorious festivity, for some reason this year I wanted to take a picture with Mr. Johnson. By this time, more visibly frail, he spent a great deal of time sitting than standing and walking. A wheelchair was his main mode of transportation. When asked about taking a photo with me, Mr. Johnson happily and graciously agreed. He struggled to stand but did so anyway.

I did not know then that would be the last Christmas party he'd attend at his headquarters on the tenth floor. I also did not know that I had taken a picture with the entire Johnson family, including Mrs. Johnson and Linda, standing behind us on different sides talking. It's true what they say. A picture is worth a thousand words.

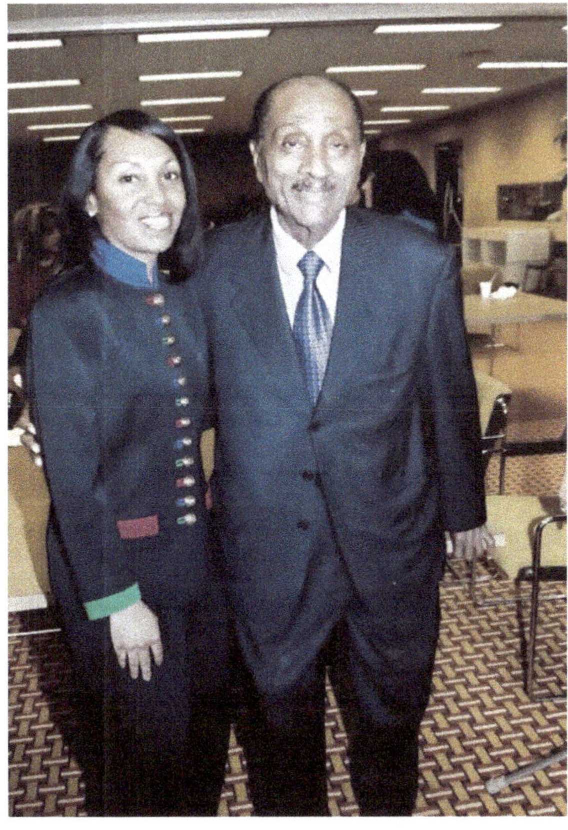

FIGURE 2: The author with John H. Johnson at company Christmas party in 2003 on the tenth floor at Johnson Publishing Company. Margena A. Christian's personal photo. 

# INTRODUCTION: IN REMEMBRANCE

On August 15, 2005, more than 2,000 people packed the sanctuary and overflowed to the front plaza of Rockefeller Memorial Chapel on the campus of the University of Chicago to say goodbye and to celebrate the life and legacy of pioneering magazine publisher John H. Johnson.[1] A who's who showed up to reflect upon how the eighty-seven-year-old media magnate educated, inspired, and uplifted African-American people, and the world at large, through his magazines *EBONY* and *JET* in an effort to illustrate the beauty of his race.

Attendees and guest speakers included the Rev. Jesse L. Jackson Sr., Chicago's Mayor Richard M. Daley, Illinois Gov. Rod Blagojevich, nationally-syndicated radio host Tom Joyner, and Christie Hefner, president and CEO of Playboy Enterprises.[2]

U.S. Sen. Barack Obama, the man Johnson did not live to see make history as the first African American and forty-forth president of the United States, spoke during the memorial. Obama explained how Johnson belonged to a small group of people who managed to touch the world through his work in publishing and as a businessman. Obama lauded Johnson for how he used his magazines to educate his race socioculturally and intellectually about their rich history. "If we are lucky, most of us expect to lead lives that leave an imprint on those who love us," said Obama. "Only a handful of men and women leave an imprint on the conscience of a nation and on a history that they helped shape. John Johnson was one of them."[3] Fortunately, Johnson did live to see Obama make another type of history when he first documented on the pages of *JET*, how, in 1990, the twenty-eight-year-old, second-year law student was named president of the Harvard Law Review, becoming the first black to hold the position in its more than 100 years of publication at Harvard Law School.[4]

At the service, former President Bill Clinton, Johnson's close friend and fellow Arkansan who presented Johnson with the Presidential Medal of Freedom, the nation's highest civilian honor, in 1996, escorted Johnson's widow, Eunice, into the church. Clinton told the packed-audience how his late friend "had a vision of keeping hope alive" by showing his race positive images and "faces of hope."[5]

As I write this book, it's been thirteen years since Johnson, made his transition at Northwestern Memorial Hospital in Chicago.[6] Johnson's million-dollar marble crypt sits next to a lake at the Oak Woods Cemetery in Woodlawn on Chicago's South Side. Inscribed high above its top in gold leaf above the elegant doors is a saying Johnson was noted for: "Failure is a word I don't accept."[7] [8] Oak Woods covers 184 acres and has four small lakes, one of which–Symphony Shores at Symphony Lake–is considered one of the prestigious sections of the cemetery.[9] [10] [11] It is fitting that this is where Johnson rests, because he tread new ground and opened doors that had been previously closed to African Americans in the media, in business, in advertising, and in beauty.

Established in 1854, Oak Woods Cemetery has a history as storied as many of the people resting there. It is a bit ironic how Olympic track great Jesse Owens, Chicago's first black mayor Harold Washington, anti-lynching crusader and suffragist Ida B. Wells, the Father of Gospel Music Thomas Dorsey, the Queen of Gospel Albertina Walker, and famed guitarist-singer Roebuck "Pops" Staples are among the other notables resting at Oak Woods—all of whom Johnson once prominently featured in his magazines and/or covered during a time when mainstream media did little to celebrate achievements of blacks.[12]

Ironically, something else more telling about this cemetery is how after the end of the Civil War, more than 4,000 Confederate prisoners that had died at Camp Douglas were reinterred there and at the Chicago City Cemetery, which closed in 1866 due to constant flooding. They are buried beneath an elliptical plot, called Confederate Mound, which is a 30-foot granite monument with a bronze statue of a Confederate soldier standing on top. It is recorded as the largest in the Western Hemisphere.[13]

During his life, Johnson earned thirty-one honorary doctorate degrees, including one from Harvard University and another from Howard University, where the John H. Johnson School of Communications was named in his honor in 2003 after he contributed $4 million to the school's capital campaign, which sought to raise $250 million during a five-year initiative.[14] [15] Sadly, the dream of having a school that he so admired bear his name was buried with him and would not come to fruition. In October 2016, Howard University named its school of communications after Cathy Hughes, a former Howard University staff member and founder of Radio One, when

Alfred C. Liggins III, president and CEO of Radio One, donated $4 million like Johnson did thirteen years earlier.[16] [17]

This unfortunate turn of events some eleven years after his death did not cast a dark cloud on the countless other accomplishments Johnson earned. Among his esteemed recognitions, and one forever etched in stone, was him being awarded the Presidential Medal of Freedom. Among the ten others honored that year included Civil Rights activist Rosa Parks, Chicago Archbishop Cardinal Joseph Bernadin, and James Brady, the former White House Press Secretary under President Ronald Reagan who was by Reagan's side during an assassination attempt that left Brady permanently disabled.

Upon bestowing the honor to Johnson, Clinton said, "He gave African Americans a voice and a face, in his words, 'a new sense of somebody-ness,' of who they were and what they could do, at a time when they were virtually invisible in mainstream American culture."[18] The citation went on to add how he was considered "one of the world's greatest pioneers in media, founding the landmark magazines *EBONY* and *JET*" and how he "lived a life inspired by his own advice to act with responsible daring never to accept failure."[19] [20]

Lerone Bennett Jr., who attended Morehouse College with the Rev. Dr. Martin Luther King, Jr. and *JET* Associate Publisher and Executive Editor Robert E. Johnson, cited Johnson's impact upon the Civil Rights Movement. Bennett revealed that Johnson was a "major benefactor of the Freedom Movement" and how he "gave more money quietly to Civil Rights leaders than anyone else" he had known. He pointed out how Johnson was one of the largest contributors to former Chicago Mayor Harold Washington's campaign, and how his magazines "ran more major stories on the King Movement than any other major magazine," citing this as a prominent reason why Dr. King wrote a monthly column for *EBONY*, "something no other magazine can say."[21]

Talk show host and author Tavis Smiley expressed how Johnson "was unapologetically Black" and how "his abiding love for Black people was always on display—both literally and figuratively."[22] Johnson was not ashamed of his race or heritage though others looked down upon his people and overlooked their accomplishments in history. Johnson sought to correct this oversight by educating his race and showing them a different side of life. He did this because he was aware that to ignore one's history would result in self-hatred where a person might even reject his racial group membership because of shame.

Long before his death, notables reached out to show Johnson their support. Many were touched by his work and mission by daring to share their unheard stories, which challenged stereotypes that others placed on African Americans. Prolific writer Langston Hughes, one of the early writers for Johnson's first magazine, *Negro Digest,* was moved by Johnson's mission. He took time to pen a short note in "Letters and Pictures" to the Editor for the 1945 December issue of *EBONY*. The poet wrote that he thought "*EBONY* is terrific!" The poet went on to say, "I like it very much and hope it goes places!"[23] And while it was going places, Hughes also made a contribution to the magazine's editorial side by recommending Griffith Jerome Davis, a Morehouse College graduate who was one of Hughes' students there and a former photographer with the *Atlanta Daily World*, Atlanta's oldest African-American newspaper. Davis made history as *EBONY*'s first full-time staff photographer.[24] An early work that he won fame for was the August 1948 cover story with singer Nat King Cole, one of Johnson's former high school classmates at both Wendell Phillips and DuSable, and his new bride, Maria Ellington, detailing a photo diary of their week-long honeymoon in Acapulco, Mexico. Davis died of cancer in Atlanta at the age of seventy. Johnson ran a full-page story, along with an image of Davis and Hughes holding a copy of *EBONY* while reviewing its layout, to honor Davis' 1993 transition.[25] [26]

Throughout the years, three top executives at Johnson Publishing Company were Morehouse College graduates, including *JET* Managing Editor Robert A. DeLeon. A surprise came Johnson's way on May 23, 1972, when Morehouse bestowed upon him the honorary degree of doctor of laws. Before christening Johnson a "Morehouse man," it was stated, "Let it be mentioned here that Johnson Publications are more than mere news magazines. They report news but they also describe the achievements of black folk and show the way out of the racial dilemma in the United States."[27]

On the occasion of *EBONY*'s fortieth anniversary, Pulitzer-Prize winning poet Gwendolyn Brooks shared how the monthly with the glossy cover gave blacks "a new respect for themselves because they saw things that they were doing all over the world."[28] Congressman Louis Stokes, in recognition of the momentous occasion, explained how Johnson used *EBONY* to be "at the forefront of the black man's struggle for political and social equality in this great nation."[29] Stokes' comment acknowledges how Johnson used the magazine to recognize the plight of Africa, African Americans, and people of the African Diaspora.

Harvard University psychologist Dr. Alvin Pouissant, in lauding the fortieth anniversary, praised Johnson for allowing his race to see a positive reflection of self. "Just to see a black magazine with black people in it and talking about things of interest to black people, whether it was Joe Louis or whatever, that in itself was a great uplift."[30]

Legendary figures in politics, music, and sports constantly spoke about the influence of Johnson's work with *EBONY*. Congresswoman Shirley Chisholm explained that being on the cover of *EBONY* "alerted the world that the first black woman had, at long last, been elected to the highest legislature in the land, the United States House of Representatives."[31] This historic event of being a cover subject showed black people that they "can and do make the news," and allowed the white press to "realize the importance" of her election. "It gave the others the cue to talk to me," she said.[32]

Former Brooklyn Dodger Roy Campanella was put on the cover of *EBONY* and remembered that moment and the implications of having others see an African-American baseball player in such a lofty position. "I felt it meant something to the entire black world that I was on *EBONY*'s cover. It meant that we were making progress—not just for ourselves, but for everyone."[33] During the time when Campanella was first on the cover of the June 1956 issue, segregation and racism were still rampant and mainstream media rarely discussed this or showcased African-American accomplishments.

Campanella went even deeper in terms of the magazine's impact, stating how it educated not simply people but baseball owners. He said:

> We were not allowed to stay with the team at hotels in the South…Some of the cities we played in, we had to stay in private homes and arrange our own transportation to the field. We had to go through things our teammates didn't. The regular writers didn't know how we got to the park or what we did off the field. But *EBONY* was there and let everyone know what we were going through—about the racism. That's why the Dodgers built Dodgertown, so we wouldn't have to run into

> segregation and so the team could live together. The Dodgers definitely had their eyes opened by the articles in *EBONY*. And that's how the public learned how tough it was for Jackie and Don and me.[34]

Baseball great Hank Aaron and performer/activist Harry Belafonte believed *EBONY* encouraged African Americans to embrace self-love and their blackness. Aaron, who later became vice president of the Atlanta Braves, said, "*EBONY* gives every black in this country the hope that you can make it if you work hard and do what you have to do. It made me feel like I was 10 feet tall."[35] Belafonte believed the presence of *EBONY*, especially when it came about, was of vital importance to blacks and the nation. He said, "For the first time, it gave blacks the opportunity to see their culture displayed, and whites the opportunity to gain insights to the hopes and aspirations of blacks in this country in a way that was free of stereotypes."[36]

Instilling racial pride and self-esteem came by way of *JET* as well. Johnson was remembered by boxing legend Muhammad Ali because his publications were groundbreaking. "Creativity knew no limit in his more than sixty years in the industry, on which he has left a permanent impression," Ali said. "He will be remembered for his good business skills, determination, and wit. In the field of publishing, John Johnson was 'The Greatest.'"[37]

Comedian/activist Dick Gregory recalled how Johnson "put a face on black folks around the world." Gregory said there were stories but no pictures on African Americans in print media. *JET* and *EBONY*, he said, "told the world there were black lawyers, doctors and medical associations. *JET* and *EBONY* told us about the social part of black as well as the economic side. The one person who was the most influential on African Americans receiving their rights was Mr. John H. Johnson! He made us Human!"[38]

Legendary actor Sidney Poitier, who made history as the first black man to win an Oscar for Best Actor in a Leading Role for his role in 1964's *Lilies of the Field,* reflected upon how Johnson's doing the impossible has allowed those after him to see that anything is possible. The Academy Award-winning actor said:

> In the wake of his most remarkable life, Mr. Johnson has left an astonishing amount of evidence for every African American

> child to see that creative imagination and entrepreneurial instinct can carry them, as well, to the highest reaches of success. Mr. Johnson is the perfect example that one's dreams should always be nurtured by one's passion.[39]

Denzel Washington, the only African-American man to win two Oscars, one for best actor in 2002's *Training Day* and best supporting actor in 1989's *Glory*, discussed the educative nature of Johnson's presence as a publisher and how Johnson was so busy documenting everyone else's life that his own was often ignored.[40] Washington explained:

> Mr. Johnson was a pioneer who was way ahead of his time. He was bold and determined, and just a great leader who I don't think has been recognized the way that he should have. Needless to say, he was a great man who taught so many of us so much just by sharing our world with us.[41]

Washington wasn't the only person to realize that Johnson was not often given the respect or accolades he deserved. The week of his death, ABC News anchor Peter Jennings died of complications from lung cancer a day earlier on August 7, 2005. It seemed hard to believe that Johnson was barely a footnote on news broadcasts or special reports at the time of his death.

The Rev. Jackson wrote a commentary about how he found it disrespectful that TV networks could so easily dismiss Johnson's passing with virtually no coverage. Jackson's commentary reminded the world how African Americans were portrayed in the media. He said:

> Back then we were Aunt Jemima, Amos and Andy, Little Black Sambo. We were the popping eyeballs, the exaggerated lips, the grotesque stretched-out fingers and legs. We were the minstrels, the jesters, the babbling idiots. Those demeaning, degrading images were everywhere except John Johnson's magazines. In those slick images, week after week and year after year, we saw beautiful Black people, who were successful and living well. Week after week and year after year, John Johnson changed our minds. We changed our minds about

> ourselves. We developed pride and aspiration. And we developed resistance, a condition of fierceness that could not be denied, as we saw the pictures and read the stories of Emmett Till, Rosa Parks and so many others. The best chronicle that exists of America's human-rights struggle lies in the files of *EBONY* and the Johnson Publishing Company.[42]

Rev. Jackson wasn't the only person who used the print media to express disapproval about little to no coverage about the death of this pioneering publisher. Pulitzer Prize-winning writer E.R. Shipp said she was "angry though not surprised" that the mainstream media did not take this opportunity to honor the legacy of this media giant. She said:

> He, like Wilbert Tatum of the Amsterdam News here in New York, took issue with those of us who worked for the mainstream (aka "white") press. They challenged us in that tradition of the labor song, 'Which side are you on?' Johnson is largely how many black editors, producers, corporate executives, civil rights activists, politicians, playwrights, novelists, entertainers, athletes—even Bishop Desmond Tutu—got to where we are by giving us that 'sense of somebodiness,' cultivating our dreams and celebrating our successes.[43]

Roland Martin, then executive editor and general manager of *The Chicago Defender*, observed how Peter Jennings' death a day before Johnson's garnered many different accolades and widespread media coverage. He, too, was disappointed that Johnson was not remembered properly. Martin explained:

> I think when you look at the impact of one individual who was able to connect Africa with African Americans, who was able to present a picture of African Americans that to the date was — at that point had not been seen, who founded *EBONY* on the basis of *Life* and *Look*, yet those two magazines are no longer in business, yet he is still the number one magazine in his industry...It is so difficult to capsulize John H. Johnson. And so it is so important that we know his history, we know his story.[44]

In addition to the lack of media coverage, noticeably absent from his funeral were many of the celebrities who were celebrated in Johnson's magazines long before mainstream media gave them attention. Throughout his career he was criticized for doing soft news because his magazines were heavy with entertainment. Actress Diahann Carroll, the first African-American woman to have a primetime TV series on NBC, *Julia*, whose career began as an *EBONY* Fashion Fair model at age fifteen and later married a *JET* managing editor, Robert DeLeon, did not hold her tongue with the disgust she felt because of the lack of celebrity presence at his funeral.[46 47]

Johnson, as she pointed out, helped to build the careers of just about every major black with coverage in *EBONY* and *JET*. So, where were all the stars now, Carroll questioned? She was not alone. "Where was Oprah?" was what many wondered when leaving the funeral. In fact, a press release, issuing a public statement about the man who allowed her to grace the covers of both *EBONY* and *JET* throughout the years, was not circulated either.

Martin was the loudest voice heard in his criticism about Oprah Winfrey. The Houston, Texas, native called the media mogul out for not issuing a statement about the publishing giant or showing up at the funeral. Martin said:

> I do not consider him to be the greatest black publisher in the history of our industry. I consider him to be one of *the* greatest publishers. I think if there was a Mount Rushmore of the media magnates, I believe that John H. Johnson's bust would be alongside Henry Luce, David Sarnoff, Bill Paley, Ted Turner, and the other icons of our industry.[48]

Winfrey, who explained that she was in Hawaii at the time and did not receive word of his passing until days later, was unable to attend the funeral. Winfrey also said that her staff did not contact her about getting a quote because she "normally doesn't make public statements." She made it clear how troubled she was about being criticized as if unconcerned about the media giant's passing, saying, "I am furious at the allegations because it's just not true. It's not true and it's unfair."[49]

*The Chicago Defender* claimed to have tried to get a statement from Winfrey to use in a special edition of a sixty-four-page commemorative edition about Johnson. The column, headlined, "Oprah's silence on John H. Johnson confounds many," said that the *Defender* attempted six times to get a comment or a testimony from the talk show host but got "the run-around every time." Soon after the paper came out, Winfrey called Martin. "As I said in the column, she was very respectful—but she was clearly angry and upset with what I wrote," Martin told *Editor & Publisher*. "I told her, we made every available effort to get a comment from her."[50]

Winfrey explained how she sent flowers and a note to Johnson's widow, Eunice, and daughter, Linda Johnson Rice, offering to even provide a copy of the note and confirmation that the flowers had been received at Johnson Publishing Company headquarters. She also revealed her plans upon returning from summer hiatus in September to air a tribute to Johnson and singer Luther Vandross, who died July 1.[51]

Johnson Rice said this in a press statement issued to *The Defender*, following Martin's concerns:

> Ms. Winfrey said she sent flowers and a note to the chapel and we have no reason to question her statement. She called me yesterday and explained that she had sent the flowers and a note. Unfortunately, they did not come to my family's attention and we were unaware that they were delivered. No one has been able to locate her note or flowers, but I do want to thank her for her supportive expression of sympathy and kind words of tribute to my father. We thank her and look forward to the upcoming tribute to my father's legacy on her show. We also thank *The Chicago Defender* and their executive editor, Roland S. Martin, for all of their truly wonderful commemorative efforts in saluting the life of my father.[52]

A couple of months before Johnson's death, Martin met with him and his daughter, Johnson Rice, but he vividly recalled the first time he met his Alpha Phi Alpha fraternity brother in 1990. Martin was an intern at the *Houston Defender*. "When John H. Johnson came through the office, I mean, it was as if royalty was there, because that's how so many people looked at him and held him with such high regard. Clearly one of the greatest giants we have ever seen in this industry, and his impact goes far beyond the pages of *EBONY* and *JET*."[53]

CHAPTER 1

# MOTHER TO SON

***"She always believed in me. It's very important in life to have someone who believes in you. It helps you to succeed and get through bad times and makes you feel you can overcome difficulty. I always knew my mother was in my corner."***

***John H. Johnson***

Anyone who met John H. Johnson knew how much his mother meant to him. She was the air he breathed and the queen of his heart. Gertrude Johnson Williams believed in the trinity: the Lord, her son and all education. Johnson often casually mentioned his mom during staff editorial meetings, reflecting upon some of the morsels of knowledge she sprinkled into his life's journey. From the serious to the not so serious moments about his life growing up in Arkansas, he seemed to have a story for every occasion. Without fail, when Johnson spoke, everyone listened no matter where he shared a story. One that stood out most was when he spoke about how he came to be—his very existence.

Mrs. Williams, as his mother was called, had a couple of miscarriages before she successfully conceived.[1] When he spoke about the difficulty she encountered trying to conceive and carry a child, one could tell that Johnson knew his birth was in divine order. It was as if he sensed that he was put on this earth for a reason and that his mother's "talk with God" had everything to do with it.

Williams was a God-fearing woman who prayed without ceasing. Saddened by the previous loss of children, she did what she knew best. Williams had a talk with the Lord. She prayed to God and finally conceived in 1917, a time when the Great War, World War I, was taking place and race riots were high due to segregation and white rule in the South. She made a vow and told God that if this child lived, "she was going to devote her life to having a better life...and education was part of that."[2]

He loved and adored his mother simply for being who she was but especially for giving him life and for keeping her promise to God. Johnson witnessed firsthand how his mother's attitude and actions honored her promise—covenant if you will. He witnessed the great lengths she went to in order to make a way out of no way for her son.

The path was never smooth for the woman born Gertrude Jenkins. To understand Johnson's past was to understand what motivated him as a businessman and as an adult. He wanted to make his mother proud and he wanted to take care of her. She entered this world on August 4, 1891, in Lake Village, Arkansas.[3] Her parents were young when she was born after slavery and of the second generation of freedom. At the time of her birth, lynchings for colored people (as blacks were called back then) were daily in the decade of Plessy v. Ferguson and Jim Crow laws. Education was limited for blacks so it should come as no surprise that she only completed the third grade, but she refused to allow her limited schooling to interfere with her offspring's educational advancement. Williams did not depend upon the traditional school system to later educate her son about seminal life lessons and the importance of hard work. She taught him these things herself and did so in earlier years while she was holding down jobs in the fields and in kitchens. Employment as a domestic came later when she relocated to Arkansas City, Arkansas.[4]

On January 19, 1918, in Arkansas City, Arkansas, Gertrude became a mother for the second time and gave the child the birth name of Johnny Johnson. He entered the world in the last year of World War I. A parallel that he often marveled about was how he founded the monthly publication *EBONY* in 1945, the last year of World War II. As he saw it, "critical turning points in history" seemed to shape his life.[5] For it was during World War I, a time when black America and white America were forever altered, that the Great Migration took place with Southern blacks moving to the North.

Growing up in a small, river oak town, with a population of only six hundred people, Johnson's world centered around a sawmill. His home was right by the levee with the Mississippi River within walking distance of his tiny shotgun, three-room wooden house made with a tin roof.[6] It had no inside plumbing, so he used an outhouse, which was common for black people in those days. White people were the exception to the rule and had running water; however, there was one black man who had it all in town.

He was a builder who constructed most of the homes for white people. By standards then, this man was considered wealthy because he had a toilet and the fact that he owned a car left no doubt that he was beyond privileged and lived well. Johnson recalled how as a young boy he and other children would play with this man's daughter, Willie Mae, on Sundays. Simple things were the cause for attraction, with the kids being most fascinated with the family's toilet. He laughed at how he and the other black children would go to flush it, amusing themselves by wondering where the water went.[7]

Johnson bore an uncanny resemblance to his mother, a mocha-colored woman, about 4'11" in height, with bow legs like him, who was always careful about her appearance. "I never saw my mother with gray hair," Johnson once chuckled during a meeting in the ninth floor conference room on the executive level at the headquarters building. "She either had it colored or wore a wig." As he got older and even as his health rapidly failed, he did exactly as his mom did and was never seen with gray hair. The little remaining hair he had on his head in later years were always colored, evidence left behind as his balding edges exposed the dye on his scalp, giving away his secret. He didn't care. As long as his hair was black, the rest was minor.

When he discussed his mom, which he did often, it seemed as if he were an only child. In actuality, he had a half-sister. Few knew that before his mother married his father, Leroy, a sawmill worker, she was briefly married to someone else and had a daughter named Beulah Lewis, fourteen years Johnson's senior.[8] He never got to know his sister well because most of the time while he was growing up, she was away in a neighboring town serving as an educator. In those days if a person finished high school, teaching school was an option. Johnson had a profound respect for teachers. One reason might have been that his sister was one. Another reason is that in his youth, he witnessed how the most respected blacks in Arkansas seemed to have been ministers and teachers.

Johnson was eight years old when his dad died in 1924 during a sawmill accident. Not remembering much about him except that he had dark skin, a well-groomed mustache and stood about 5'11", Johnson observed that his biological father traveled often with his work having him follow levee camps up and down the Mississippi.[9]

Growing up in a two-parent household, for the most part, he did understand that it was his mother who was always the dominant force in the house even after she later married a man named James Williams, who worked as a grocery deliveryman at a bakery, following the untimely death of Leroy.[10]

Unlike most women today who remarry and let the stepdad discipline a child, Williams was the one who handled her son and let it be known. If there was a problem between Johnson and his step dad, they always communicated those thoughts through her. Discussions were an important way to avoid any confusion even if it meant having a third party translate. James Williams, who died in 1961, later served as superintendent of Johnson Publishing Company, which his stepson founded in 1942 with the founding of *Negro Digest* magazine.[11]

Johnson's defining years were shaped by his mother's resilience and her God-fearing nature. And, as did all African Americans during this time, the mother and son endured discrimination and poverty with regularity in the segregated South. She powered through and raised her younger child and only son so that his desire was fueled to transcend the obstacles and limitations placed on him solely as a result of the color of his skin. Perseverance was mirrored throughout Johnson's early life by his mother's strong belief in God, which helped him to understand that all things are possible and he could succeed even as the odds appeared stacked against him. Johnson once said in a 1985 interview that his mother taught him in order to earn success, one must prepare by working hard, having commitment, and having faith. "You have to believe that things are possible. If there is a secret, the secret is in all those things," he explained.[12]

Johnson's formative years were also shaped by self-determination, because he was compelled to make something of himself, for he did not want to disappoint his mother. He couldn't let down himself either because failure was a word he simply didn't accept as a result of his mother's teachings. He said he constantly repeated what he wanted in his life because early on he learned that words hold power. Failure was a word Johnson considered himself to be "at war with the word and all its variations."[13] Having his mother by his side reaffirmed to him what was possible, but he also found a technique to talk himself into remaining hopeful.

He revealed the following:

> I used to lock myself up in my office and say the word success out loud, over and over, like a Buddhist monk chanting his mantra. I used to say to myself, 'John Johnson, you can make it. John Johnson, you can make it. John Johnson, you can make it. John Johnson, you can make it.' When things got real tough, I'd call my mother and she would say, 'You can make it.'[14]

Johnson saw education as a way out of poverty despite being marginalized as a poor, black man in Arkansas. He learned to do for himself because he couldn't afford to wait for someone else to help him. Purposeful about moving beyond the pits of despair to the pinnacles of hope and power, Johnson's attitude reflected a steadfast resilience and fortitude that would enable him to later found more than magazines but ignite movements where African Americans were educated about themselves and learned to be proud of their rich heritage, tradition and values.

Hard work, as was an understanding of a higher power, was instilled in him by his mother, whom he often said was his rock as she laid the foundation through actions with her nonstop prayer and firm belief in knowledge. No stranger to putting in what was necessary to go the extra mile, he learned the value and importance of hard work not by talk but through actions. For instance, one of Johnson's earliest memories took place in 1927 when he was only nine years old.[15] That's when he and his mother were leaving church, a place they attended regularly every Sunday, when they learned of the traumatic moment when the Mississippi River broke a levee 25 miles from where they lived. They were instructed to run for the levee. They had no clothes. No money. People couldn't even take pets. Johnson recalled how more than 800,000 people were displaced and how this was considered one of the worst floods in American history.[16] That unsettling moment was the first time he truly thought about survival for himself and his mother as they spent six weeks on the levee before the water went down.

First hand he saw how people of all races worked together to assist each other in the midst of turmoil. He noticed how blacks from Arkansas City, as well as his own family members, appeared to labor more than others. These qualities informed Johnson about the attitudes of his family members, because these were examples that demonstrated to him how he came from a lineage of survivors and fighters. He saw how all the houses floated away in the twenty-feet deep water.[17] The Red Cross came in sea planes and brought blankets, water and food. They also informed all the people that if they could find their house, the Red Cross would offer assistance in fixing it up and refurbishing it. If a house couldn't be found, a new one would be provided. Little Johnny secretly hoped that his home wouldn't be located so he could get a new place. "I said a prayer every night," he said, recalling how he longed for a safe haven much better than the one in which he resided.[18] His prayers went unanswered and his tiny home, where snakes and other rodents crawled around in before being cleaned up, was found and moved back to its original location. That moment became significant to the young Johnson for several reasons. He learned that houses could be moved. And Johnson developed a lifelong respect for the Red Cross.

At that time in Arkansas City, people walked everywhere they needed to go and they had no telephones. If someone from far away died and word needed to be given to a family, the person with the information would call the town's only grocery store. Then, the store owner would send an errand person to someone's house to deliver the message. Even without basic necessities and things that people today take for granted, Johnson always believed he had a good life because he never knew there was anything better.

Prejudice and discrimination were common in his world but his mother made certain to keep him away from it as much as she could. He did his part by not going anywhere that would challenge the system. In the small segregated town, Williams worked as a domestic for a white doctor known as Dr. McCampbell.[19] [20] Johnson would go to work with his mother to do errands as a way for her to keep an eye on him and make sure he didn't get into any trouble. Johnson remembered how it was common for black people to have a white person look out for them as a means of survival. "If you asked anyone in my little town if they were going to church or some other meeting, they would say, 'If I live and nothing happens,' because there was no certainty that they would live and there was no certainty that nothing would happen."[21]

Living to see another day was important and vital to one's very existence, considering this was during a time when blacks were being killed for simply being present, looking at a white person or saying the wrong thing. For instance, with the first movie theatre, or "picture show" as Johnson called it, blacks had to sit in the balcony while whites sat on the main level. They could not laugh unless whites laughed. Because blacks and whites during those times did not share the same sense of humor, if blacks were caught laughing in the balcony, they were told, "You niggers, cut out that laughing."[22]

During those times, the derogatory label "nigger" rolled easily off the tongues of whites. "We were known as Dr. McCampbell's niggers. Nobody bothered us. He was considered the protector. He was a big tall guy."[23] One day little Johnny did encounter an experience he never forgot and how being called a "nigger" rolled off people's tongue as easily as saying someone's name. There was a pharmacy downstairs from where [Dr. McCampbell's] office was and he sent Johnson downstairs to pick up a prescription. The white people who worked at the pharmacy didn't know what the kid was coming in for and immediately let it be known that, "We don't serve any niggers in here." Johnson vividly remembered running upstairs in tears and telling his mother who then told the doctor, who went downstairs and "beat up the guy and said, 'Don't ever call my niggers no nigger.'"[24 25] This was one early memory of racism that Johnson witnessed in his youth.

Williams' strong work ethic was passed along to her son. There came a time when he had to work in the fields like most poor African Americans during this time, and how working was something he learned to do before he learned how to play. "I was a working child," is how he described it.[26] This taught him about responsibility and became a quality that helped develop his character as an adult.

Johnson's imagination developed as early as his belief in the unknown. Having little money, Williams couldn't afford to buy toys with such a limited income so playing cowboy with a toy gun wasn't possible.[27] Her son instead used a stick to play with. Johnson credited this kind of early creativity with shaping his life later as a publisher, because this fostered his ability to think outside of the box, a quality that would solidify his genius as a businessman.

His feelings about growing up with so few material possessions did not make him bitter. It made him better, for it forced him to use his imagination in a way he may not have done otherwise. Johnson believed he thought his way out of poverty, because his mind was his passport to a better life. "If I can put a definition to my leap from poverty, it is my mother's determination that I would have a chance to be somebody and my own ability to analyze a situation and think my own way out of it," he said.[28]

An observant youth, it did not take him long to see who was revered in the Arkansas community where he grew up. Teachers were respected and so were those with positions in the church. Going to church allowed him to learn about a higher power in more ways than one. In fact, at a point in Johnson's life, he thought of becoming a minister, because he valued the importance of faith and how it played a pivotal role in his life and in his mother's life. As a poor youth with concerns regarding his dark complexion, bow legs (inherited from his mother) and heavy southern accent, he also saw the power and respect that pastors received. He said "the only black people who were somebodies were the ministers and the school teachers."[29]

Having a very religious mother whom he worked hard to please made it a no brainer for Johnson to place his focus on being a minister. Other, more superficial, things captured his attention about the "power" in the church as well like the fact that ministers always wore suits, were respected by blacks and whites, had the best pick of chicken pieces before the Sunday dinner, and had the "support" of the ladies.[30] An early incident as a child, while working in the fields, also served to make him believe the church was where he belonged. "One day, after hours of hard work in the blazing hot sun, I had some sort of vision which seemed to say that I had been 'called.'"[31]

That aspiration of a career in religion was quite premature for Johnson because the intentions were for all the wrong reasons. After coming to his own revelation, he had to be honest with himself by admitting that he was possibly attracted to the pulpit for everything except saving souls. Unsurprisingly, his ambitions of becoming a man of the cloth were short lived and this became revelatory almost immediately.

Johnson's life's mission would shift. But in an interview in 2000, he acknowledged that had his mom not relocated him to Chicago during the Great Migration, he would have been preaching. "If I stayed in the South, I was going to be a minister. I just wasn't going to pick cotton and chop cotton all day for fifty cents a day," he said.[32]

But Chicago played a pivotal role in shaping the young Johnson even before he and his mother made the trek up North. An avid reader even as a youngster, Johnson enjoyed reading what he described as "the militant *Chicago Defender* that black Pullman porters smuggled" into a nearby town called McGehee, Arkansas.[33] He knew there was something special about that paper and he enjoyed reading about the opportunities that were developing in Chicago and in other northern cities. He discovered a world outside of Arkansas, namely Chicago and other northern cities where blacks received opportunities for liberation intellectually and professionally; this newly discovered world was unlike the South. Reading *The Chicago Defender* gave him "an intellectual and physical thrill. I loved to touch the newsprint and to trace the contours of the screaming red headlines. I didn't know it until later, but I had been called—and found."[34]

Johnson and his mother would soon follow the call of the new world in Chicago as Williams sought the best for her son. Williams' words and actions demonstrated just how much she wanted for her son; however, even her best attempts at affording him better things in life wasn't always possible because money was scarce. When Johnson finished eighth grade, he could not continue his education. School for the black students in the Arkansas City Colored School System ended after eighth grade; students were sent off to work in the fields or those who could afford to travel, continued their education in larger cities such as Little Rock or Pine Bluff, Arkansas. Williams, however, was working on a plan to relocate to Chicago for Johnson to attend high school. Even then, the trip would have to wait. He said, "There wasn't enough money in the secret bank under the mattress to go to Little Rock, much less to Chicago." He said his mother took immediate action. She rolled up her sleeves and "redoubled her efforts cooking, washing, and ironing for whole camps of levee workers and volunteering for every extra job that came up."[35]

With finances not readily available, Williams was not deterred. She used the time to earn more money and dream a bigger dream for her son, whom she was set on sending to school up North in Chicago. This decision was twofold and made in an effort to provide him with a better life and a quality education. Due to the forces of racism, Williams decided to relocate to the Windy City in the early 1930s. This was during a time that signaled the great migration of blacks from the South to the North.

The road leaving Arkansas seemed long and uncertain for the youngster. Like most children, Johnson assumed he would play ball and be out of school for a year until his mother got things in order. His mother, on the other hand, had different plans since education and hard work went hand in hand. Her dream was for him to finish high school and she was working on making that happen. So, while she saved more money to leave Arkansas for Chicago, the determined mother made Johnson repeat the eighth grade—even though he had graduated already. "She didn't want me running wild on the streets, she said. And she didn't want me to get used to a life of menial work. To prevent that, I was going to repeat the eighth grade two, three, four times—as many times as necessary. 'You're going to stay in the eighth grade,' she said, 'until we've got enough money to go to Chicago.'"[36]

Johnson often talked about how he graduated from the eighth grade twice. While this fact was a source of shame for him as a child, it would later serve as a source of pride for him for he had something few people did—two grade school diplomas. And, the second time in eighth grade he joked about being an honor student.[37]

Johnson's desire for knowledge was being shaped as he witnessed how his mother saw education as a means to a better life and a way to be liberated and in charge of one's own agenda. Of course, he didn't like being teased by kids who made fun of him for attending school with younger students. But while he was catching hell from his peers, his mother was dealing with her own share of problems.

Williams endured criticism from neighbors and friends who didn't understand why she took on extra jobs and worked longer hours to save money so they could move to Chicago. Johnson saw his mother's determination to allow him to have a better life, which rested upon a foundation built upon education and hard work. Having her son see her actions meant more to Williams than any idle chatter or concerns from others. And as people continued to doubt her efforts, she held firm to the belief that "there was a solution to every problem."[38]

His mother's motto stayed with him in his personal and professional life. He once said during a 1975 interview for *The Saturday Evening Post* how "especially blessed" he was to have the mother he had. She taught him to be self-sufficient by showing him how to cook, wash, iron, and clean for himself. "She instilled a positive attitude in me. She always told me...every problem has a solution. I've always thought that way."[39]

These kinds of lessons shaped Johnson throughout his life, molding him into a teen and into an adult who embraced hard work. Johnson remembered something his mother once told him, which was, "Our destiny is, in large part, in our own hands."[40] His mother's unwavering certainty helped her son to learn the importance of how actions truly speak louder than words. She'd always believed that there was a solution to every problem, and that the solution was in God's hands, not humans' hands. But she believed also, and with equal fervor, that God helped those who helped themselves. "Victory," she said, "is certain if we have the courage to believe and the strength to run our own race."[41]

Before it was time for him to finish the eighth grade for the second time, his mother had earned enough money for them to go to Chicago in July 1933 during the height of the Great Depression when he was 15 years old. Being a woman of great faith, Williams revealed it more than anything when she left Arkansas without her husband, James, who didn't believe heading to the Windy City was the best plan. Her husband even tried to discourage her from moving, but she did it anyway because, as Johnson once put it, "She loved my stepfather, but she loved freedom and education more."[42]

Beulah, Johnson's sister, moved to Chicago just before they did. Having a family member already in the Windy City helped to make the adjustment a bit smoother. A former teacher in Arkansas, by this time Beulah, a skilled dressmaker, transitioned to a career in the garment district.[43]

But when she lost her job, she turned to salvation from a "prophet" who believed himself to be "God" named Father Divine. Members of his organization lived in "heaven," as he called it. After joining this movement, Beulah moved to Philadelphia and assumed her given name of Beauty Ray. Because she "renounced her worldly family and could only talk to people who accepted the teachings of Father Divine," Johnson's family never heard from or saw her ever again. "My mother broke down in tears and my stepfather cursed."[44] Interestingly enough, many years later once he founded *EBONY* and *JET* magazines, Johnson would do major stories about Father Divine, which ended up being some of the company's most popular articles during that time. He had a dual agenda for the coverage. Maybe Beauty Ray would read the stories and reach out to her little brother in order to make his mother happy, and Father Divine had a rock star following, which translated into major sales at the newsstands.

The love and admiration the business magnate had for his mother was often expressed and discussed by Johnson. He felt his life was positioned with a purpose and he had no complaints about the direction it had taken. "One doesn't decide when to be born. One doesn't decide who his parents will be. But I was so fortunate. I didn't decide to move from Arkansas to Chicago in 1933, my mother did, partly because she wanted me to have a better education."[45]

Coming from a small place like Arkansas City, the teen Johnson was excited about the possibilities for the future and surprised to see so many people when he got off the train in Chicago. He was surprised because he had never seen so many black people together at one time. "Black people were coming from everywhere in the South because jobs were here. Opportunity was here," said Johnson. "Education was here. And I was just impressed. I just hadn't seen that many people anywhere, black or white."[46]

Earning two eighth grade diplomas paid off in the long run for Johnson, because when he first attended the all-black Wendell Phillips High School in Chicago, he excelled so much that he was able to skip the ninth grade. A move like this certainly had an impact on his intellectual confidence and sense of pride. He knew his mother's prayers were powerful, because she demonstrated trust with actions where she constantly told her son how much she believed in him and showed him the importance of having confidence in his abilities. Her dedication and tireless efforts were early lessons, which would later fuel Johnson's desire and belief that he could overcome any obstacle. "She always believed in me. It's very important in life to have someone who believes in you. It helps you to succeed and get through bad times and makes you feel you can overcome difficulty. I always knew my mother was in my corner."[47]

Relocating from Arkansas to Chicago wasn't easy for Johnson and his mother. The first year alone, in 1933, they were constantly changing addresses because, though she was a domestic worker, she had a difficult time finding a job to even clean homes. Their first place was at 422 East 44th Street (off King Drive then known as South Parkway). They later moved to 5610 Calumet Avenue and 5412 South Parkway.[48]

Without the extra income from Williams' husband, from 1934 to 1936, they received public assistance, welfare. Johnson often discussed how those were humiliating and humbling moments for him because he felt so ashamed. He told a story of how in those days he ran around with a group of young people, who would sit around and watch the welfare trucks, which delivered assistance in the form of food and not with money. Johnson recalled how the truck would drive up to his house and someone would say, "They're going to your house," and how he would say, "That's not my house." The truck would drive up to someone else's house, and he would say, "That's not my house. We all knew the trucks were going to our houses, but we were just too ashamed to admit it."[49]

Eventually Johnson's stepfather was able to move with the family to Chicago. He received a Works Progress Administration (WPA) job and Johnson received a job with the National Youth Administration. "We moved on from there to better times and better jobs, but it was the first step, and it was better than welfare. It gave me some dignity because you performed some work for what you were getting."[50]

Treating people right was something else his mother instilled in him—and Johnson followed his mother's teachings once again to transform the world around him. He said:

> People have the capacity to change but we have to have the capacity to bring about change. And one of the things that brings it about is education. That's what my mother believed. You have to be well educated. And you have to treat people decently. You can't call them names and then expect them to support you.[51]

Surrounding oneself with like-minded people was something else his mother impressed upon him. When times got difficult later in Johnson's life, he sought spiritual guidance and words of encouragement from one of his mentors, Dr. Mary McLeod Bethune, founder of Bethune-Cookman College, whom he met as a student during one of her National Youth Administration events.[52] That connection made with Bethune during Johnson's youth would prove viable as an adult when the entrepreneur faced challenges as a new publisher in 1942 with his publication Negro Digest. Bethune provided her former student with encouragement by telling him not to give up when things got tough. "Hang on. Have faith. Keep trying. The project is too good to end. The Lord wouldn't want it to end," Bethune would share with Johnson.[53] His mother, as his biggest cheerleader, also let him know "as long as you're trying, you're not failing."[54]

Williams' strong belief in education for her son was just one trait she encouraged. Common sense and discernment mattered as well, as demonstrated by Johnson's mother, who never went beyond third grade and yet she was the most educated woman he felt he'd ever met. She was courageous. She was daring. She believed that you could do anything you wanted to do if you tried, and she gave her son that that belief, that hope, and it was the kind of thing that guided him most all of his life.[55]

Johnson understood that his mother did not rely upon a formal, traditional education system to teach him. The way he constantly mentioned the teachings of his mother indicated his absolute deference in her. That belief inspired a saying that Johnson was well known for, which was, "Failure is a word I don't accept."[56] And, surprisingly, Johnson had no shame in mentioning that it was born out of something he told a young man before he fired the gentleman for using the word failure.

Johnson explained, "Nothing personal, but I'm too insecure myself to have people around me who believe that failure is a possibility. Failure is a word I don't accept...Failure: I was at war with the word and all its variations. The word I wanted to hear, then and now, was success."[57] What a person puts out in the universe has a profound impact whether it is realized or not. He knew and understood the power of words. Putting them on paper mattered but uttering them into the universe mattered just as much.

Faith was something Johnson believed to be spiritual and also mental, because for him the two weren't separated. He felt that a lot of it is psychological because a person must believe in self. He understood that if a person believed that he/she could make it, that person could make it. It was about mind over matter. "And I think most people don't really believe they can make it," he said. "You see, sincerity is contagious. They say that the difference between an amateur and a professional is sincerity. Professionals believe in what they're doing."[58]

Williams poured her hopes and dreams into her only son, but as she got older, she managed to find time to do things she enjoyed. Once moving to Chicago and well after her son founded Johnson Publishing Company, Williams organized clubs and social organizations. A life member and publicity chairman of the National Association of Colored Women's Clubs, she also founded her own Gertrude Johnson Williams Civic and Charity Club.

She was also a founding member of the Emmanuel Baptist Church, where she served for 24 years as treasurer. It was at that church that she met a young man, Jesse L. Jackson Sr.[59] Johnson often laughed while recalling how his mother took a liking to Jackson.

She asked her son if he had any jobs at Johnson Publishing Company. "I told her I did not have any jobs at the time," he said. Then he added, "My mother looked at me and said, 'Boy, I'm your mother. I'm going to ask again.'" Needless to say, Johnson found a job for Jackson at the 18th and Michigan location of Johnson's company. This job provided Jackson, then a married father of two small children, with his first job when he came to Chicago "penniless, unemployed and unknown."[60]

Johnson often told the story of how he saw bigger things for Jackson and encouraged him to get out of the office and do sales. Eventually, the man Jackson affectionately called "Godfather" planted the seed for him to become a world leader, by encouraging him to start something that he could call his own, which led to the creation of Operation Bread Basket, which later became Operation PUSH.[61] Jackson received more than a job at Johnson Publishing Company. Johnson offered him the same hope that Jackson would later preach about to the world.[62]

Johnson held the utmost respect for his mother and continued to take her advice and turn to her when he had doubts. In the early days he admitted he relied on her almost to a fault. That's the only person who knew his personal thoughts and struggles about his uncertainties along with the many obstacles he battled during times of trials. He said, "She was a security blanket. I always felt that no matter what difficulty I had, even as a child and as I grew up, that if I talked to her, she would make me feel better about it."[63]

Her way of handling situations that Johnson encountered as a child stood out to him. Though he had an older sister, it was as if he was an only child because he was being raised without his sibling around. And, he might have been his mother's only son, but Mrs. Johnson did not coddle him. He said this about his mother's tough love:

> She didn't kiss my fingers—you know, like when kids burned their fingers and the parents kissed the hurt away—she didn't do that. She reasoned it away. She pointed out to me. She was a great believer in religion and faith. Faith has played a very important role in my life, faith in myself, faith in the belief that

> people will respond to a service they want and can't get anywhere else.[64]

He also said she disciplined and wasn't above using a "switch" to give him a spanking if he got out of hand.[65] Her tough love and sacrifices paid off. He talked to his mother on the phone every day as an adult. She witnessed her son start three magazines, build an eleven-story headquarters on Michigan Avenue, become the first black person named to the board of Twentieth Century Fox film corporation, assist under the leadership of three presidents, create a cosmetics company, launch Chicago's first black-owned radio station, start a book division, launch the nation's first black weekly syndicated TV celebrity interview show, and be named Most Outstanding Black Publisher in History by the National Newspaper Publishers Association. In a 1975 issue of Reader's Digest, Williams said, "Sometimes, I'll be thinking about the long way the Lord has brought me and my son. And I'm just washed with tears of happiness."[66] Two years later, on Sunday, May 1, 1977, Williams died after slipping into a coma at Chicago's Michael Reese Hospital. She was eighty-five.[67]

Observing the relative scarcity of black writers, eleven years later in 1988, Johnson announced the Gertrude Johnson Williams Literary Contest, named in honor of his mother and aimed at stimulating an interest in writing with a $5,000 top prize along with publishing of the story in *EBONY*.[68] His mother's legacy carried on and prompted the writing career of former English teacher Sharon Draper, who beat out more than 4,000 others after winning the contest in 1990. Encouraged to enter the contest from a challenge by a former student, she had never had anything published before submitting the short story, "One Small Torch," about child abuse. "Almost immediately after the publication in *EBONY*, things started happening. All of a sudden I was a writer," Draper said. Not only has she since gone on to become a New York Times best-selling author and five-time winner of the Coretta Scott King Literary Awards, the Ohio native also was named in 1997 National Teacher of the Year, one of the highest awards an educator can receive, by former President Bill Clinton. [69] In 2008, during the historic election of former President Barack Obama, for the first time Johnson Publishing Company launched a digital version of the competition. Shortly thereafter, the contest eventually ended.[70]

Throughout the years, Johnson provided his mother with some of the finest things that money could buy like cars, a chauffeur and even a maid. Her office was on the sixth floor of the headquarters building at 820 S. Michigan Ave. and remained intact exactly how she left it when she died. A picture of her, wearing a yellow suit, sat on her desk and her son had fresh roses delivered in her office every week. As time went on, the photograph started to fade due to the sun's bright rays. Still, her son continued to show his dedication to her long after her death and he made provisions for the honor to continue even after his death. "I've left instructions that the office is to be left that way as long as Johnson Publishing Company lives," he wrote in his autobiography.[70]

FIGURE 3: Gertrude Johnson Williams enjoys a 1973 Chicago dinner gala with her son. Courtesy Johnson Publishing Company, LLC. 

CHAPTER 2

# BUILDING AN EMPIRE

***"I picked a name out of the air, and Johnny Johnson became John Harold Johnson."*** ***John H. Johnson***

What's in a name? It forms one's identity and in it possesses a story. Some more obvious than others. This was no different for the man that the world would come to know as John H. Johnson, the architect of the empire known as Johnson Publishing Company. He was given the birth name of simply Johnny, named in honor of his mother's close friend Johnnie Ford, whom she promised she'd name her next child after. She did not give him a middle name.[1]

How Johnny became John Harold is yet another testament to the role Providence played in his life. Sometimes it is the least likely person who will step into one's life and end up changing his/her world for the better or for the worst. The person who did this for Johnson did not look like him and had he not been open to believing that not everyone who isn't your same race is against you, he might have missed an opportunity to grow. Being born and raised in the segregated south did not afford him many chances to know white people on a personal or even humane level. All he saw was the oppressive nature and how African Americans were treated. He knew that not staying in one's place could possibly mean some sort of tragedy and even death.

When Johnson first moved to Chicago, he attended Wendell Phillips High School and took journalism classes because he loved to read. He became fascinated with the news after first encountering *The Chicago Defender* while still in Arkansas. That fire was lit when he was a kid and still burned inside him when it came to the news. It didn't take him long to become the editor of the *Phillipsite*, the school's newspaper, and sales manager for the school yearbook, because

Johnson enjoyed writing and had values instilled in him that reflected principles of self-determination and faith.[2]

After Wendell Phillips High School burned down in January of 1935, Johnson was later transferred to DuSable High School, located in the well-to-do Bronzeville area with a mostly black population. Robert Sengstacke Abbott, founder of *The Chicago Defender*, was instrumental in having the school renamed in honor of Jean Baptiste Pointe DuSable, a black Haitian frontier trader and trapper known, in 1779, as the first settler in Chicago. Some of his new classmates at DuSable High School included people who would go on to make great accomplishments such as music legend Nathaniel "Nat King" Cole and comedy legend John "Redd Foxx" Sanford.[3]

Poorer than most fellow students, life was difficult for Johnson because he seemed to stand out as a country boy by comparison to everyone else. Matters were made worse for him because he was shy and bowlegged, which is considered sexy now but was a point of ridicule then along with his thick, Southern drawl. He said in his 1989 autobiography:

> They thought my bowlegs were hilarious. I've heard it said that bowlegs are sexy. They weren't sexy to my classmates, who ranked them slightly below a social disease...If your classmates laugh every time you stand up to recite, if they follow you, shouting, 'Look at that bowlegged guy in his mammy-made clothes,' if this happens every day and you have no friends or money and you're alone in a strange city, you begin to feel put upon.[4]

And, of course, Johnson didn't like this so he figured the best way to fight back would be through the one thing his mother constantly encouraged—education.

Williams' early actions and attitude stressed to her son the importance of education and being determined, both of which helped to carry him through times when fellow students weren't so kind. Always making a way out of no way, his mother, at the time, worked for a woman whose husband was close to her son's size. After gentle persuasion, his mom was able to get her son some of the man's old suits. "Almost overnight I became one of the best-dressed students at the old and the new Wendell Phillips," recalled Johnson.[5] Those early habits of wearing a suit remained with Johnson throughout his life. He was never seen by employees without wearing a suit, a tie and dress shoes.

One person who entered his world and gave it new meaning was a woman named Mary Josephine Herrick. Her presence was felt in Johnson's life during a pivotal moment. She stepped into his space during a period when he had distrust toward white people. Herrick, who was white, taught civics at Chicago's predominantly African-American Wendell Phillips High School and later she transferred and taught at DuSable High School from 1935-1961. Surprisingly she was an early person who made an indelible impression upon his life in 1933, shortly after he and his mother arrived in Chicago.[6]

As an educator, Herrick had developed a reputation for her work on the city's South Side that some perceived to be good, while others looked upon unfavorably due to their racist views about whites and blacks. This same woman would be the person Johnson would later consider as one of "the most important teachers" in his life.[7]

To understand Herrick, one had to first appreciate her essence and character. Her actions inside of the classroom and outside of it were unparalleled. Johnson recalled how Herrick would invite students to her house for tea and was the first white person to invite him into her home "on a social basis."[8]

Most Chicago educators who taught on the South Side were white but taught classes filled with predominantly black students in the 1930s. Herrick gained a reputation for being different than the other educators. She ended up becoming the first teacher who taught Johnson and his classmates about the Motherland, Africa. Herrick worked outside of boundaries of Eurocentric education. When this is viewed within the context of social justice, she saw there was an intellectual injustice. She was looking at her students and looking at the books she was given. She knew they didn't see themselves in educational materials and realized the impact it must have on them being unable to see themselves.[9]

Johnson understood the value in what Herrick taught and how she wanted the best for her students, no matter what race they were. He said, "The true story was not in the books, but Mary J. Herrick taught it. She told us we were descendants of the ancient people who had created major civilizations in Africa. She challenged us to prepare ourselves for the next lap of a great race."[10]

It was brave of Herrick to step outside of herself and dare to structure lessons that would have meaning for her students during a time when racism was high. That did not stop her though. She took students to municipal buildings and courts to teach them civics and government. This opened up their world because many black youths during this time then seldomly left their neighborhood. Johnson said about Herrick:

> She showed us a world we didn't know. She also took me into her home. You can't imagine how that gave me confidence...Mary Herrick was the first white person who ever showed a real interest in me. She let me know there were good white people in the world, and that is so important for young blacks to learn.[11]

Johnson described Herrick as an educator who "taught as if her life—and our lives—depended on it. She was the first white person I'd ever met who was completely free of racial prejudice."[12]

Born May 14, 1895, Herrick was a lifelong civics teacher in the Chicago Public Schools (CPS) from 1922 to 1965. Actively involved in the teachers' union movement, she was the first editor of the Chicago Union Teacher, the official newsletter of the Chicago Teachers Union, and vice president of the American Federation of Teachers. She signed the original Chicago Teachers Union charter in 1937, amalgamating five small unions into Local 1 of the American Federation of Teachers.[13] Herrick was also a researcher who wrote the 1970 book The Chicago Public Schools: A Social and Political History. Some considered it probably one of the finest in the history of a big city American public school system ever written.[14]

Herrick, a Phi Beta Kappa graduate of Northwestern University and the University of Chicago, was not surprised by Johnson's later success. In a 1975 interview, Johnson's former teacher described him as "a good student who plugged away and was quietly impressive. He always set out to do something and did it. That's something that many grownups can't learn in a lifetime."[15]

A little lady who stood about five feet tall, she was so beloved by her students that when Harold Washington was elected Chicago's mayor in 1983, he and other Herrick former students from DuSable High School organized a 1984 dinner in her honor and declared an official Mary J. Herrick Day in the Windy City.[16] Herrick, who never earned more than a salary of $9,000 a year during her teaching career, said she chose to teach at black schools because she needed "an interesting job that also had something to do with changing the inequalities and injustices of the world."[17] She died at eighty-nine, a few months after being honored that year, and Johnson included a small write-up about her life in the census section of *JET*.[18] Johnson said this about her longstanding impact:

> The letter alone killeth but the spirit transforms disadvantaged youths and giveth new life. There's nothing wrong with public education that more resources, more love and more...Mary Herrick's can't cure. And our most important task is to duplicate the nurturing, transforming environments that made it possible for unsung and underpaid teachers and administrators, black or white, to perform the educational miracles of yesterday.[19]

With Herrick and others at DuSable, Johnson's senior year, in 1936, marked a time of discovery and lessons that would change the path of his life in more ways than he ever would have imagined. Johnson was the editor in chief of the Phillipsite newspaper, president of the student council, leader of the student forum and president of the French Club. Working to better himself so that students would no longer laugh at his southern ways paid off in a major way. Practicing for hours in the mirror on how to speak and carry himself, he soon found that he was the only student who had the nerve and courage to stand up and speak in front of others. What was once his disadvantage, speaking with a heavy southern drawl, ended up becoming his advantage after Johnson worked on his speech. As the junior and senior class president, he graduated with honors in May 1936 while being the only student speaker at the commencement.[20] His speech, titled Builders of a New World, dealt with "the task that lies before us," which was "excellence linked to service" and purpose.[21] He was especially excited to learn that *The Chicago Defender* announced the 206 student graduates along with his distinction as student speaker.

During this time, Johnson's accomplishments caught the attention of Harry H. Pace, president of Supreme Liberty Life Insurance Company, which was the largest black-owned enterprise in the United States at this time. While Johnson won a tuition scholarship to the University of Chicago, he didn't have enough money to cover other expenses and attend the university because he didn't have a job.

The eighteen-year-old Johnson was approached by Pace, who attended an event where Johnson and other top high school students were honored. Pace was curious about Johnson's plans beyond high school and after learning about Johnson's dilemma with funds for college, Pace offered him employment and a scholarship to go to college part-time. Johnson started the job on September 1, 1936 where he was hired as an office boy at $25 a month.[22] Within a couple of years, Johnson elevated himself from office clerk to Pace's personal assistant where he worked on the house magazine, *The Supreme Liberty Guardian*.[23] Later, he left college to work full-time when he was promoted to editor where his job included taking copy to the printer, reading proofs, and ensuring that the photographs were in order.

Though not earning a college degree, Johnson also later briefly studied part-time at Northwestern University. Gaining entry into the University of Chicago and Northwestern University wasn't easy back then, especially for an African-American person, and it remains a challenge to enter both even today for financial and academic reasons. Ultimately, Johnson chose working over going to school because having a job was considered a "glorious thing to behold" in an effort to help his family. "I went to college for a while and even studied journalism at Northwestern, but I can't even remember the name of my teacher now. I benefitted mostly from on-the-job training," he said.[24]

His time at Supreme Life helped him to not only to be mentored by Pace but also the general counsel at Supreme Life, Earl B. Dickerson, an activist and a Chicago alderman. Seeing people who looked like himself allowed Johnson to believe that what once seemed impossible was possible. Black people could do for self and not have to work for others. Johnson said:

> I had an opportunity there to observe black people running a business. For the first time I believed that success was possible for me in business. Up to that point, I had seen lawyers,

> ministers and doctors, but I had never seen a successful black businessman. And here I was working for a company, which was the largest black business in the North at that time, and I saw black men making big decisions. I saw them moving around with dignity and with security and it inspired me. It made me know that my career could be in business and that success was possible.[25]

In 1936, Johnson's identity was also altered through his name. This is when his beloved teacher Herrick personally encouraged him to change his birth name from Johnny to John because she felt the new name was more fitting for a maturing young man. At this time, she also suggested he have a middle name, so Johnson decided upon Harold, a name which he said he picked out of the air.[26]

FIGURE 4: Johnson is shown as a young man.
Courtesy Johnson Publishing Company, LLC. 

Another person, as mentioned earlier, who helped to shape Johnson's youth and his journey toward building an empire was an African-American educator named Dr. Mary McLeod Bethune. President Franklin D. Roosevelt, in 1935, asked educator Bethune to work under his administration where she was appointed Director of the Negro Division of a New Deal program called the National Youth Administration (NYA). The appointment made her the highest-ranking African-American woman in the federal government during this time. Her role with the NYA helped African-American youth find employment and opportunity during the Great Depression in 1929.[27]

One of those youth happened to be Johnson, who had a part-time position with NYA where he published a magazine, titled Afri-American Youth, in addition to organizing events for young people. He was able to not only earn money, but publishing Afri-American Youth, which was a mimeograph, allowed him to explore his interest in journalism and help bring money into his family's home so that they could get off welfare.[28]

In his autobiography, he described Bethune as "short and black as polished ebony. She was not what the world considers beautiful, but she had so much soul force and authority that when she walked into a room all eyes were pulled to her as if to a magnet."[29]

Bethune, who later founded the historically black Bethune-Cookman College in Daytona Beach, Florida, remained a constant in Johnson's life, affectionately considering him one of her "boys," even as he scaled heights to become a pioneering publisher. When things got tough in the early stages of his career while publishing *EBONY*, due to great adversity because of his race and lack of finances, he recalled what Bethune once told him: "The darker the night, the brighter the stars." These words carried him throughout his life.[30]

As a maturing young man, Johnson recalled how he was too poor to date, so he would study, because he was determined to be the best. Studying helped him to shift his focus and energy to something other than what he was lacking. In order for this to happen, Johnson educated himself by finding books that would boost his self-esteem. Reading self-help books became the solution for him. A few of his top picks included Dale Carnegie's *How to Win Friends and Influence People* and Napoleon Hill's *Think and Grow Rich.* These were the books that allowed him to work on his being and taught him ways to improve his self-image. "Faith, self-confidence and a positive mental attitude" were the basic messages Johnson recalled as the central themes.[31]

He worked on his speech by practicing conversations and selling approaches. At first students laughed at him, but Johnson didn't get discouraged because he was determined to do well and had enough confidence to see himself through. Eventually, he won his classmates over, as they stopped laughing at him and began lauding him. Johnson recalled that moment in high school that became the turning point in what he was taught:

> The sweetest emotions in the world is watching scorn turn into admiration and awe. I learned something else that I've never forgotten: There is no defense against an excellence that speaks to a real need. This brings back, at a new and different level, to the advantage of the disadvantage. If I had been rich with a lot of friends, I wouldn't be where I am today. It's not satisfaction but dissatisfaction that drives people to the heights. I was goaded, I was driven to success by the whip of social disapproval.[32]

Social disapproval drove him to success and is how he turned a negative into a positive—a theme of his life. Johnson used experiences meant to tear him down as avenues to uplift himself to a higher level. He started educating himself further with works that included books by Booker T. Washington, W.E.B. DuBois, and Langston Hughes. He was laser focused and didn't have hobbies or play sports because education was his roadmap to a better existence. Johnson said "the food and drink" of his life was trying to succeed. He was too busy trying to "think" his way out of poverty so he had no time for sports—not even taking gym—in school.[33]

As he got older and eventually became a self-made millionaire, Johnson still never found solace in hobbies. He was a man of tradition and didn't like straying too far from his roots. "I've always been interested in getting ahead, in watching for new opportunities, in reading books on how to improve myself, books on how to be a public speaker and on how not to be afraid of things that I'm afraid of," he said in 1985 during an *EBONY* interview.[34]

Johnson said he never learned to play golf, for example, because at that time when he would have learned to play the expensive hobby, black people were not permitted to play on courses in major cities. He recalled how a mutual friend, who wasn't black, once told him, "'Johnson, you're never going to get anywhere until you learn how to play golf.' And I said, 'I'm already where I want to be. Golf might mess me up.'"[35]

Work was the only thing he seemed to know how to do. Even taking lengthy vacations was something Johnson hardly ever did in his entire life. Work was his hobby. He enjoyed being a publisher and businessman so much that it didn't feel like a job. There's a saying that if you find your passion, you'll find your purpose. Johnson recalled someone once questioning him as to why he didn't take long vacations. He said, "I asked them, 'What do you do when you're on vacation?' And they said, 'Anything you want to do.' And I said, 'I do that every day.'"[36] Learning was a lifelong process for Johnson. Simple lessons taught him the most, including that there's an advantage in every disadvantage, something he learned from his mother. One major disadvantage that became an advantage was his life's course. Had there been a high school for him to attend in Arkansas City, Johnson said he wouldn't have ever left to go to Chicago. "I've thanked fate for that gift many times."[37] It is clear Johnson believed there was a greater reason and purpose behind everything that happened the way it did in his life.

Regarding his personal life, Johnson didn't have much luck with the ladies in 1940. "I was not, to put it mildly, one of the great catches" because he didn't come from wealth.[38] He purchased his first car that year, a light brown Chevrolet and met an attractive Talladega College student, Eunice Walker, who was on vacation in Chicago. Born to a prominent "first black" family of the South, her father, Dr. Nathaniel D. Walker, was a physician and her maternal grandfather, Rev. Dr. William H. McAlpine, "was one of the founders of Selma University and the National Baptist Convention." Her mother, Ethel McAlpine Walker, was a high school principal and taught college as did Eunice's only sister. Her brother, Dr. William M. Walker, also had a medical degree along with another brother.[39] Needless to say, she was often told to date on her level and align herself with one of the "young black professionals …most likely to succeed."[40]

After a year of dating, the couple eventually wed the following year in 1941. Johnson said Eunice stood out from the other people he dated because she was "a good listener, sympathetic to my ambitions. She made me feel that maybe I would be somebody one day."[41] Their honeymoon consisted of driving from Alabama, visiting a friend in Atlanta for a few days before planting themselves into a residence in Chicago. In addition to earning a degree in sociology with a minor in art at Talladega, Eunice earned a master's degree in social work from

Loyola University in Chicago. She later studied interior design at the Ray-Vogue School of Design (now called the Ray College of Design at the Illinois Institute of Art-Chicago), and she was a lifetime member of Delta Sigma Theta Sorority, Inc., a black Greek-lettered sorority founded in 1913 that is renowned for its mission of service.[42]

Even though Johnson never completed college himself, at the time of his death, he received thirty-one honorary degrees from institutions, ranging from Ivy League schools such as Harvard University to Northwestern University to renowned Historically Black Colleges and Universities such as Howard University and Morehouse College.[43]

FIGURE 5: An honorary Doctor of Laws degree is bestowed upon Johnson in 1998 during a commencement ceremony at Harvard University by University Marshal Dr. Richard M. Hunt. Courtesy Johnson Publishing Company, LLC. 

In addition to attending college and working, while at the University of Chicago, he— along with nine other men on his line—was inducted into the Alpha Phi Alpha Fraternity, Inc.'s Chicago-based Theta chapter in 1937. As a member of "the first intercollegiate Greek-letter fraternity established for African-American men" in 1906, he also served as president of the Theta chapter from 1939-1940.[44] When Johnson started his publishing company, he belonged to the Xi Lambda chapter, considered one of the organization's "power" graduate chapters. There, his fraternity brothers recalled how he hired "a lot of Alphas" at his company but would not employ a person unless he was an active member.

Johnson, who attended monthly fraternity meetings until his health began to fail, was an active member of the organization until his death. An entire issue of *The Sphinx*, Alpha Phi Alpha's national magazine, was dedicated to him for the sixty seventh anniversary convention issue. The publication had a story where he was crowned the reclamation king of Alpha Phi Alpha's Xi Lambda's Chicago graduate chapter.[45] Realizing the chapter needed a boost in reclaiming members who were no longer active, Johnson was approached to help members become financial once more. He hosted a dinner at his Johnson Publishing Company, raising more than $1,000 in dues during 1973. Johnson was also lauded for helping to contribute to most of *The Sphinx* magazines when the national headquarters was based in Chicago at 4432 Dr. Martin Luther King Dr. and editorial offices at 4728 Drexel Blvd. Under the supervision of Johnson Publishing Company art director Herbert Temple and with photo supervision by Basil O. Phillips, the company employees would work after hours to assist Johnson and his fraternity.[46] An Alpha Phi Alpha award—along with various other honors—hung from the wall behind Johnson's chair in the conference room on the eleventh floor suite where Johnson held editorial meetings. A life member, more than 40 fraternity members filled the lobby of the Johnson Publishing Company headquarters to sing the national hymn and "Amazing Grace" following his Omega service while he laid in state as a part of his fraternity's funeral ritual.[47]

Johnson was also a member of Sigma Pi Phi Fraternity's Beta Boule Chicago Chapter and a Prince Hall Freemason. On July 3, 1958, assisted by Past Masters of Wisdom Lodge No. 102 and others, assembled a lodge and conferred the degrees of Entered Apprentice, Fellow Craft and Master Mason upon Johnson, stating how he "contributed much to the race through publications and dissemination of the culture and progress that has been made."[48]

A staunch advocate of racial unity, Johnson was a member of the Urban League and became a member of the National Association for the Advancement of Colored People (NAACP) at the age of 18. He was vocal about the importance of uplifting and not putting others down. "I never knocked anybody. I never knocked Farrakhan,"

Johnson said. "I never knocked the NAACP. I never knocked anybody. We need everybody trying to help us win complete equality. We are part of the civil rights movement."[49]

Giving back was important to him. While working at Supreme Life, his philanthropic philosophy took form because he worked with what he described as "community minded" people. They felt it was important if you were doing well to give back to the community. This wasn't viewed as a way of getting anything out of it or taking a tax write-off. His mentors taught him that giving to others had a deeper meaning. "If you have the money and you're doing well, do something to help your fellow men. It was instilled in me by the people there [at Supreme Life] and by my mother. And so, I joined a number of organizations and I enjoyed being there and helping to make a difference in a number of things."[50]

Johnson never asked for acknowledgement about the financial contributions he quietly made to help others. Giving back was part of his fabric. It was something he was taught and it was something well learned. Johnson explained his philosophy about this:

> The credit comes from within. I feel that I've been blessed to some degree of success and that I have an obligation to give it back in some way to the community. I've tried to do it through community. I've tried to do it through education. I've tried to do it through community groups and organizations and I've tried to do it through politicians who did not have the normal support that would come from the white corporate community. But I'm not giving for them as much as I am giving for myself, for an inner feeling of peace and satisfaction, for the knowledge that I have given back some of what has been given to me. And here again, this goes back to my mother, who believed that you would be blessed if you contributed to good causes and if you were unselfish in your relationship with your fellow man.[51]

Keeping with his values of giving back, when Johnson and his wife were unable to have biological children, they adopted a two-week old son, John Harold Johnson, Jr., in 1956. The couple returned to the same Illinois adoption agency two years later to adopt a two-week old daughter, Linda Eunice Johnson.[52] One Christmas he treated his family to a mountaintop home in Palm Springs, California, where he was the only black to purchase property in the area. Actor Steve McQueen had a mountain pad nearby and comedian-actor Bob Hope was Johnson's neighbor down the street.[53] When Johnson made history as the only black to make the Forbes 400 in 1982, Hope was one of the few celebrities on the list.[54]

Johnson's residence in Chicago was a condominium at the Carlyle at Chicago's 1040 Lake Shore Drive, located in the prestigious Gold Coast; but despite the perceived trappings of success, Johnson was more ordinary than not.[55] He often described himself as someone who "runs scared all the time, someone who is never quite sure of anything until it happens, and who has never been able to forget the time he was on the welfare rolls of Chicago."[56] Never forgetting his roots is what many could argue as a quality that kept him grounded no matter how much success he amassed.

Johnson recalled the early lessons that his mother taught him about being independent. Even when he had money and opportunities to have others wait on him hand and foot, he preferred to do things himself. Success did not change him when it came to some day-to-day activities. For instance, he didn't have a personal chef. He once said that at night he would eat a bowl of cereal if he got hungry, but he did find cooking to be helpful. "It's a form of therapy and relaxation and it goes back to the self-sufficiency my mother taught me. She wanted me to be independent, so she taught me to cook, to wash clothes, to iron, to clean up behind myself."[57] He usually had his Executive Aide to the Publisher, Raymond Grady, pick up Kentucky Fried Chicken every weekend. And Johnson looked at an awful lot of television. On Sundays, for instance, Johnson would devotedly watch Apostolic Church of God mega pastor Bishop Dr. Arthur M. Brazier followed by Lakewood Church mega pastor Joel Osteen on television. Word had it that Johnson used to go to church without fail as his company continued to grow, but he found it necessary to stop after people kept asking for money.

Others moving across the Chicagoland area were even surprised to see him grocery shopping for himself. In fact, once a woman asked why he didn't have someone shopping for him instead of rolling around the basket and pulling items from shelves himself. Johnson simply told her "I like to do it myself." When she mentioned how she was certain that he at least had a chauffeur, he told her, "'No, I like to drive myself.'" On the subject of caring for himself, he said:

> I think people assume that money or success takes away the basic human element in people. I don't know what it does for other people, but it doesn't take away my human element. The things I liked to do when I was poor—and there were a lot of things I didn't like to do when I was poor—but the things I liked to do when I was poor, I still like to do.[58]

Grady, whose duties included sometimes being a driver for Johnson, died in 2016. But for the most part, Johnson drove himself to work. It wasn't unusual to see him in the morning, creeping up Michigan Avenue in his blue Cadillac with the silver running board underneath. He often told the editorial team about the days when he recalled the only automobile company that would sell to blacks was Cadillac. That's why so many black people had the automobiles and considered those to be the status of luxury.

Until the day he died, whenever he drove, it was his Cadillac with the license plate that read 268. Low number license plate numbers were a rarity and only given to the extremely wealthy in Chicago. The three digits were clear indicators of influence in Illinois. Considering Johnson's wealth, it was not alarming to learn in 1999, according to a Chicago Tribune article, "There were only 900 three-digit standard-issue plates for passenger cars in the state, and the vast majority of those were on Cadillacs, Lincolns, Jaguars, Mercedeses and similarly high-priced vehicles."[59]

It was an honor for Johnson to hear people whose opinion he respected tell him how he did not let wealth change him. Johnson shared the following:

> From the time I got past minor luxuries, like being able to eat and sleep and drive a good car without worrying about where the money was coming from, I haven't worked for money. Since then I have worked for the challenge of it, for the joy of accomplishing a goal I set out to accomplish. Some money, some material wealth, has come, but it is not something I sought.[60]

Johnson wanted his life to be a model for others to see that anything is possible with confidence and hard work. The same success stories that were showcased in his magazines could have pulled inspiration from the publisher, who knew the importance and value in African Americans seeing others who looked like him succeed against the odds. He said in a 1975 interview:

> When a young man comes to me today, I tell him he should be able to do better than when I started thirty-three years ago. I tell him to set small goals for himself and gain confidence. Start a grocery store, not a supermarket! He must get into something he's interested in. I can only urge him not to be hostile, or be against everything. That's what my mother told me many years ago, and that's what I've lived by.[61]

The businessman was grateful to be a Chicagoan and never had any regrets about residing in the Windy City. "Black people have done better in Chicago than anywhere else in the country," he said in 2000. "More than anywhere else, Chicago has been a mecca for black businesses...I have loved every moment of my life in Chicago. I think it is the best city in the world."[62]

Because of his concern for helping others who resided in low and moderate-income housing, he was one of the major investors in Chicago's Lawless Gardens apartment complex on the South Side. By 1989, he owned ninety-seven percent of the development.[63]

A difficult moment in the philanthropist's personal life came when his only son, John Jr., died at the age of twenty-five in 1981 after a long illness with complications stemming from sickle cell anemia. John Jr. made his transition at the University of Chicago's Wyler Memorial Hospital where his parents established a $30,000 annual hematology research fellowship in 1983 to support sickle cell anemia and related blood cell diseases. A former photographer whose images appeared in *EBONY* and in *JET*, John Jr. married at the age of eighteen and liked to do "dangerous things" such as racing cars, skydiving and skiing.[64] "I learned a lot about courage and patience from John," Johnson said in the eulogy he wrote to his son. "He loved life but knew he was destined not to have much of it. So he lived each day to the fullest."[65] After his son's death, Johnson committed himself to having more stories about adoptions and helping to raise awareness as well as working to find a cure for sickle cell anemia.

Johnson's economic power and influence with the African-American population made him a person that politicians wanted to get to know. Though some believed he was Republican, Johnson was considered an independent. However, he once said in 1995, "I don't think conservatism spells doom for black people. I'm still a Democrat, but on financial matters I'm a conservative Democrat. I want to conserve what I have and build on it."[66] Frequently he was a guest at presidential inaugurations, White House state dinners, and held several national service appointments.

He had spoken with every U.S. president from Dwight Eisenhower to Bill Clinton, a fellow Arkansas resident who was his dear friend. Former President Clinton presented him with the Presidential Medal of Freedom, the highest civilian honor of the United States, in 1996. When Johnson died in 2005, Clinton escorted Johnson's widow, Eunice W. Johnson, into the funeral and never left her side.

*EBONY* twice endorsed Adlai Stevenson in his bid against Eisenhower. Stevenson's roots in Illinois had something to do with Johnson's preference, and Johnson admitted to being "leery of a general in the White House," though his fear was unfounded.[67] When Richard Nixon was vice president, he took Johnson on a goodwill tour of nine African countries in 1957 and to the Soviet Union and Poland in 1959.[68] At least twice, however, he personally voted for Nixon while *EBONY* did not endorse him or anyone else. Johnson admitted to being concerned about the sincerity of Kennedy in 1960 and his stance on civil rights, so he backed Nixon in 1968 and in 1972, thinking "the Republican candidate would follow a productive, middle-of-the road course, maintaining and improving gains for the black population."[69]

He did have *EBONY* endorse Lyndon Baines Johnson against Barry Goldwater in 1964. Johnson cited, in a 1975 interview, that President Johnson was his favorite. "Lyndon Johnson impressed me with his sincerity on civil rights. He was easy to know and talk with. LBJ wanted to treat people equally. He sat up nights thinking of ways to do it."[70] When Johnson visited the president at the White House, they even took a picture of the president holding a copy of *JET*. Johnson said about that day:

> As a matter of fact, when I was at the White House with Lyndon Johnson and I agreed to everything he wanted me to agree to, he said, 'Well, let's pose with a picture of *JET*.' I said, 'Gee, Mr. President, I don't have one.' He went in his back pocket and pulled one out. He said, 'I happen to have one.' We took a picture with *JET*.[71]

At a White House stag dinner for President Johnson, Johnson recalled once being asked to offer him advice. He said he rose and said, "Mr. President, my mother's name is Johnson; my wife's name is Johnson. I have never had any success in giving advice to Johnsons, and I am not going to try to give any to you."[72]

FIGURE 6: Johnson talks with President Lyndon B. Johnson, who holds a copy of JET magazine, during a White House visit in 1964. Courtesy Johnson Publishing Company, LLC. All rights reserved.

President Johnson named him a Special Ambassador to head a delegation representing the United States at independence ceremonies of the Ivory Coast (Kenya) in 1963. Three years later President Johnson made him a member of the National Selective Service Commission.[73] Johnson said in 1985 that he believed President Johnson was the president who did the most for civil rights. "It was President Johnson, if we are talking about moving blacks ahead, of breaking new ground, of ensuring civil rights," he said. "Although I had great respect for President Kennedy and others, if I had to name one president, it would be Lyndon Johnson."[74]

In 1961, President Kennedy appointed Johnson to head a four-man delegation as special U.S. ambassador to the Independence Ceremonies of the Ivory Coast. Kennedy and Johnson even posed for a picture together, holding a copy of *EBONY* with Frederick Douglass on the September 1963 special issue cover.[75]

FIGURE 7: Johnson presents President John F. Kennedy with a special copy of *EBONY* in 1963 at the White House. Courtesy Johnson Publishing Company, LLC. All rights reserved.

When Chicago Mayor Richard J. Daley died in December 1976, it was in early January that affluent and powerful black Chicagoans felt the time was right for a black mayor. John Sengstacke, publisher of *The Chicago Defender,* along with the Rev. Jesse Jackson and 40 other businessmen and political figures gathered at the Johnson Publishing Company headquarters for a meeting hosted by Johnson. That dream of a black mayor would not become a reality until seven years later when Harold Washington would become mayor.[76] Johnson, it was later revealed, "quietly" contributed $63,000 to Washington's 1983 campaign and "was the largest single contributor."[77]

Oddly enough, no matter how Johnson seemed to have assimilated as a man of wealth, he was never really comfortable around white folks. "No matter how I try I just can't seem to relax with white people. Maybe it's Arkansas in my background but I guess I always have my guard up," Johnson confessed to Ben Burns, the white top-ranking, early executive at Johnson Publishing Company.[78]

He didn't like eating around white folks, especially fried chicken and watermelon. In 1949 when Johnson purchased a three-story building at 1820 S. Michigan Avenue, some said a dining room was built as a way to monitor employees in an effort to see if they would return from lunch to work in a timely manner, but the truth of the matter was that the dining room, during that time, was for him probably more than the employees. Johnson said, "I just don't feel comfortable eating with white people. I can't relax."[79]

FIGURE 8: Johnson and his wife, Eunice W. Johnson, greet Chicago Mayor Harold Washington during a celebration of the city's 150th anniversary. Washington, who became Chicago's first Black mayor, attended high school with Johnson. Courtesy Johnson Publishing Company, LLC. 

Johnson was not only concerned about stereotypes in his publications but he was especially concerned about living up to any preconceived notions of how black people stereotypically do things. This included what they ate. For instance, when Eleanor Roosevelt came to the company for a luncheon after the visit was arranged by editor Milton Smith, her choice of meal did not go over well with

Johnson.[80]

Guests were often given a pre-meal selection of filet mignon or fried chicken. Years later, a lobster tail was added to the menu. It seems that Mrs. Roosevelt loved fried chicken and this is what she requested. Since *EBONY*'s food editor at the time, Freda DeKnight, was celebrated for her famous fried chicken, this seemed like a winning combination. But it wasn't. Not for Johnson anyway. "Fried chicken! No way!" Johnson said upon being told of her desired menu preference. "No, we just can't do that," he added. Smith then said to Johnson, "But I was told she's really partial to good fried chicken and Freda makes the best. Why not serve her what she likes?" Johnson insisted that she would not eat fried chicken at his company and she didn't. Instead she was served steak.[81]

Forever cautious about how he was perceived, there were many instances where he was forced to swallow his pride and do things he rather not had. A shrewd African-American businessman during the 1940s, he knew that getting ahead often meant using someone from another race to do so. When it came to advancing his goals, Johnson let nothing stand in his way, not even his pride.

This was demonstrated in 1955 when he wanted to expand office space by purchasing an old funeral home, Hursen, at 1820 S. Michigan Avenue. The owner refused to sell to "colored" buyers and even refused to take $60,000 for the property from blacks.[82] Johnson said, "I could have reported it to the NAACP. I could have marched around the building. I could have reported it in the magazine. But I wanted the building."[83] He explained, "I had a choice of protesting, getting violent, or persuading a white friend to buy it for me. I chose the last alternative and it was very simple."[84]

*EBONY*'s white founding editor, Burns, revealed in his memoir how he and Irwin J. Stein, a white advertising manager at Johnson Publishing Company, were called upon by Johnson to take part in the purchase of the building as well. Johnson described Stein as "one of the most honorable men" he'd known and hired Stein, noted for his management skills, with the understanding that he would "train a black to take his place" once he educated the person about the white advertising world. Johnson, according to Burns, tagged along with the men, pretending to be a building maintenance person there to check the heating and air conditioning.[85] Burns said this about the moment in his 1996 memoir *Nitty Gritty: A White Editor in Black Journalism*:

> Our white advertising manager, Irwin Stein, and I became bit players in Johnson's maneuvering; we rather than Johnson himself became the prospective buyers, supposedly representing a white publishing syndicate that wanted to keep its planned expansion hush hush. The Hursen people were informed that Stein and I wished to have our building maintenance worker inspect the heating and air conditioning system, and Johnson dressed for the occasion. Despite higher bids from Negro would-be buyers, Johnson's rock-bottom offer of $52,000 was finally accepted because he was presumed to be the 'white buyer.'[86]

Johnson recounted the story of the purchase by saying:

> My white friend told the owners that he represented a large Eastern firm, and that he was sending their Negro maintenance man over there to take a look at it. I became the Negro maintenance man. I put on old clothes, took a flashlight with me and told the owners that my boss sent me over. I looked that building over from top to bottom and decided it would be fine. My white friend bought it for me and we moved in. We had little trouble after that.[87]

The three-story structure was sold with Johnson's white attorney, Louis Wilson, closing the deal.[88] To Burns, Johnson was perceived as less than honest. As a white man Burns did not understand why Johnson resorted to some of the tactics that he did in order to obtain certain things. As a black man, Johnson resorted to creative strategies to find ways to have things that were denied to him simply because of his race. Johnson was not a con artist; he was surviving and getting ahead by any means necessary. "I felt good," said Johnson. "I knew I had bought the building. If I had to do it over again, I would. I stooped all the time to get what I wanted."[89] He said in 1974, "I have often been angry about racism, but never bitter. Bitterness is not helpful for solving problems. I find ways around racism."[90]

Johnson said in 1985, when he amassed a business empire that included, at that time, Fashion Fair cosmetics, three radio stations, three magazines, a book publishing company and a TV production company, that he did not have any unfulfilled desires "I don't know any other job in the world I would rather have than the one I have

now. My only ambition is to keep it. I don't think there are any more mountains I want to climb—I just want to stay on top of the one I'm on."[91]

# CHAPTER 3

## MESSAGE IN THE MOVEMENT

***"When I see a barrier, I cry and I curse, and then I get a ladder and climb over it." John H. Johnson***

Johnson never stopped dreaming. Even when his dreams appeared to be coming true, he always wanted more not only for himself but especially for his race. Stumbling blocks were nothing new to him, but November was considered his "signature" month, because it was "magic" in "tribute to the god of November."[1] This is why he founded most of his publications, including *EBONY* and *JET* magazines, during this month.

On November 2, 1987, it was no different. Luck, along with his preparation, summoned his name once again. That year he was the only African-American inducted into the prestigious Publishing Hall of Fame. The great-grandson of slaves ended his speech by telling the audience how dreams unite us all: "For it is the most enduring element of our faith that men and women are limited not by the place of their birth, not by the color of their skin, but by the size of their hope."[2]

Born during the last year of World War I, which started the Great (black) Migration to the North, America was segregated and restricted when Johnson entered this world.[3] Due to sociocultural racism, European Americans' views were valued and voiced at the sociopolitical and historical expense of African Americans. This marginalization contributed to millions of African Americans, between 1910 and 1970, leaving mostly rural areas in the South and traveling to industrial cities in the North and Midwest.

Johnson's family was no different because his mother moved her son to Chicago so he could receive a high school education. Chicago was a great attraction for African Americans, who were provided with more opportunities—education being one. The Windy City's appeal was described like this:

> Cities like Chicago…contained established African-American communities dating from the years before the Civil War. These communities also suffered from racial discrimination, with blacks limited in where they could live, shop, and work. Nevertheless, compared with their counterparts in the South, black Chicagoans enjoyed better schools, greater access to other public facilities and leisure activities, voting rights, and the ability to live from day to day without suffering the indignities of Jim Crow.[4]

Growing up in Arkansas City, Arkansas, Johnson said there were no newspapers or radios in the area in which he lived. Though, one of the first publications he recalled seeing in Arkansas was the African-American newspaper that inspired him in so many ways—*The Chicago Defender*. During the Great Migration, many African Americans were educated and informed about job opportunities in Chicago after discovering the pioneering newspaper. Through his discovery of *The Chicago Defender*, Johnson realized there was a world beyond Arkansas City because while reading it, he was able to see the world had more to offer, although his world only showed the restrictions of African Americans because of racial group membership.

*The Chicago Defender* was important for Johnson because for the first time, he saw a newspaper about his people, which served to be "reflective of the sociocultural realities and life experiences that are indigenous to that group."[5] This awareness would later inform his educational philosophy, which examined agency and the significance of people doing for self as well as helping those who looked like them.

The 1930s and 1940s were turbulent times for race relations in America. Blacks were not treated equally and endured Jim Crow laws enacted between 1876 and 1965. There was an absence of positive, informative news about black people. Johnson observed this. He saw how blacks struggled for simple courtesies from others, such as the right to be addressed in a respectable manner and not be called "boy," "girl," or "nigger." Racial tensions were high and so was the desire to keep the black man "in his place" by denying him basic rights and opportunities to advance himself for the better and to excel in a country where systemic racism is embedded in its very fabric.

"It was in this world that *Negro Digest* was conceived," Johnson once said about his first magazine. "It was a world where the primary need, almost as demanding as oxygen, was recognition and respect."[6] During this time, people of color were commonly referred to as "Negro," so when Johnson decided to start the magazine, the titled reflected this. *Negro Digest*, noted as "a magazine of Negro comment," was born November 1942. The 7 ½″ by 5″ magazine featured news and journal articles.[7] He said the idea to start the monthly condensation of Negro-oriented articles in magazines and newspapers would "increase [Negroes] respect and add to their knowledge and understanding."[8] This would be the first magazine of its kind, a commercial magazine solely for African Americans.

Johnson was a business man first and foremost. He saw a void and filled it after observing how black newspapers were "primarily concerned for the rights of all people, particularly black people," but that "no one was dealing with black people as individuals."[9]

Training to become an astute businessman came through early mentoring while working with Harry H. Pace, the prominent attorney who was the founder of the Chicago-based Supreme Liberty Life Insurance Company and who had offered Johnson a job upon his graduation from high school. The work Johnson did at Supreme would change his life—especially after Pace requested that Johnson complete another task for him, compiling articles about black news.

In addition to being a prominent attorney and business owner whose company was the product of a $27 million merger of three Black companies, Pace was also a magazine publisher.[10] With W.E.B. DuBois, Pace first published, in December 1905, *The Moon Illustrated Weekly*. DuBois described it as "a new race consciousness to the world and [to reveal] the inner meaning of the modern world to the merging races."[11] A weekly, it focused on people, places and events that interested African Americans in the United States, but it also included articles about South Africa, Liberia and Barbados. It only lasted a year.[12]

Pace was a very fair-skinned man who completely identified with blacks though his identify was often questioned. He was mistaken for being white and the time came when he quietly distanced himself from his race. Pace's son and daughter attended the University of Wisconsin, fell in love and had serious romantic relationships with whites. When it was time to get married, Pace knew that the in-laws of his children would not welcome the thought of meeting blacks, so Pace opened a law firm in downtown Chicago. He also moved from the predominantly south side to River Forest, which was predominantly white in the 1930s.[13]

For fear of having anyone know the truth about his identity as a black man, Pace would not take any black newspapers home with him. This turned out to be a blessing in disguise for Johnson, who was charged by Pace with giving him a digest of what was happening weekly in the black community so that Pace could speak intelligently with those coming in and out of his office. Johnson explained:

> It was this problem that transformed my life. For, from my perspective, God, history, fate, life—choose a word—was challenging me, testing me, offering me prizes beyond my wildest imagination when I was faced with a crossroads problem that couldn't be solved by a traditional means.[14]

Pace allowed Johnson to subscribe to any newspapers so that he could be well informed and pass along the knowledge to him. This turned out to be a winning situation for them both because it combined their love of business with journalism. Johnson said:

> For me, as well as for Pace, journalism was a skyscraper value precisely because it combined the ultimate business challenge with the ultimate social challenge. A magazine—and we were both interested in magazines—could not survive if it wasn't based on sound business principles. But sound business principles alone would not ensure its survival. That was the dilemma and nobody in black America had solved it.[15]

After compiling news and information about blacks for Pace on a daily basis and receiving constant feedback at social gatherings about the importance and value in the articles Johnson selected, Johnson thought to do his own publication. The only problem was that not many considered it to be a good idea. Pace, on the other hand, shared Johnson's sentiment and also believed Johnson was moving in the right direction. Timing was also important and things seemed to line up.

Ben Burns, a white editor at *The Chicago Defender*, first met Johnson in Earl B. Dickerson's second floor office at South Parkway and 35th Street, the headquarters of Supreme Liberty Life Insurance Company, when Burns and Johnson were doing political campaign work; Dickerson was legal counsel at Supreme. Johnson worked as an aide to Dickerson, then an alderman. According to Burns, during his and Johnson's campaigning for congressional candidates Dickerson and William L. Dawson in the summer of 1942, Johnson approached Burns about starting a new Negro magazine since he had editing experience.[16]

Deciding to start his own magazine wasn't something Johnson admitted to deciding upon immediately. He said that while going out to social events and sharing stories about what he learned, that's when he said it occurred to him "that I was looking at a black gold mine."[17]

Johnson, who was four years younger than Burns, had the goal of making money while Burns was hardworking and ready to roll up his sleeves. It seemed like a perfect fit. Born on Chicago's Jewish West Side, the man born Benjamin Bernstein was a journalism student at New York University when he joined the Communist Party.[18] Burns, who spent hours reading books and articles about black Chicago, was ever grateful that Communists, through a prominent leader and black man named William L. Patterson, provided Burns with his initial introduction to the black press.[19] Burns worked with Patterson when Patterson was co-editor of Chicago's *Midwest Daily Record*, sponsored by the Communist Party.[20]

One major problem in which Johnson was fully aware was that black magazines had a history of failure due to lack of financing. *The National Reformer*, a monthly, appeared in 1838. It was owned by the American Moral Reform Society of Philadelphia and an anti-slave agitator and leader was the editor. The organization was interracial but because of the black editor, it was considered Negro though more whites than blacks read it. Another publication, *Free Northern Negroes*, was an editorial magazine founded in 1833.[21]

David Ruggles, an abolitionist who helped more than 600 slaves to freedom in the North, including Frederick Douglass, published the first African-American magazine, a quarterly, in 1838. Ruggles owned and edited the New York journal titled *Mirror of Liberty*.[22] Frederick Douglass failed as publisher with the magazine *Douglass' Monthly*, successor of his *North Star*. It only survived five years and ended in 1863 due to delinquent subscribers.[23] A publication called *Negro Word Digest* was founded in New York City in 1940 but it went out of business. *Racial Digest* was published in Detroit in 1942.

"When I learned that another *Negro Digest*, with exactly the same title as the sanguine Johnsons', had died after several issues, I began to believe that Johnson was pursuing an idle dream, and I conveyed my pessimism to him," said Burns, who referred to Johnson's dream of starting a successful black publication as a "scheme" because Burns was skeptical and could not dream the impossible dream like Johnson for his race.[24]

Another early magazine that did not fare well was published in Philadelphia in 1906 by Thomas Swann and was even called *EBONY*.[25] Johnson took imitation and turned it into innovation, crafting models of African-American publications that, like himself, succeeded against the odds.

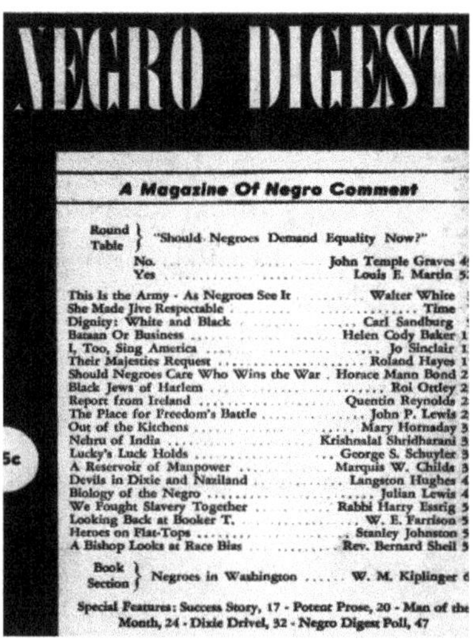

NEGRO DIGEST

A Magazine Of Negro Comment

5c

Round Table } "Should Negroes Demand Equality Now?"

| | |
|---|---|
| No. | John Temple Graves |
| Yes | Louis E. Martin |
| This Is the Army - As Negroes See It | Walter White |
| She Made Jive Respectable | Time |
| Dignity: White and Black | Carl Sandburg |
| Bataan Or Business | Helen Cody Baker |
| I, Too, Sing America | Jo Sinclair |
| Their Majesties Request | Roland Hayes |
| Should Negroes Care Who Wins the War | Horace Mann Bond |
| Black Jews of Harlem | Roi Ottley |
| Report from Ireland | Quentin Reynolds |
| The Place for Freedom's Battle | John P. Lewis |
| Out of the Kitchens | Mary Hornaday |
| Nehru of India | Krishnalal Shridharani |
| Lucky's Luck Holds | George S. Schuyler |
| A Reservoir of Manpower | Marquis W. Childs |
| Devils in Dixie and Naziland | Langston Hughes |
| Biology of the Negro | Julian Lewis |
| We Fought Slavery Together | Rabbi Harry Essrig |
| Looking Back at Booker T. | W. E. Farrison |
| Heroes on Flat-Tops | Stanley Johnston |
| A Bishop Looks at Race Bias | Rev. Bernard Sheil |

Book Section } Negroes in Washington ...... W. M. Kiplinger

Special Features: Success Story, 17 - Potent Prose, 20 - Man of the Month, 24 - Dixie Drivel, 32 - Negro Digest Poll, 47

FIGURE 9: The first issue of Negro Digest in 1942. Courtesy Johnson Publishing Company, LLC. 

Johnson modeled his 1942 scholarly journal *Negro Digest* after the white mainstream publication *Reader's Digest*. The name's inspiration, like so many other things by Johnson, was a nod to a publication already in existence. Articles in that first issue of *Negro Digest* were written by Langston Hughes, Charles Himes, Gwendolyn Brooks,

Richard Wright and Zora Neale Hurston. Johnson made it no secret how he took magazine blueprints from others and created his own. Negro Digest was the same size as *Reader's Digest.*[26] *EBONY* was an offshoot of *Life*. *JET* was an offshoot of *Quick*, a pocket-sized news weekly first published by Cowles Magazines Inc. in 1949 and ended in 1953.[27] "An editor must begin with that which has already been established and make modifications to obtain the type of publication he desires," Johnson said during a private interview with Dorothy Deloris Brown on August 25, 1969, in Chicago.[28]

Money, Johnson understood, would be his stumbling block toward starting a publication, especially one geared toward people of color. It also didn't help that every magazine prior to that time failed. "The problem here was not my density but a general climate of doubt surrounding black publications. Most people had seen *Reader's Digest* and *Time*, but nobody had seen a successful black commercial magazine. And nobody was willing to risk a penny on a 24-year-old insurance worker and what people told him at cocktail parties."[29]

*Abbott's Monthly* was published by the *Chicago Defender* in October 1929. It failed due to the stock market crash and Great Depression.[30] With the examples of failed publications surrounding him, Johnson knew he didn't have the capital to proceed and no one was willing to invest in an African-American man's idea, as this was the time when Jim Crow ruled the North and South with segregation. A venture like this was difficult to finance, because even African Americans who had the money were reluctant to offer assistance.

Looking for the financial backing, Johnson asked art editor/cartoonist Jay Jackson and Burns to invest in his company with "$1,000 each and split the profits three ways."[31]Burns recalled not even having $500 to buy into the partnership. "I refused, however, in the belief that *Negro Digest* would not succeed with a couple of novices at its helm and for lack of five hundred dollars in my threadbare bank account," he said.[32]

Pace, the president of Supreme Liberty Life Insurance, was among the many businessmen who were hesitant to stand behind him and invest in a publication. With no investors, Johnson relied upon the inner determination that helped him pull through tough times as a kid with his family in Arkansas.

Burns thought Johnson was being unrealistic. Like ebony and ivory, the two were always a study in contrast. Past evidence had proven that black magazines could not do well due to lack of finances and here Johnson was wanting to start one anyway. Burns said he once asked Johnson, "How are you going to sell a quarter magazine when the Negro papers are just getting through by the skin of their teeth on a dime?" Johnson told him, "You know there's a war on. Big things are in the air and we can get in on them if we make the right moves. The magazine can't miss." Burns later admitted that "he was right and I was wrong."[33]

Having no place left to turn, Johnson shared the story of how he knew his mother had just bought new furniture. He asked her to assist him. And, after much prayer and deliberation, she agreed to allow him to use her furniture for collateral so he could get a $500 loan from a finance company.[34] Johnson didn't have the burden of paying for office space. Attorney Earl B. Dickerson, dubbed the Dean of Chicago's black lawyers during this time, had a law office he never used in the Supreme building since his main office was downtown.[35] Johnson was allowed to use the space. And, needless to say, despite the naysayers, *Negro Digest* was an immediate success.

Johnson's hiring Burns as the first editor shed light on an interesting perspective of Johnson as a person. For as much as he claimed to have distrusted white people because of the racism he grew up seeing in Arkansas, the fact that he had a white man help him start pioneering publications for blacks showed how he secretly subscribed to the notion that maybe white folks are more competent. Johnson would often say in editorial meetings, "Some people think the white man's ice is colder." Perhaps he would have known best, for Johnson was willing to take a chance with a Jewish man, a known Communist, to help him start his first publication during 1942. Johnson picking Burns also demonstrated yet another shrewd business move on his part by employing someone with experience in editing and understanding black publications. Then Burns would go on to become founding editor for *EBONY* and *JET*, both magazines noted as cornerstones in black America.

This was during the time of the Red Scare, a promotion of fear of a potential rise of communism or radical leftism.[36] Some might argue self-loathing on Johnson's part as a black man with southern roots and even the notion that white folks have a greater intellect would explain Johnson's bold decision to ask Burns to partner with him. Why did he not ask a black person to start the publication with him? During this time, most black writers worked at *The Chicago Defender*. There weren't any editors who looked like him in Chicago during the 1940s.

For Johnson, it seemed that everything was about convenience and utilizing what was within reach and closest at hand. On one end while he did not fully trust white people, it was interesting that he trusted Burns, a white man, enough to allow him to help start what would go on to become pioneering magazines in black history. At this point and time, Burns was that person because of Burns' connection with Pace, one of Johnson's trusted mentors.

Johnson also had somewhat of a connection with Burns in that Johnson did briefly attended Northwestern University where Burns earned a master's degree in journalism. After graduating from the Medill School of Journalism at Northwestern, Burns worked his way up to the copy desk of the *Daily Worker*, the oldest and best-known Communist newspaper. Then, for a short period, he worked at the first and only Communist daily in Chicago, the *Midwest Daily Record*.[37] Burns said in his memoir:

> From the first day we met in Dickerson's office, Johnson had known full well of my Communist background, having been privy to Dickerson's frequent strategy sessions with William L. Patterson, my party sponsor. But he never questioned my leftist politics when we commenced working together on *Negro Digest*. Despite my Communist affiliation, he needed me at that particular time for what I could bring to his young venture.[38]

By the mid-1930s there was much unemployment with many people having to resort to welfare, including Johnson and his mom. They received aide from 1934 to 1936.[39] During this time he noted that for people residing on the South Side of Chicago, the "only people preaching hope were the communists and the followers of Father Divine." Johnson said some of his friends became members of the Communist Party. "I shunned the party because it wanted to destroy the system. I didn't want to destroy the system. I wanted to join it so I could change it and make it more responsive to poor people and blacks."[40]

Burns' tenure at two Communist daily papers included work with renowned writer Richard Wright, covering racial news and issues. At the *Midwest Daily Record*, the only Negro on staff was Patterson, who with his experience of living in Moscow, became their political "commissar" in interpreting political right and wrong.[41]

In his off-hours at *The Chicago Defender*, Burns helped Johnson. The November 1942 issue of *Negro Digest* "appeared, based on templates Burns borrowed from *The Chicago Defender* and containing reprinted articles written by Carl Sandburg, Walter White and Langston Hughes, among others."[42]

In the summer of 1942, Burns was hired as a fill-in editor at *The Chicago Defender* and simultaneously worked there while doing part-time work to help start *Negro Digest.* Burns started as managing editor and two years later was promoted to executive editor. Burns' name was not first printed anywhere in *Negro Digest* until the June 1944 issue where there was information about his race relations and his experiences as a merchant marine.[43] The staff was small; Johnson and his secretary were the only full-time employees at the time. In addition to finally adding Burns' name on the masthead as associate editor, Johnson included E.M. Walker, initials indicating his wife, and G.J. Williams, initials indicating his mother.[44]

Johnson's name was added as publisher on the masthead of *Negro Digest* after a year. And when the company published a one hundred twelve-page book called *The Best of Negro Humor in 1945*, it was credited with both Burns and Johnson's names. Langston Hughes provided the introduction for the book, which included some of Hughes' "simple stories" along with a collection of stories "published in the first years of *Negro Digest*," ranging from politics to the military.[45]

Not surprisingly Johnson had concerns about his readers knowing Burns' race. Burns said Johnson was "fearful that self-demeaning Negroes, seeing a well-crafted product and lacking faith in their own talents, would be apt to mutter disparagingly 'Must be some ofay behind it.'"[46] When the company moved into a new building in 1949 and in the past, Burns was given an office "relegated to a spot not readily seen by outside visitors."[47]

Some often believed that Burns gave himself too much credit in the history of Johnson Publishing Company. It wasn't for Burns to decide. The fact remained that he was the founding editor and only white editor to ever helm *Negro Digest*, *EBONY* and *JET* magazines. He also made history as the only white editor-in-chief of the leading black newspaper, *The Chicago Defender*.[48]

Johnson recognized early on that those who knew about Burns often feared that he would try to take Johnson's company from him. He felt insulted that people had "a lack of confidence in black entrepreneurial skill and a lack of information on the steel inside John H. Johnson."[49] Johnson was also concerned about people believing something so absurd when he had complete ownership. "For how could any White person 'take' the company from me if I owned all the stock and if he or she didn't work with or near the money?"[50]

Starting *Negro Digest* required quite a bit of elbow grease. Johnson thought of the idea of advance subscriptions, offering charter subscriptions at a rate of $2. This was a $1 off the regular subscription rate. Some 3,000 subscribers had an early interest. "I've never been able to do it again. But the letter I wrote was most unusual," he said. "Blacks who could hardly read had *Esquire* magazine on their tables. They were buying encyclopedias to impress their friends. The letter I wrote said, 'A friend of yours told me about you. You try to keep abreast of Negro issues and developments.'"[51]

Burns recalled that the letters were "patriotism mixed with commercialism in the appeal." There was a request for subscriptions to be sent to black GIs by relatives back home. Johnson and his wife, Eunice, mimeographed the initial mailing of some twenty thousand letters to potential subscribers.[52] *Negro Digest* made its debut in November 1942, at a time when there "were no generally circulated Negro magazines."[53]

Money was often a central concern so Johnson found innovative ways to get the job done in an effort to advance his business. The shrewd Johnson initially had *Negro Digest* printed by Progress Printing Company with them believing it was part of a job from the insurance company. Johnson said, "When I went to the printer's office and told him that 'we' were thinking about publishing a magazine, he assumed that I was talking about myself. Since he assumed that the magazine was either owned or backed by the insurance company, he started working without worrying about how I was going to pay him."[54]

But when the composing room supervisor realized the work was for something other than the insurance company, Johnson had to come clean. According to Burns, "Johnson confessed his trickery and then, by guile and persuasion, convinced Gabby [the nickname of the printer] that since he had already set most of the *Negro Digest* copy, he might as well finish the job. He swore that he would somehow manage to pay the printing costs."[55]

Historically, as previously mentioned, it has been well documented that Johnson received the $500 to start *Negro Digest* by borrowing against his mother's new furniture. There's nothing wrong with controlling one's narrative and Johnson certainly was a man in control of his destiny and how his story was written. In Burns' 1996 memoir, he challenged the narrative. Burns revealed: "Johnson raised some cash by borrowing policyholder lists from the insurance company, where he still worked, and soliciting charter subscriptions at two dollars a year, even while *Negro Digest* was as yet a figment of his imaginations. He later said he paid for that mailing with five hundred dollars borrowed on his mother's furniture."[56]

No matter how he got his start, Johnson did what he felt was necessary to achieve his goal. After all, what made him a good publisher was that he was a great businessman. Johnson believed that he made the right decision so that his first publication would be a success. While *Negro Digest* immediately drew comparisons with the mainstream *Reader's Digest*, the scope was distinctly different. "*Reader's Digest* tended to be upbeat, but *Negro Digest* spoke to an audience that was angry, disillusioned, and disappointed. You couldn't digest that world without digesting the frustration and anger," he said.[57]

Magazines of protest were popular. Some included *The Messenger* (1917-29), *The Crusader, The Emancipator.* W.E.B. DuBois' Crisis was the first to attain a circulation of more than 100,000 in 1910 for the National Association for the Advancement of Colored People (NAACP); however, DuBois resigned as editor and from the NAACP and the publication's circulation dropped from 9,500 in 1919 to 8,000 in 1934.[58] *The Opportunity* was founded in 1923 by the Urban League. These were journals that stayed afloat in the early 1940s due to membership dues and not subscriptions.

*Negro Digest*'s approach was different in that it was a compilation of articles from scholarly magazines and newspapers from the black and white press. This publication would simply reprint articles from both black and white media, because Johnson's goal was to escape the radical label that most black publications were known for during this time. Johnson wanted *Negro Digest* "to set a moderate tone, which remained the mark of his publishing ventures for years to come."[59] Johnson served as the managing editor where his name was the only on the masthead. Burns once more disputed this fact in his 1996 memoir, stating, "Although Johnson had no role in editing *Negro Digest*, in spite of his title of managing editor, in later years he embellished his personal success story by claiming to have edited the *Digest*." Burns challenges that he "single-handedly put the magazine together."[60]

Johnson paid Burns, his first employee, $25. Burns claims to have "did all the editorial work and makeup on the first issue at home," at his kitchen table.[61] For whatever reason, his name did not appear in the masthead of *Negro Digest* until August 1944, where he was listed as associate editor.[62] After a year of publication, Johnson eventually changed his own title from managing editor to publisher.[63] The first issue, though 5,000 copies were initially printed, sold out. An additional 5,000 were printed and they did the same. Within a year, *Negro Digest* was selling 50,000 copies a month.[64]

African Americans responded favorably to the publication, because they were able to read intelligent stories, from a range of topics, about themselves. Johnson saw a need and he met it; supply and demand are the basic principles of any decent businessman and that was the DNA of Johnson. Early contributors of the section called *If I Were a Negro* included stories by businessman Marshall Field and actor Orson Welles, both paid only fifteen dollars for their contributions. By July 1943, less than a year after its start, it was proclaimed "the biggest Negro magazine in the world, barring none"[65]

Of the magazine's popularity, Johnson explained it this way. People were "hungry for information about themselves."[66] Readers were proud to have something where they could read others' work and contribute if they so chose. "We dealt with any books that would come out about Blacks, any governmental reports that would show us in any kind of favorable light. So in general, I think it met a need that was not being met and I was rewarded in having a great many people buying it and it became an overnight success."[67]

The interesting thing about Johnson was that he stepped into the unknown. He conceived of what was possible. People he greatly admired did not believe that the magazine would be a success because history had proven that black publications didn't have the financial means to stay afloat. Burns said this about Johnson's resilience and determination:

> He remained undaunted by discouraging predictions of his downfall, including a warning from NAACP executive and *Crisis* editor Roy Wilkins that 'you'll never make it.' In his ambition to make *Negro Digest* a viable business, he was driven by his youthful indigence and privation as I was by my striving to find a better life. He never slowed in his pursuit of wealth even when after twenty years in business, he finally attained it.[68]

Johnson discussed how he sought advice from Wilkins and did not leave with the type of backing and encouragement he hoped for. Johnson said in 1985:

> I remember spending some of my last money to go to New York to talk to Roy Wilkins, who was then editor of the NAACP magazine, the *Crisis,* which was really the only viable black monthly magazine, although it was not commercial. And Roy said, 'Save your money, young man. Save your energy. Save yourself a lot of disappointment.' And I guess one of the great moments of my life was when Roy called me and said, 'You know, I think I gave you some bad advice.'[69]

Getting money to start *Negro Digest* was just one adversity Johnson encountered; he also had trouble getting a distributor to supply the magazines to newsstands and stores. "The first thing the distributor said was 'we can't distribute any colored books.' I said, 'If you knew the colored magazines would sell, would you distribute them?' The distributor said, 'Why sure.'"[70] Johnson, always finding a way to be clever, had 20 people from the insurance company go to south side newspaper stands and request *Negro Digest.* Since the newsstand owners did not have the magazine, they had to call the distributor to request it. But potential customers asking for the magazines wasn't enough. Johnson went the extra mile and made sure the distributor knew the magazines could sell. The young entrepreneur took money from the bank and gave it to his friends, who went to newsstands buying all the magazines. "We made sure we never went to the same dealer. The only way to create demand was to buy," he said.[71] Newsstand owners asked Johnson for more magazines, which he provided by supplying them with the ones that his friends bought. In a year's time circulation increased to 50,000.[72]

During a time when so many others tried and failed in any attempts to start black publications, Johnson made it work. How did he succeed against the odds? His explanation was uncomplicated. He reasoned it this way:

> First, I think the timing was right. Secondly, I think the market was ready. Thirdly, I think I was able to learn from their mistakes. I recognized that if you are going to travel a long distance, you can't burden yourself with a heavy load. So I had low overhead. I went in for the long haul, and I went in with a determination that nothing and nobody would get in the way.[73]

Johnson was a man of his word and had laser focus. Negative thoughts were cancerous to him. Noted for his saying, "failure is not an option," Johnson started using this phrase, which demonstrated the power of tenacity instilled in him by his mother, when he encountered a negative employee. "The first person I dismissed from the company was a person who told me that I couldn't make it. And I said, 'I'm too insecure about myself to have somebody around me telling me I can't do it.' And so, even today, I think that to believe in something, to have the commitment, is really more important than the money. If you have enough belief and enough commitment, you'll find the money somewhere."[74]

Quickly proving the naysayers wrong when he started *Negro Digest*, Johnson was ready to start a second publication, a picture magazine named *EBONY*. *Negro Digest* was doing so well that he was grossing $24,000 monthly on 100,000 copies. He took money and invested it in his next magazine.[75] He didn't waste time with his plan for his second effort. "We had already made a success of our first magazine, *Negro Digest*, and with the war over, and the boys coming home, I judged it was time for another magazine. The returning servicemen were looking around, trying to see what their opportunities would be and what their life would be like."[76]

The difficulty he encountered while trying to start *Negro Digest* did not deter him from wanting a picture magazine that mirrored *Life* magazine. He was also aware of competition from other publications like the magazine *Our World*, which was published from 1946 to 1955. "*EBONY* wasn't the only Negro magazine in the early days. There were many which failed. My big competition was *Our World*, which had a lot of white money behind it and a smart black lawyer as publisher."[77]

As a businessman first and foremost, Johnson realized that anywhere there was a need, marked an opportunity for him to fulfill it. He wasn't looking to start a magazine that would stir up or ignite anger with blacks but one that would motivate them. Johnson used agency to advance his purpose and uplift his race. "The surveys showed that *Life* magazine was a favorite with Negroes, as we were called then, and I decided to use the *Life* format for my new magazine. *EBONY* became a great success, but what I am most pleased with is that *EBONY* helped make black people proud to be black."[78]

With his energy used to propel *EBONY*, Johnson made the decision for *Negro Digest* to end in 1951 with the birth of his third publication, a newsweekly called *JET*. However, *Negro Digest* re-appeared in 1961. The second time around it was devised as a publication for young black militants, who were concerned with social, political and literary matters. *Negro Digest* was described by *Time* magazine as "a strenuous voice of black power. Writing that is roughly eloquent mingles with writing that is just plain rough."[79]

During a 1998 speech in Chicago where Johnson addressed six hundred Harvard Business school grads about surviving success, at the Harvard Business School Global Alumni Conference, he spoke about the power of the pen, especially when it came to doing business. *Negro Digest* had a story called "If I Were A Negro," in the same section Welles and Field had written for in one of the first issues. Since Eleanor Roosevelt, wife of Franklin Delano Roosevelt, was often criticized for her activities with blacks, Johnson reached out to have her write for a section called "Freedom: Promise or Fact," where prominent white people shared their thoughts about if they were black. [80]

It was Roosevelt's participation that was a turning point in Johnson's career. He recalled how blacks were told to wait on equality until after the war ended, but Johnson wanted to know if his prominent white subjects were black, would they feel the same way? Would they want to wait on equality if they were a negro? Roosevelt's agreeing to do the article was a pivotal point in his career for *Negro Digest*, which sold for twenty-five cents and earned him sixteen cents.[81] He said at the Harvard Business School Global Alumni Conference:

> I never heard the word entrepreneurship when I was getting into business, but I always believed in never give up and never take no. I wrote to people like Eleanor Roosevelt and asked them to do an essay titled, 'If I Were A Negro.' Twice Roosevelt had her secretary write me back that she was too busy. Then I wrote one more letter and said I'd wait until she wasn't too busy. Her secretary prevailed and Mrs. Roosevelt wrote a piece that started, 'If I were a Negro I would have great bitterness. But I would also have great patience.' Papers sort of missed the bitterness and, especially in the South, only played up the patience part. But circulation doubled to 100,000. Now what if I'd stopped with two letters?[82]

Roosevelt wrote the October 1943 cover story, "If I Were A Negro: First Lady Sees Negro Struggle Part of World Battle of Beliefs." Newspapers in the North picked up on how she said she would have great "bitterness" if she were a negro while newspapers in the South picked up on her adding how she would have "great patience." What Johnson himself learned from being patient is that first of all, you don't need to be introduced to people. Have enough confidence in yourself to go directly to the source. "I don't do referrals" was his motto. He said he "read between the lines" and Roosevelt never said she couldn't do the story. She was just "busy" when he made initial attempts to contact her to do the story. Johnson remained patient and when Roosevelt spoke at a hotel in Chicago, that was his chance to make another attempt to reach her. Johnson sent her a telegraph. Patience and persistence paid off for him.[83]

Ironically, Roosevelt would later become the first First Lady to get inducted into the Alpha Kappa Alpha Sorority, the first Greek-lettered sorority established and incorporated by African-American college women in 1908.[84] Johnson was a member of Alpha Phi Alpha Fraternity, the first intercollegiate Greek-letter fraternity established for African-American men in 1906, which is the brother organization for that sorority.[85] During a 1944 visit to the White House where the sorority was recognized for its human rights strides, the bond between the sorority and former first lady was made. This is when she accepted honorary membership.[86]

Three years after founding *Negro Digest*, it nearly ended because of the government's paper control during World War II. It seemed as if

Johnson had violated Regulation L-244 by exceeding his 7.43 tons per quarter usage.[87] Since the government controlled paper, in order for a person to have even gotten it for his magazine, he had to have signed something stating that he understood Order L-244. He was "ordered to cease and desist publishing," but to do so would mean the end for *Negro Digest*.[88] The real problem came because Johnson signed the Order, which stated he read and understood the rule. He recalled, "The bureaucrat who signed the letter came down hard on the Catch-22 provision. He wanted to know how I obtained additional tons of paper. He used the ugly word 'collusion' and hinted at penalties or worse for willful violation of the code and—this was the stinger—impeding the war effort."[89]

Further problems ensued as no attorney would represent a "Negro" during this time so Johnson relied upon his high school oratory skills and astute business knowledge to plead his case in a court of law by representing himself.[90] Johnson's strength and resilience allowed him to forge ahead for more than just his magazine but for the advancement of his race's history in the media. He once recounted:

> I spoke from my heart. I told the five members of the board present how hard I'd worked to start my magazines and how much it meant to me personally and to black people in general. I told them I needed a production of 100,000 copies to keep my organization intact and to permit me to discharge my debts until the inevitable victory of our brave soldiers permitted the lifting of paper restrictions.[91]

Johnson delivered a passionate plea to save *Negro Digest*, because he knew that the magazines were a way of liberating his race from sociocultural and intellectual racism through an informal way of learning. He was not only concerned about his magazine possibly having to end, but he was also concerned about explaining the reason should that have been a reality. He said:

> I wouldn't be able to go around and explain to each member of the group who has been reading the magazine that we were denied an appeal by the War Production Board. They would assume that perhaps for some financial reason we were discontinuing publication, and this, I believe, would make it

> unusually difficult for a new magazine to begin after the war because these people would say, 'I invested my money in the *Negro Digest* and it failed.'[92]

The case was eventually won but he waited until the end of World War II, when paper restrictions were lifted, to start *EBONY*, a monthly magazine, in November 1945. It was "produced with a Royal portable typewriter, a pica ruler, a stack of copy pencils, scissors and a bottle of rubber cement on the kitchen table" of Burns' Jackson Blvd. apartment in spring of 1945.[93] There were "only three names on the masthead," Johnson said. He was listed as editor and publisher while Burns was executive editor and Jay Jackson was art editor.[94]

Picture magazines weren't anything new. A few others tried to do this. *Flash* magazine, a weekly news picture magazine selling for .10 cents, was founded in 1937 and ended in 1944. It was published in D.C. and in Chicago. L.V. Williams, its founder, saw the magazine reach a circulation of 58,000 before it ceased publication. *Newspic*, founded in 1940 and ending in 1947, also was a news picture magazine. It was founded by Edward C. Jinkins of Birmingham, Alabama. And yet another picture magazine was called *Color*, founded in 1944 and ending in 1956. None of them lasted due to lack of funds.[95]

Though *EBONY* appeared to have been an overnight success, that was far from the truth. There were lean years that proved tough for Johnson with limited resources, but he made the most of those moments. Recalled Burns about the early days:

> The seminal years of *EBONY* were not easy ones financially despite all the 'success story' publicity about the magazine that appeared in white media. Often paydays were uncertain as the still green publisher learned that circulation revenue was very slow in arriving from distributors and often was not quite enough to meet the mounting printing bills. But the agile Johnson ducked and dodged deftly as creditors closed in on him like sharks.[96]

It's important to note that Johnson was considered one of the country's greatest publishers not because of his journalism skill set, it was because of his strengths as a business man. He certainly understood the inner workings of publishing, but had he not had the business acumen that he possessed, his empire would have imploded early on like so many others who made attempts at starting magazines.

Johnson himself later explained how those struggles brought out the best in him and forced him to find his way. He explained it this way:

> It was during this period of frantic growth and improvisation that I formulated my basic approach to publishing. We had only a handful of employees at the time, and I had to write stories, edit copy, sell magazines and negotiate with angry creditors. This was a valuable experience, which I recommend to all magazine publishers. By dealing with all facets of the production process, I developed a total approach to magazine publishing. And since that time, I have always evaluated one part of the publishing process in terms of its impact on the whole.[97]

Finding black magazine writers and editors in the mid-1940s was another problem, because the only major magazine was *The Crisis.* Gordon Parks and Gordon Coster were among the "first-rate" photographers later listed on the masthead.[98]

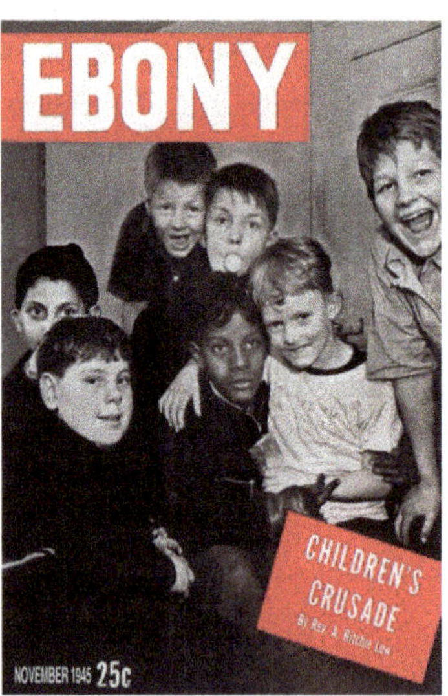


FIGURE 10: The first issue of EBONY in November 1945.
Courtesy Johnson Publishing Company, LLC. 

Burns claimed he did not know of any blacks with magazine experience and *Life* only had one black staff editor named Earl Brown. Yet Burns managed to find Harlem, New York, resident Allan Morrison, who had magazine experience and was initially approached about joining *Negro Digest* but came aboard because of the popularity of *EBONY*. Another early writer was a white woman named Kay Cremin, who first began as an editorial assistant for *Negro Digest* before moving to *EBONY*. The Wheaton College graduate had an honorable mention in a *Negro Digest* competition, Should Negro Students Attend Mixed or Negro Colleges?[99] "She was qualified, we were an equal opportunity employer—and we hired her," Johnson said.[100] Others eventually hired were Robert Lucas and Freda DeKnight, the woman responsible for starting the magazine's popular cooking section, "Date With a Dish."[101]

Employees were expected to rise to Johnson's high standards. For anyone who ever worked during John H. Johnson's tenure, they can tell you how he was a stickler for people arriving to work on time. He was known for even sitting in the lobby, near the front desk, so that anyone arriving even a minute late would have to sign the desk pad and have it documented in his/her record. Cremin, according to Burns, was eventually terminated for being a "bad example" for arriving late to work.[102] Another white writer was Mark Harris, who went into academia and wrote a novel, *Bang the Drum Slowly*.[103]

As *EBONY* continued to expand, there were challenges finding "competent staff" based in Chicago, according to Burns. To help produce the magazine in the beginning, Burns said that "in desperation" he "turned to my leftist contacts in journalism...Johnson knowingly agreed to my suggestions to retain or employ some of my radical friends, even if my own Communist background made these people suspect and even though all of them were white."[104]

The magazine's staff and freelancers were multiracial at its inception but later editors and writers were recruited from the "Negro press" and eventually became all black. Johnson had to convince many to relocate to Chicago. Robert E. Johnson, Lerone Bennett Jr. and Ariel Strong left the *Atlanta Daily World*, while Clotye Murdock came from the Cleveland *Call & Post*. Alex Poinsett and Hans J. Massaquoi joined the staff along with Nieman Fellow Simeon Booker, who came from the *Washington Post*.[105]

When it came to locating images and finding someone able to do the job, there were no black photographers on *Life*, *Look*, or any other nationally-circulated magazine's staff. Burns used this as his rationale for hiring white photographers to do most of the early issues of *EBONY*. However, they were lucky and managed to land Gordon Parks, whose pictures ran in most of the first issues of *EBONY*. But, the magazine was slow to make an offer to Parks, who was later hired full-time by *Life*. *EBONY*'s first full-time staff photographer was a man named Griffith Davis, a former GI who attended Morehouse College and took images as a hobby. He was referred by poet Langston Hughes and had no formal training. He eventually left and ended up in Liberia with the State Department.[106]

Many of Burns' white friends, his "leftist contacts" as he referred to them, agreed to take photos for a fraction of what they would normally ask from mainstream publications because they saw the magazine as a "worthy cause."[107]

Six months after *EBONY*'s first issue was published, the white advertising manager, Irwin J. Stein, was listed on the masthead. Johnson tried to hire staff from black newspapers but the magazine was still new and, according to Burns, these people weren't willing to leave their jobs to join a company that was just starting. As a result, Johnson agreed to hire Stein, another of Burns' leftist friends, when he couldn't find people from his own race, willing to take a chance with the new magazine. Eventually, thanks to the National Urban League, as years progressed, Johnson was able to hire people recruited from the civil rights organization.[108]

Simeon Booker, who made history in 1952 by being the first black editor at the *Washington Post* before coming to Johnson Publishing Company in 1953, was the Washington Bureau Chief for *JET* and *EBONY* magazines for more than five decades, having handled coverage on 10 presidents before retiring in 2007. He was the longest-serving editor in the history of Johnson Publishing Company.[109]

Johnson hired photographer Moneta Sleet Jr., who had worked at *Our World*, once considered *EBONY*'s major rival, until the magazine went bankrupt in 1955. As a photographer at Johnson Publishing Company with *EBONY*, Sleet made history as the first black photographer and first black man to win a Pulitzer Prize in 1969. His powerful image of Coretta Scott King, holding her young daughter, Bernice, in her lap at the funeral of slain husband, Rev. Dr. Martin

Luther King, Jr., signaled a defining moment in the Civil Rights Movement era.[110]

Setting *EBONY* apart was something else that was carefully crafted and designed by Johnson. An advertising trade organ called *Tide* had an editorial that praised *EBONY* for "taste and restraint to avoid the taint that afflicts so much of the Negro press."[111] Burns said, "The 'first-only-biggest' formula of *EBONY* stressing black accomplishment was in Johnson's eyes the needed antidote to so much negative news and a whiff of cheer and inspiration in the lives and dreams of ordinary African Americans."[112]

Later in the magazine's history, sections like "Speaking of People" and a section in *JET* called "Newsmakers" highlighted and introduced those who made history as the first. This same trio formula, "first-only-biggest," was a staple with many articles published in *JET* and in *EBONY*.[113] If someone was the only person to have accomplished something that was considered pioneering, and the biggest often dealt with money and business. "The first, the only, the biggest" was a formula sure to produce results.[114]

An early blow came to Johnson's *EBONY* publication in May 1946 by way of a $100,000 libel suit by boxing great Joe Louis. White mainstream publications discussed Louis' financial problems that were mainly claimed by his estranged wife. Johnson used the same information that others reported and placed Louis on the cover of the magazine with the headline, "How Joe Louis Spent $2,000,000."[115]

The story discussed how he spent his money on "slick chicks," poor investments and camp followers. The issue did surprisingly well. This meant big sales for the company, but Louis wasn't pleased because apparently just before *EBONY* hit the newsstands, he and his estranged wife were on friendly terms. Johnson said Louis believed the magazine "attacked his manhood and his honor."[116]

Burns claimed that a sports writer at a black newspaper challenged Louis about the claims in *EBONY* and when Louis denied them, the reporter encouraged the boxer to file a lawsuit. "For a magazine six months old to be slapped with a libel suit was very nearly a knockout blow," said Burns.[117] Johnson was disappointed with the action taken by Louis. "I was embarrassed, not only because of the threat to the new venture but also because I truly admired Joe," said Johnson.[118]

Johnson sought the advice of Burns and Charles Beckett, a newly hired business manager, during a "crisis meeting" to figure out how to handle the sticky situation. During the conversation, Beckett suggested Johnson handle the lawsuit by issuing an apology in the magazine. Burns, on the other hand, wanted Johnson to stand by the story because to issue an apology "might encourage future threats and intimidation from other public figures anxious to keep their indiscretions out of our pages."[119] Ultimately, Johnson revealed that neither he nor Louis were seeking a "public fight," so during a conversation with Louis, the boxer suggested that if Johnson agreed to issue an apology in the magazine and pay his attorney fees, the lawsuit would be dropped. And it was.[120] In fact, the last issue to be printed on flatbed presses, October 1946, included the apology.[121]

Problems didn't stop there. Trying to locate a company with flatbed presses able to keep up with the demand of *EBONY* became a concern along with "bigoted printers," recalled Burns. He said the following about those times:

> Shopping desperately for a printer with rotary equipment, Johnson was spurned repeatedly, in part because open press time was still at a premium as a result of postwar shortages. Telephoning one of the biggest printing houses in Chicago, W.F. Hall, Johnson insisted that the company at least do him the courtesy of sending a sales representative to see him, implying that Hall might have turned him down initially because *EBONY* was a Negro publication.[122]

Johnson was a businessman and he had a way with words, drawing upon the early experiences and lessons that helped him win confidence as an Arkansas teen finding his comfort zone in Chicago. Having W.F. Hall print his publications came with hurdles and the standard initial rejection, but just as Johnson did not believe that failure was an option, he also knew that where there was a will, there was a way. And Johnson had his way by doing his homework and doing research.

Prior to a meeting with a sales rep at the company, Johnson learned from the Chicago Urban League that W.F. Hall was experiencing low employee morale from the black workers, who were arriving to work late or not showing up at all. Armed with this knowledge, Johnson was able to explain to the sales rep that having the employees work on black publications could potentially change their work habits because this would foster a sense of pride and make them want to arrive to work on time as well as show up to do the work.[123] This strategy helped Johnson secure W.F. Hall during a time when they had no interest in producing anything for people of color.

However, the battle was just beginning before Johnson would eventually win the war. News reports were kicking up steam about black soldiers dating white girls in Germany in early 1946. Burns hired a French photographer, Ilya Gregory, to take pictures. This seemed to be a difficult accomplishment, considering white Army officials objected to racial mixing, but somehow Gregory delivered. He took pictures of black soldiers with German women "at parties, on the beach, and in private necking sessions."[124] The images were held at the Canal Street customs office for clearance because they were deemed "salacious," and, according to Burns, despite his and Johnson's "contention that many similar photos were being circulated in the United States, the customs inspectors refused to budge until we hinted at a charge of discrimination."[125]

Those images were eventually cleared but Johnson soon discovered, with the very first issue under his new printing company, that W.F. Hall wanted to censor his magazine. It turns out that the men working the presses were angry about the story, seeing black men with white women. "There are some pictures some of the fellows are hot about. And you know with the unions and everything, well, we've got to be careful," Burns recalled a rep at W.F. Hall, telling him with Johnson eventually removing any objectionable photos.[126]

An added problem came because most of Johnson's transactions had to be made in cash. His funds were low by the 1950s and he owed the printers. They tried to use this to their advantage with more attempts to censor, including a picture of a white woman shining a black man's shoes though this woman was the wife of a shoe shiner.[127]

The printer refused to run the picture without being paid. Reluctantly, Johnson did pay up, but it wasn't until the printing company saw the power of Johnson's almighty dollar that the censorship requests stopped. Burns explained:

> In time the printers' attempts to censor *EBONY*'s contents diminished somewhat, no doubt influenced by the fact that the monthly check from Johnson to Hall had risen to more than

> $100,000. *EBONY* became too big an account for the printer to risk losing. Still attempts to censor the magazine continued, but now they came from advertisers rather than printers.[128]

A decade after the picture incident with that printer, Johnson became their second biggest client. Not one to forget his struggles, he sent the printer the same picture to print, which they did this time with no questions asked and no problem.[129]

*EBONY* made history in July 1947 when it became the first black magazine audited by the Audit Bureau of Circulation. In the final quarter of 1946, peak net paid sales totaled $309,715, making it the largest circulation of any black publication in the world.[130]

Being the first, the only, the best, people with physical deformities and interracial relationships were staples guaranteed to peak readers' interest in *EBONY* and in *JET*. For as controversial as interracial relationships and blacks passing as white seemed to be, those were stories readers seemed to enjoy most. Those types of subjects, appealing to what many deemed as sensationalism, increased circulation "by as many as 50,000 copies."[131]

A popular, yet highly controversial issue dealt with Father Divine, the flashy Harlem preacher who thought himself to be "God" and was married to a white Canadian woman. Her story was called "Life With Father" and given a byline by Mother Divine. Johnson moved with the story given his only sister cut herself off from his family to become a member of Father Divine's "heaven" and because his popularity would guarantee a soar in magazine sales.[132]

Another top feature story was "Five Million U.S. White Negroes," written by Roi Ottley. It addressed how increasing numbers of race mixing resulted in blacks being so light-skinned that many passed for white. The story mentioned how "nearly 82 percent of the Negro community have some white blood" and how "between 40,000 and 50,000 Negroes 'pass' into the white community yearly and between 5,000,000 and 8,000,000 persons in the United States, supposed to be white, actually possess a determinable part of Negro blood."[133]

Other cover stories that were top sellers were up close and personal and at home pieces. That formula proved a winner early on with stories about Lena Horne and even a story by Jackie Robinson called "What's

Wrong with Negro Baseball," which was actually ghostwritten by its black sports writer A.S. "Doc" Young, who later wrote the 1963 book *Negro Firsts in Sports*, published by the company's book division.[134]

Then there were other taboo subjects that *EBONY* dared tackle like marijuana and STD's effects on those in the black community. Articles about numbers rackets were discussed and a gangster story was even written as told by bandleader Earl Hines. "How Gangsters Ran the Band Business," the title, did well on the newsstands, but with names and nightclubs being pointed out, that kind of detail and those allegations were a problem for those being singled out. It turns out that a gangster referenced in the story had someone pay Johnson a visit and the tough-as-nails publisher wasn't too happy about it. "'Aw, there's nothing to be scared about. They don't shoot newspapermen,'" Burns told Johnson. "'That's what you think. I don't know whether they do or don't—and I don't ever want to find out,'" was Johnson's response to Burns.[135]

Gangster stories subsided until a story about Chicago gambler William "Flukey" Stokes Sr.'s son, William Jr. "Willie Wimp," ran in the March 19, 1984, issue of *JET*. Willie Wimp picked up his dad's ways of the streets but was murdered that year at the age of 28. The "pimp in a coffin story" is what it became known as, showing the deceased gambler sitting upright in a $7,000, custom-made Cadillac Seville coffin, wearing a wide brimmed hat, hot pink suit and holding five $100 bills.[136]

Johnson figured out a formula and it worked. Through the highs and lows, the heavy loads that came his way only made him stronger, and he didn't bite his tongue when he said how he was pleased with every step of the way along his journey. He explained: "I wouldn't change anything, because I would be afraid to. So many things happened along the way, maybe by accident, maybe by Providence, and I just don't think I would change anything. If you are pleased with the end result, you shouldn't worry about what happened along the way."[137]

FIGURE 11: The first issue of *JET* in November 1951. Courtesy Johnson Publishing Company, LLC. All rights reserved.

# CHAPTER 4

## BLACK MAGAZINES MATTER

***"I say that white magazines and white newspapers are written for white people. They do not have us in mind even when they write about us. They don't have the commitment…My line is to help black people."***

***John H. Johnson***

Whoever holds the pen determines how the story is written. The media influences the shaping of culture through information, images, and words. Most lives mattered in the 1940s, or so it seemed. As a rule, people of color were portrayed stereotypically, especially black people. During this era, stories in the mainstream media about other races appeared carefully crafted and centered around achievement and enlightenment. On the other hand, when it came to articulating stories about the lives of African Americans, they were ignored or, if told, the articles focused on negativity that did not seek to educate or advance the race. These kinds of stories fostered a sense of hopelessness and helplessness in terms of how African Americans viewed themselves and their abilities.

What one sees, one believes. If one doesn't see it, one has no reason to believe it. The concept of anything other than what is presented will seem foreign. *EBONY* and *JET*, along with other publications founded in the 1940s by Johnson Publishing Company, were staples in African-American communities, because this race of people was marginalized but Johnson made the race prominent, a priority. They were no longer invisible. They mattered. Their stories mattered because Johnson showed how their lives were worthy of being documented in history like other races.

Johnson took the time to show contributions, large and small, made by blacks, in fields ranging from politics to education, religion to fashion, entertainment to sports and science to health. Before 1942, with the founding of Johnson's *Negro Digest* magazine, black people did not see themselves in mainstream print publications unless there was a connection to crime, poverty, or intellectual inferiority. That absence created an unspoken and widespread belief that black people seemingly did not exist, because they were not important enough to study or to write about in the context that they were human, intelligent, and contributors to this society.

The night Barack Obama made history at Chicago's Grant Park by being elected the forty fourth President of the United States on November 4, 2008, of the estimated crowd of 240,000 and millions of people around the globe who observed this momentous occasion on television, many knew this signaled a time of change. An African-American man did something that had never been done before.

It is not insignificant that the first exclusive interview and photoshoot that Obama agreed to do for a national magazine was with *EBONY*. The following day after his victory, Obama came to Johnson Publishing Company and posed in the studio on the first floor of the house that John H. Johnson built at 820 S. Michigan, which was directly across the street from the exact location that the newly elected president gave his victory speech on that historic night. It was as if synchronicity was at work. What are the chances that the first black man to be elected president would have this moment happen across the street from Johnson Publishing, the first building in Chicago's renowned Loop area to be "exclusively designed and constructed by a black-owned corporation." [1]

*EBONY* subscribers received the January 2009 collector's issue, the first-ever with a gold *EBONY* logo, which went on sale December 9, 2008, and named Obama Person of the Year. This special edition sold the most copies in the magazine's sixty-seven-year history, according to a February 12, 2009, press release issued by Johnson Publishing Company. Newsstand sales topped 405,000, more than double an average month, the press release stated.[2]

It was fitting Obama chose *EBONY* to grant his first exclusive print interview and photo shoot to chronicle his rise as leader of the free world. Many observed how this move and decision demonstrated in nationally and globally the value and importance of this historic

African-American publication. As a black man, Obama wanted this celebrated magazine to share his story. Obama, like so many others, remembered how people who looked like himself could only learn about others who looked like him on the pages of the monthly magazine *EBONY* and/or *JET*. The weekly *JET* magazine recorded his journey as an Illinois senator and his bid for the presidency, but when examined more closely, *JET* documented his tracks further back than that.

The February 26, 1990, issue of the weekly magazine first showed Obama's picture and wrote how the then twenty-eight-year-old, second-year law student made history by being elected the first black president of the *Harvard Law Review* in more than 100 years of publication at Harvard Law School. He told *JET*, "I wouldn't want people to see my election as a symbol that there aren't problems out there with the situation of African Americans in society. From experience I know that for every one of me, there are a hundred or a thousand black and minority students who are just as smart and just as talented and never get the opportunity."[3]

The would-be president was right. The mass media, controlled by European Americans, is a critical source of information that is often incorrectly provided about African Americans and their image. This public image influences public perception and is capable of reinforcing and/or establishing opinions about African Americans. Ownership in the media controls what is presented. It's no secret that African Americans are significantly underrepresented in the newsroom and as publishers. As long as blacks don't have a seat at the table when it comes to decision making, stories and images will always be subjected to scrutiny, inaccuracy, and unfavorable coverage that portrays this group as inferior to other races.

African Americans learned they had a voice on a national and global level because Johnson saw to this. Someone of African-American descent learned from reading that February 26, 1990, issue of *JET* how a law student, whose skin color was black, made history. This magazine provided hope and illustrated possibility by showing what was achievable. However, when viewed through the lens of mainstream media, this reality was presented in a manner that revealed otherwise. Appropriately so, after Obama made history once more as president, a full-circle moment, if you will, he returned to his roots with those same two publications, which wrote about him before the world at large even knew he existed.

For years before Obama made history, Johnson was showcasing a race of people to the world. His magazines stood in contrast to what was being shown. For example, *Life* was a picture magazine that depicted the endeavors of ordinary people, yet African Americans were scarcely included. One would never think people of color did normal things like graduated from college, raised a family, or got married because those kinds of articles for people of color were not written about in *Life*. Black people were not considered valuable enough to mention with any semblance of humanity or compassion. Blacks were seen as lesser—so much so that they did not exist.

This exclusion might not have been obvious to mainstream America, but it was definitely noticeable for African Americans and their relationship to the media. Not seeing stories and images reflective of blacks made it difficult to value any history pertaining to the race, for many would be inclined to think they did not have anything of significance to share and thus the void. Johnson saw otherwise and how this lack of seeing self was creating self-negation for his race. Johnson said the following:

> You do need visible successful models. I think it's important for a black person to see another black person, someone like himself, who is doing the thing that he wants to do. It lets him know, particularly in a country like ours, where you read so much about racial barriers and difficulties, that in spite of all of those difficulties, it is still possible to make it. That's very important for black people to know.[4]

The media plays a vital role in shaping culture and defining the world. If certain stories are shared while others are ignored or presented negatively, this makes it easy for the world to believe that some races are more intellectually inferior than others. The very name *EBONY* even fostered a sense of pride for its audience. Readers quickly saw the importance in something as simple as a title. Johnson's wife, Eunice, chose the name, *EBONY*, because it means black.[7]
But when *EBONY* was founded in 1945, for every positive letter that was written about the magazine and its name, there were just as many negative ones with people taking offense to being called "black" because they considered it to be a disparaging term. Johnson told the

*New York Times*, "Quite a few people wrote letters and wondered, 'Why are you calling us black? We're not black. We're Negro.'"[5]

Johnson said a critical moment of acceptance of the name came on March 6, 1957, the day Ghana became an independent African nation. "It was good to see a black man who was president of a country," Johnson said. "It was good to see black people operating on the highest government levels. And I think from that moment on, we were black."[6]

Had Johnson conceded and used Negro in the title, it would have proven to be outdated at this point when some people prefer to refer to themselves as African Americans while others take more of a liking to being called black or people of color. And Negro didn't carry the idea of pride the way *EBONY* did.

A reader from North Philadelphia, Pennsylvania, named Mrs. Daniel Thompson, penned a letter that was published in the April 1946 issue of *EBONY* where she discussed how the title was refreshing to see because of what it implied and what it stood for. Another reader from Providence, Rhode Island, named Helen McMillan, said that other Negro publications aroused hatred in her, but seeing *EBONY* made her feel racial pride because it demonstrated that education of all people is the key to real brotherhood, as she believed.[7]

Johnson gave voice and presence to African Americans. He saw a need that wasn't being met. People were not being fulfilled because they felt incomplete without seeing themselves so he created an opportunity to alter the course of media history since no one was trying to make black people feel good about themselves. That's what Johnson thought they needed to see—and not to just read it in a book. "I thought blacks needed a better image of themselves. We needed to see and to know what other members of our race were doing."[8]

He not only told but showed that their stories were of importance and had value. Johnson knew that people become mirrors of what they see. If something isn't shown, people will think it is not possible or it does not exist. African Americans achieved and accomplished just as much as any other race and Johnson set out to show this in print. He knew the only way their stories would be told with an appropriate, cultural sensitivity was by a member of the same race. There is a language, a culture, and a history that members of the identical race share. This makes it feasible to present information in a way that inherently understands the culture.

Johnson once described *EBONY*'s perspective as a positive approach to everything. Johnson said his goal was to seek out good things, even when everything seemed bad. He reasoned, "You know the old saying, 'It is better to light a candle than to curse the darkness.' We light candles. We look for breakthroughs. We look for people who have made it, who have succeeded against the odds, who have proven somehow that long shots do come in."[9] This was his rationale for the positive approach, though things were far from equal or at peace between whites and blacks when his magazine was started.

In 1975, Johnson recalled how when he got his start in 1942 with *Negro Digest*, the black press was an organ of protest. It dealt with lynchings and had to take a negative perspective. It had to expose and protest injustice. He said *JET* and *EBONY* were recording achievements and that was the difference. Johnson explained:

> If a black man can be elected mayor of Tuskegee, we are arriving. We pioneered in this kind of black journalism. The black press today, in general, is not a protest medium, nor is it attempting to be one. Instead, it deals with people and at the same time shows a strong and bright future for blacks.[10]

Surprisingly, just because these publications were for blacks and the publisher was black, many of the early editors and writers were not. Robert E. Johnson, the late executive editor of *JET* who was black, said they employed "token whites" because it was difficult to find whites who had knowledge of black history. "White writers are not hired to write white news," he explained.[11] Ben Burns, who was white and Jewish, was far from a token in the company's history. He is the man who became the founding editor of *Negro Digest*, *EBONY* and *JET* magazines. Some believed he gave himself too much credit for the role he played in helping to launch the historic publications, while Burns felt justified in claiming his legacy though overlooked because people assumed he was black. He was even invited to submit a bio for inclusion in Who's Who in Colored America.[12] Burns was described by Johnson as "a hard worker with a flair for colorful and somewhat spicy journalism." Johnson also stated "he made a major contribution in the first phase of our development," as chronicled in chapter three of this book.[13]

Though the publications were created for African Americans, with the popularity of Johnson's magazines, publishers of all races began to take notice. By the 1950s the Good Publishing Company, based in Fort Worth, Texas, was considered the second largest publisher of black magazines. Its first owner, Horace J. Blackwell, an African-American clothing merchant, died in 1949. The man who purchased the company in 1951 after Blackwell's death was George Levitan, who was white and Jewish. His magazines included the following: *Sepia*, formerly known as *Negro Achievements*, was a picture magazine that was modeled after *Look* and *EBONY*; *Bronze Thrills*, which told true stories, was formerly known as the *World's Messenger*; and other publications, including *Jive, Hep, Soul Confessions,* and *Soul Teen.*[14]

Some began to question the ownership of Johnson Publishing Company, believing it was possibly white owned like Levitan's company. The early staff of Johnson's magazines were indeed racially mixed as previously mentioned. During an interview with the *black weekly* called the *Los Angeles Tribune*, *Our World* founder John P. Davis, a black man who co-founded the National Negro Congress in 1935 and was a one-time leftist like Burns, stirred the pot by saying, "*EBONY* reads like a white man's idea of what Negroes want in a publication." Davis then mentioned that *EBONY* "has a white man high on its staff, one Ben Burns."[15]

In an early issue of *EBONY*'s Backstage column, the article explained that the staff was interracial but that Johnson "is the brains and money behind this enterprise with no strings attached." The column ended with how the staff was "hired on ability not color," going against what Robert E. Johnson once claimed as tokenism.[16]

Some questioned the early influence of other races in helping Johnson to write stories and edit pieces about blacks. There was one instance when Levitan, who was based in Texas, came to visit the company and met Burns. Upon seeing Burns' white face and realizing he was also Jewish, Levitan exclaimed to Burns, "I knew it. I knew it! I knew there must be a Jew somewhere behind this setup!"[17]

No matter the early writings of people like Burns, *EBONY* and *JET* magazines were socially and culturally grounded to meet the needs of African Americans and were created by a member of the same race. Learning about African Americans during the 1940s when Johnson started the publications wasn't possible, because this kind of information was scarce. The order of the day usually reflected negative aspects of African-American life. Like Ralph Ellison's *Invisible Man* novel suggested, black people did not seem worthy of existence as three-dimensional beings when it came to the press.[18] Johnson answered that call and filled the void in terms of negative portrayals or exclusionary practices set against African-American representation. His informal, culturally grounded way of teaching adults was liberatory, because it showed African Americans that they do matter, they do exist, and they are not deficient.

By practicing this, Johnson created a mirror, which became liberatory in that African Americans felt a renewed sense of strength, pride, and belonging in a world that more often than not showed they didn't matter, didn't belong, or couldn't belong. If a person's mind is imprisoned and confined to limitations, he will never experience freedom. Carter G. Woodson's thesis about mis-education in his seminal work *The Mis-Education of the Negro* discussed the way Eurocentric education promoted and placed a value on their ways over other cultural values and views.[19] This type of teaching produced a negative self-image and a denial of one's true self, which fostered low racial self-esteem and racial pride.

After the landmark 1954 Brown v. Board of Education United States Supreme Court case, in which the court declared state laws establishing separate public schools for black and white students to be unconstitutional, some people believed the Supreme Court abolished "Negroes as well as segregation," Johnson once said.[20] Specifically, they believed in the dissolution of all black institutions but not all white institutions. *Life* and *Look* magazines were white publications noted for being picture magazines about American life, most noticeably white life. *EBONY* was similarly modeled after *Life* magazine in size and as a picture monthly. The difference was Johnson used his magazine to document black life.

Johnson was amazed at the number of people who were anxious and often asked when *EBONY* would go out of business when separate but equal schools were abolished. His response indicated that Johnson saw the need for inclusion in a diverse world. "Why should *EBONY* go out of business? Real integration, not to mention the increasing black and Hispanic populations in the major cities, will produce a society that looks more like *EBONY* than *Life*."[21] Eventually, *Life*, in 1972, and *Look*, in 1971, both went out of business, but *EBONY* remained standing and remains in existence today. "Integration didn't put us out of business. *Life* and *Look* unfortunately went out of business, but we didn't," he said. "We try to show our heritage, our pride, and what's coming for all of us."[22] Johnson knew he was on to something when his magazine stayed in business. "Imagine a white magazine with the same format as mine going out of business and me staying in business. Now, I've got to know something."[23] Johnson also marveled at how his magazine remained large during a time when pressure was on him to change its size, which he eventually altered in 1982.[24]

People often commented that *EBONY* and *JET* magazines are racist because they cater to African Americans. Most Americans believe blacks have come such a long way, especially after Obama's election as president. With this perceived advancement of this race by others, these people believe there's no need to have separate publications anymore. In their minds the playing field has been leveled and there's not a need for *EBONY*.

Johnson's magazines, however, had their own identities, which were reflective of African Americans and those in the African Diaspora. The publications championed the cause of setting standards and turning up the heat in raising awareness about a race of people previously viewed as invisible like the character in Ellison's book that spoke about being overlooked by other races in society.[25] Under Johnson's leadership, the publications never lost their identity of turning up the heat through fostering education and knowledge.

Some argued a concern about these types of publications is that they polarized and did not speak to everyone in the race. Johnson disagreed. Be it a select few or a majority, African-American publications serve a purpose and are essential to the race's self-reliance. Out of ignorance, some counter with thoughts that there are no publications exclusively for whites. There's no need for any magazines to be exclusively for whites because every mainstream publication that excludes blacks makes it quite clear, through its limited coverage, that African Americans are an afterthought when it comes to representation in print.

Documentation of the history of African Americans and those from the African Diaspora was recorded to show the positive historical contributions. Eurocentric history did not acknowledge the history of African Americans or make linkages between others. During this time

Johnson addressed why African-American publications are necessary. He explained to the *Detroit News* in 1990 why he fought to keep his magazines dominant:

> *EBONY* is needed more now than it ever was. Racism is rampant and the barriers are still there. True, there have been a lot of successes. We've moved forward, but the worst thing we can believe is that everything is all right now. I have one of the largest, most successful businesses in the United States, but not one day goes by that I'm not reminded that I am black. I'm still fighting—just like the next guy…What these other publications are dealing with are the black superstars who have crossed over. Even when they do a story about one of us, it's because white people want to know more about that person. I doubt if they go digging around for heroes in the black community. That's what we do.[26]

He re-defined the history of African Americans from an African-centered viewpoint by re-educating the race on their accomplishments and historical significance. Johnson also showed there was purpose in what he started and continued to do so by using *EBONY* and *JET* to document his race's own history in a culturally grounded way, which was necessary to promote racial pride and esteem to counteract the practice of mis-education created by European exclusionary practices.

During an interview with the *Houston Defender* in 1990, Johnson addressed those who questioned the viability of African-American publications. He stated:

> I say that white magazines and white newspapers are written for white people. They do not have us in mind even when they write about us. They don't have the commitment. They also don't have the knowledge. Even black writers for white publications—though there are exceptions—conform to the policies of the publications or they couldn't keep their jobs. There's always a policy; let's not kid ourselves. You have freedom of the press, but you also have a policy, a direction, and a line being followed. My line is to help black people.[27]

His magazines had a mission to address the whole person. For instance, during 1942 when Johnson founded his first magazine, *Negro Digest*, racial tensions were high with African Americans being denied basic rights as human beings in all areas of life simply because of the color of their skin. Johnson noticed racism influenced biased reporting in mainstream media. He said the following:

> In that period there was an almost white-out on positive black news in white-oriented media. There was an unwritten rule in the South in this period that a black's picture could not appear in the press unless in connection with a crime. There was no consistent coverage of the human dimensions of black Americans in the northern newspapers and magazines. It's hard to make people realize this, but blacks didn't get married on the society pages of major American dailies until the late sixties.[28]

Johnson is indicating his recognition of the media contributing to the perpetuation and societal issues of racism by the way it portrayed African Americans in the media. As Woodson's *The Mis-Education of the Negro* discussed, there's no shared history for African Americans and people from the African Diaspora because they are being taught from a singular Eurocentric lens.[29] The promotion of European ideas, values, and views over the ideas, values, and views of others will lead to self-hate. African Americans were being fed images and information through someone else's lens that put them at a disadvantage because of the way information was systematically excluded about the history and contributions of themselves.

African Americans had a strong desire to learn who they were and where they came from. In his autobiography, *Succeeding Against the Odds*, Johnson said:

> You would have assumed that we didn't finish school, because the white press didn't deal with our educational achievements. You would have assumed that we didn't get married, because white press didn't print our wedding announcements or pictures of black brides and grooms cutting cakes. You would have assumed that we didn't die, because it didn't deal with our funerals. Back there, at the ending of World War II, the idea

> and the dream were on the defensive in the media and the streets. There were no black mayors in major cities then, in all seriousness, that blacks were biologically incapable of playing on the Brooklyn Dodgers and the Chicago Bears and the New York Knicks. This was the situation in 1945.[30]

In explaining society and its psychological impact due to mis-education, Johnson described it by saying the following:

> In a world of despair, we wanted to give hope. In a world of negative black images, we wanted to provide positive black images. In a world that said blacks could do few things, we wanted to say they could do everything...Words and pictures, black words and pictures, and a holistic presentation of the black image, showing professionals and entertainers, athletes and doctors and preachers and women and men and children, everybody: This was the idea.[31]

Johnson set out to show African Americans are not intellectually inferior to their European counterparts. And as long as African Americans wait for other races to tell their story, they are at the mercy of those who decide to portray them any way they see fit. If a publication doesn't show a race of people in positions of power, those people will not believe this can be accomplished. Nobody understands the needs, desires, trials, and triumphs of someone other than self, believed Johnson. Had Johnson not founded *EBONY* and *JET*, the civil rights efforts of the Rev. Dr. Martin Luther King, Jr. wouldn't have been recorded. People across the country wouldn't have known what was happening. *EBONY* and *JET* were more than magazines but a movement. The movement came through the message of transporting their stories and news all over the world.

African Americans found new significance in seeing "self" reflected in the media with *EBONY* and *JET*. Johnson recognized the importance of properly educating his race when he said, "We needed a new medium—bright, sparkling, readable—that would let black Americans know that they were part of a great heritage."[32] But if their history is no longer shared or documented, they will once again become re-educated into believing that the history of other races is the only ones that matter and has meaning.

In 1980 it was reported that 20 percent of *EBONY* and *JET* readers were white, which Johnson wasn't too pleased about. "If we get too many, I won't be preeminent in my field. I'll be out there competing with the white magazines for advertising."[33] A decade later in a 1990 interview with the *New York Times*, Johnson's sentiments were the same though by this time 12 percent of the readers of *EBONY* and *JET* were white. "This is more than I would like to have," he said. "I want to be king of the black hill, not the mixed hill."[34]

Five years earlier, Johnson expressed his thoughts about the future of black and white media. He said that unless the races came together, there would always likely be a need for news and publishing outlets that cater to both. Johnson explained:

> I think our country is so constituted that white media will always give the majority of their space and support to white people and that black media will give the majority of their space and support to black people, who are largely excluded from white media. Now, until these two races are meshed or merged or integrated, or whatever term you want to use, you will need both black and white media. If we somehow reach a point in this country when race will no longer be a factor and there will not be a need for black magazines and white magazines, then *EBONY* will simply serve all the people. And, as I have often said, I think *EBONY* would be a greater success than any of its white competitors simply because black people have had more experience studying and meeting the needs of whites than white people have had studying and meeting the needs of blacks.[35]

Though he championed integration early in his career, Johnson's later perspective was even more inclusive. People should be free to choose what works best for them. He reasoned, "A man ought to have the right to live with his own people or in an integrated community, whichever he wants. I don't think we're ever going to rid ourselves of prejudice. What we are striving for is to prevent that prejudice from being translated into acts of discrimination."[36]

CHAPTER 5

# MORE THAN MAGAZINES

***"When Martin Luther King first began marching, there were no television cameras, there were no White reporters. The only way he got his message across, in the beginning, was through JET."***
***John H. Johnson***

*EBONY* and *JET* magazines were the publications that people looked to when hoping to learn more about black people and their culture, their lifestyle, their world. The newsmagazine *JET*, which chronicled all facets of black life weekly, was considered a magazine of record. It was such a valuable and credible source that it was deemed "the Negro Bible" by comedian and actor Redd Foxx, who attended high school with Johnson.[1] By readers it was called "the little black Bible." Another well-known phrase often attached to the digest-sized newsweekly was "if it wasn't in *JET*, it didn't happen," based on a conversation from a character in one of Maya Angelou's plays.[2] That's how much people relied upon the reporting from the small book with big news.

Cowles' publications had a mini-magazine called *Quick*. Johnson created the counterpart to that magazine in 1951 with the birth of *JET*. *Quick* eventually went out of business, but *JET* survived and by 1975 it had a circulation of 650,000.[3] *JET* magazine's focus as a journal of black America served a specific purpose as a non-formal mode of education. It was a textbook, if you will. "*JET* gives a summary of all the important things in the world that are happening to black people," Johnson said. "No one had done that before. It was an immediate success and continues to be a success. We're giving people something that's not available anywhere else. It's convenient. You can put it in your pocket."[4]

Both *EBONY* and *JET* were the gold standard for excellence in crafting, telling, and sharing stories by and for African Americans. Johnson dared to discuss stories that others would not touch. Johnson said:

> Some people and some media tell part of the story of the black community some of the time. We are committed to telling all of the story—the good and the bad, the trials and triumphs—all of the time. We are a magazine of record and a magazine of the whole. If it happens in the black community, if it happens to the black community, if it matters to the black community, it happens to us and it matters to us.[5]

In a time when some publications were thermometers, often observing its competitors to see what was pertinent, *EBONY* and *JET* were thermostats that set the tone, turned up the heat, led the way, by telling the world what was critical to them as a race. The stories that unfolded on the pages made some people uncomfortable, but they served their purpose. The articles engaged readers and observers alike in dialogue, stirring emotions and moving people to take some form of action in one way or another. Johnson said:

> We didn't follow the parade; we were out front, beating the drums and pointing the way. Our series on 'Black Power' preceded the first call for 'Black Power.' We were the first major magazine to say that the race problem is a white problem ('The White Problem in America'). We were the first major publication to say what almost all historians say today, that Abraham Lincoln had the racial limitations of most of his contemporaries ('Was Abraham Lincoln a White Supremacist?')[6]

The spine of *EBONY* magazine in 2010 included the mantra, "It's more than a magazine. It's a movement." This is the saying coined when a story about John H. Johnson was being penned in the section Legend of *EBONY* magazine. Words and images mean nothing if they don't illicit a response from readers. The publications generated conversation in and out of the boardroom, on the streets and even in the White House. The medium might have been magazines but movement came from the messages written and the images shown on the glossy pages. Johnson revealed:

> From the beginning, I considered the company as a vehicle for building and projecting the image that had been distorted by media oriented primarily by non-blacks. I felt then that America could never take its rightful place in the front ranks of the struggle for human dignity as long as millions at home were shackled by the crippling effects of damaged self-images. I felt then...and I feel now...that every man must have a wholesome image of himself before he can demand respect from others.[7]

As time progressed and needs changed, people worked to balance a busy life that left some with little time for much reading in a fast-paced society. Johnson did not want to allow anyone the excuse of being unable to catch up on the latest news. He decided to use the pocket-sized *JET* magazine as a means of helping transmit what was happening for people in a hurry.

Initially it was 5 ¾" by 4" when the newsmagazine was founded in November 1951. Its name was even a reflection of its target audience. "The word jet was tailor made for my purposes. A talking word that sounds its message, jet means on one level a very dark velvet black," he said. "And it means on another level fast, as in the airplane. From these dictionary definitions, it is but one step, and not a long one at that, to the black American definition of 'a fast black magazine.'"[8]

The Publisher's Statement in the first issue acknowledged Johnson's desire to make reading more convenient for its audience. The creation of *JET* was the start. He acknowledged how the world was moving along at a faster pace with more news but less time to read it. Including information in a weekly news magazine, in a handy, pocket-sized form, was Johnson's solution.

The premier issue of *EBONY* was dated November 1945 and featured six little boys on the black and white cover. What made this stand out most is that all of the kids were white with the exception of them embracing one black boy, who is positioned in the middle, the dominant place on the cover. *EBONY* fulfilled the African Americans' desire to be recognized and respected through the use of inclusion. That first issue of *EBONY* had an image and a story that addressed what was possible in a 1940s segregated world. A. Ritchie Lowe, a white pastor, penned the cover story about his efforts to end racial bias by taking blacks in Harlem to Vermont farms for their annual vacations.[9]

Johnson Publishing Company, fortuitously, always had a front-row seat in the foretelling and trailing of black history. *EBONY* and *JET* had a unique, bird's eye view in that they were documenting and witnessing the trials and triumphs of a race of people whose history did not exist because it was ignored and not documented to this extent before. The names of the magazines would soon become significant throughout the world. In fact, *EBONY* "would become so successful that the word would also mean the magazine published by and for black Americans."[10]

*EBONY*'s name was also selected for business reasons as well. Johnson explained in 1985:

> We decided on *EBONY* because of a patent office rule that you can't protect a name if it is simply descriptive of goods or services. My wife finally came up with the idea that *EBONY* meant fine wood, mostly black wood. And we thought that if we could take the word *EBONY* and give it a magazine meaning, we could be protected in the patent office.[11]

*EBONY* came to symbolize all facets of black life, especially placing a lens on accomplishments in an effort to make black people proud of themselves, to see that their stories were worth telling because their lives matter. Johnson said:

> We wanted to emphasize the positive aspects of black life. We wanted to highlight the achievements and make blacks proud of themselves. We wanted to create a windbreak that would let them get away from 'the problem' for a few moments and say, 'Here are some blacks who are making it. And if they can make it, I can make it, too.'[12]

Words are impactful but images are equally as important, for what a person sees can help to validate his or her reality and even identity. In creating *EBONY*, Johnson wanted a picture magazine to allow black people to see themselves as well as read about how their very existence and lives contributed to shaping society and history. "The best arrangement is to combine them in the most effective way. Together they are sometimes more powerful than they are separate."[13]

In presenting words and pictures about black life, Johnson also made it a mission to be honest and transparent in what was presented. He did not document their world through rose-colored glasses. Learning comes from truth that has been critically reflected upon and evaluated. The transparency that he demonstrated and examined with his work had a mission in its message. This is what Johnson discussed:

> We intended to highlight black breakthroughs and pockets of progress. But we didn't intend to ignore difficulties and harsh realities. We intended to call a spade a spade and an ace an ace. And we intended to say, always and everywhere, that they are part of the same deck and can't be understood in isolation from each other. Beyond all that, we wanted to focus on the total black experience—something no one else was doing then and, I am tempted to say, now. For black people, in addition to being members of the NAACP and National Urban League, were also members of sororities and fraternities and lodges. They marched and raised hell but they also raised children and gave debutante balls and watched baseball and football games.[14]

Magazines published at Johnson's pioneering company helped to place a microscope on the plight of African Americans. For instance, the August 1975 issue was a special edition titled, "Bicentennial: 200 Years of Black Trials and Triumphs." Initially Johnson and his editorial team had concerns about commemorating this period, noted for "slavery, servitude, segregation, discrimination poverty and even death and destruction," but he decided to survey this difficult time in history that marginalized African Americans as less than human.[15] He instead used this difficult period as a teachable moment to magnify and access 200 years of history for black America. His Publisher's Statement read the following:

> Lest anyone forget, we blacks have an American history that pre-dates the Declaration of Independence and the landing of the Mayflower—not to speak of an African history that predates the coming of civilization to the nations of Europe.

> We cannot celebrate but we can commemorate two centuries of brave progress against tremendous odds. In this special issue we hope that this slow and painful progress has been made clear to all.[16]

Stories ranged from "The Black Press: Voice of Freedom," which discussed how new journals helped to shape African-American history since the 1800s to a story titled "Black Businesses: They Began Before the Revolution," which investigated how firms operated more than 300 years ago. Another story was "The Dilemma of Thomas Jefferson" that examined how he wrote the Declaration of Independence but didn't follow the principles of it.

As early as 1965 Johnson was making bold moves like the time he used the August issue of *EBONY* to tackle the roots of racism by placing a spotlight on the activities of European Americans. The cover title, "The White Problem in America," written by Lerone Bennett Jr., had a black background with a white man silhouetted on it. Johnson's Publisher's Statement thoroughly explained why he dedicated an entire issue to a theme that nobody wanted to address because racial tensions were high and solutions were low for fear of retaliation or making things worse for the "Negro." He said the following:

> In the entire history of the period during which the area of the North American Continent now known as the United States has been occupied by white Europeans and their descendants, the white man has been trying to explain away the Negro. From the landing of the first Negroes at Jamestown, VA, in 1619 to the Emancipation Proclamation in 1863, the explanation was, 'They are better off as slaves here than they were as tribesman in the African jungle.'...He was explained away again for nearly 100 years as 'not being ready yet.' He was 'protected' by the courts which legally said, 'You shall be kept separate, though equal. You are a second class citizen'...Today the explaining away is a little more difficult. Enough Negroes have proved that, given an equal chance, they can measure up to the best. Now the explaining away takes the form of, 'Things are better today than they were yesterday and will be better tomorrow than they are today. Have patience. Don't demonstrate. Everything will come about in due time.' But the time is now

> and the Negro in the pulpits, in the streets, in the schools, at the polls, in the halls of justice and in the legislative bodies of the land has emphasized that today he has earned his humanity and his full rights as a citizen. What has held him up? The unthinking white man—Mr. Charlie, Whitey, The Man—the unthinking white man who is the symbol to Negroes of all those whites who have 'stood in the doorways' to keep the Negro back. This brings us to this special issue. The White Problem in America, and its reason for being. For more than a decade through books, magazines, newspapers, TV and radio, the white man has been trying to solve the race problem through studying the Negro. We feel that the answer lies in a more thorough study of the man who created the problem. In this issue we, as Negroes, look at himself more thoroughly. With a better understanding of himself, we trust that he may then understand us better—and this nation's most vital problem can then be solved.[17]

Bennett Jr., renowned as the publication's resident historian, began his story by stating what he perceived to be the facts about this obstruction. Bennett Jr. wrote:

> There is no Negro problem in America. The problem of race in America, insofar as that problem is related to packets of melanin in men's skin, is a white problem. And in order to solve that problem we must seek its source, not in the Negro but in the white American (in the process by which he was educated, in the needs and complexes he expresses through racism) and in the structure of the white community (in the power arrangements and the illicit uses of racism in the scramble for scarce values: power, prestige and income).[18]

More stories ranged from articles such as "White Hate Groups," which examined how racists and fascists joined hands to strangle U.S. liberties. Whitney M. Young Jr. penned a story called "The High Cost of Discrimination" that dealt with how human and financial waste were a part of the nation's price for bias. Rev. Dr. Martin Luther King, Jr., who once had a regular column in *EBONY*, wrote the story, "The Un-Christian Christian," where he analyzed religious duty in racial conflicts. *EBONY* editor Hans J. Massaquoi, whose mother was German and father was African American, wrote the story "Would You Want Your Daughter to Marry One?" This piece exposed sexual fear as the root of U.S. racism. President Lyndon B. Johnson even contributed an article, "The Great Society," that told how he was committed to fight the 'American problem.'"[19]

By 1985 and with a circulation of 1.7 million, *The New York Times* featured a story to commemorate *EBONY*'s fortieth anniversary. The article discussed how it was "considered more than a magazine." It was considered an "institution."[20]

And people respected its merit and contents. The messages were resonating not only with blacks but with whites as well. The May 1946 issue of *EBONY* featured a letter from the Reverend J.B. Lux of Chicago. The managing director of *The National Catholic Monthly* wrote:

> Just finished going over the February issue. It gets better every month and I want to congratulate you. I think you are doing a fine job, not only in giving a good magazine to your own people, but in educating us whites as well. Too long have men like Doctor (Theodore) Lawless been ignored by the white population, even while they are very prompt to seek out his aid when everyone else fails.[21]

Another example of the magazine's powerful message came in an unorthodox way that few even realize. Though Jackie Robinson broke the color barrier in major league baseball by joining the Brooklyn Dodgers in 1947, it was the articles published in *EBONY* that sparked responsiveness and promoted cultural sensitivity with Dodger club owners about the unfair conditions and challenging circumstances that African-American ball players suffered unlike their white counterparts.

Baseball legend Roy Campanella stated in *EBONY* magazine during an interview that it was the articles printed in the monthly publication that really shed light on how the athletes were finally allowed to play on the same field with others, but behind closed doors and on the road, they were still very much segregated. Campanella explained that the in-depth articles in *EBONY* shared poignant reflections from baseball. Robinson and others, though appearing to have opened doors for other African-American players, endured and were continually subjected to harsh treatment in spite of being the firsts. Dodger Town, Campanella stated, was created to help ease tension and foster equality for their ball club.[22] Few people know this fact but the stories in *EBONY* helped to positively alter the course of history with that baseball team because the articles educated the team's owners about the hardships for black players. Campanella explained:

> We were not allowed to stay with the team at hotels in the South…Some of the cities we played in, we had to stay in private homes and arrange our own transportation to the field. We had to go through things our teammates didn't. The regular writers didn't know how we got to the park or what we did off the field. But *EBONY* was there and let everyone know what we were going through—about the racism. That's why the Dodgers built Dodgertown, so we wouldn't have to run into segregation and so the team could live together. The Dodgers definitely had their eyes opened by the articles in *EBONY*. And that's how the public learned how tough it was for Jackie and Don and me.[23]

The magazines were also in the forefront with civil rights coverage. The stories, people, places and events were recorded on the pages of *JET* and *EBONY*. Television footage covered certain moments and was limited during that time. *JET* was there at its inception and covered the ugly truths and harsh realities about the fight for equality from an African-American person's perspective. *JET* was often credited as a catalyst in fueling the Civil Rights Movement, hence another reason it was more than a magazine—it was a movement. Johnson said:

> When Martin Luther King first began marching, there were no television cameras, there were no White reporters. The only way he got his message across, in the beginning, was through *JET*. Simeon Booker and a guy we had named David Jackson made hundreds of trips into Mississippi, Georgia and Alabama following Dr. King before he became well known.[24]

When the teen Emmett Till was first missing in Mississippi, *JET* wrote stories about the missing Chicago youth. *EBONY* and *JET* covered the history of African Americans. The publications showed the progression of how blacks went from being called Negro to colored to black to African American. The Rev. Jesse Jackson said:

> *JET* is the only authentic national connection for the black community. The Table of Contents express the breath of concern for the black community, and the regularity of the publication gives us a national rhythm. If that publication ceased, it would be like a giant chain lost all of its critical service. His is one of the outstanding services that our race has ever acquired. It does not depend on who is mayor or who is president. It is a legitimate expression of self-reliance.[25]

As a participant and as an observer in helping to cover black history, Johnson made it known that Dr. King was the black leader he was most impressed with. "I don't even have to think about that. He was unselfish, he was unyielding and he had eternal faith."[26]

However, some conjured up rumors that black publications like *EBONY* and *JET* were not fully supportive of King and even served as informants to the FBI. In Taylor Branch's 1989 Pulitzer Prize-winning book *Parting the Waters: America in the King Years 1954-63*, which provides an account of the Civil Rights Movement, Branch makes the following claim: "The FBI did not lack friendly contacts in the upper reaches of the Negro press. Bureau officials prevailed on representatives of *JET* and *EBONY*, on the publisher of the four Afro-American newspapers, and on John Sengstacke, Robert Abbott's heir at *The Chicago Defender*."[27]

Johnson, in 2000, was asked about this claim during an interview with *Chicago History*. He called Branch's statements "ridiculous" and explained how he was surprised that someone would suggest something so baseless. Johnson said this about the accusations:

> I was shocked that someone would believe that we were against Martin Luther King. [He] relied on us more than he did anybody—*EBONY* and *JET*. Dr. King, number one, was a classmate of Lerone Bennett, who is my executive editor and has been for forty-seven years. [King] was a classmate of Robert E. Johnson, now deceased but who was head of *JET* for forty-seven years. Dr. King would call up and say, 'Fellas, the white press is ignoring us. They're not paying any attention to us. Brother Johnson, I need you to send one of your best

> writers and your best photographers down here to highlight what's going on.' The FBI never asked me to do anything. Never. Never.[28]

Johnson was committed to sharing the truth with blacks about the state of the world. People wanted to read about black entertainers and the finer things in black life and culture, but Johnson knew they also needed to understand the brutal truths about it all as well. Without force feeding anyone anything, he found a way to make teaching more palatable without appearing preachy. This was Johnson's belief:

> I go back to my mother, who persuaded me to take castor oil because she put it in orange juice. The entertainment is orange juice, but what cures people is castor oil, which is the serious material in *EBONY*. But you can't cure people who don't read your magazine. So we try to lure people in with entertainment, and once we have their attention, we try to educate and uplift them and grapple with the serious problems of the day.[29]

This new formula proved a success and was prominently utilized as audiences desired more education than entertainment. He said:

> In the early days we followed the consciousness of the times by defining success narrowly in terms of material things...We broadened the formula for success, defining it as the achievement of a positive goal or the attainment of whatever a person set out to do...This changed the weight of the magazine. Before the sixties we were perhaps 50 percent orange juice and 50 percent castor oil. For most of the sixties we were practically all castor oil. Our readers embraced the new formula. They hungered for it. They were more interested in being men and women than in being entertained.[30]

Arming readers with enough information to foster change and ignite a solidarity among people as they endured the Civil Rights Movement and its struggles, weekly and monthly information was disseminated for *JET* and *EBONY* respectively. Johnson said this about both magazines and their principles:

> Not only did we report the struggle but we also became a part of the struggle. I marched and gave tens of thousands of dollars to different arms in the movement. With and without my approval, my editors marched and volunteered for difficult and dangerous assignments…We sat in with the sit-inners, rode the buses with the Freedom Riders, braved the mob in the steps of Central High School…We were there. We told the story. More to the point, we were a part of a story that cannot be recalled or told without referring to the pages of *EBONY* and *JET* and the 2 million photographs in our archives.[31]

In a *JET* company brochure published in 1993, it included something called "A Few Words From the Publisher." Used as marketing material, this informed consumers as to how the little magazine made such big noise in sounding the alarm about issues that were relevant and concerned its audience. It said the following:

> In the past 42 years the black community has endured more changes than in the previous 400. We have seen much progress and *JET* was there. From the lynching of black Americans in the deep south, the birth of the Civil Rights Movement, to the rise of modern leaders like General Colin Powell and superstars Bill Cosby and Michael Jordan, *JET* was there. *JET* special reports chronicled the heroics of black Americans fighting the nation's wars and nature's disasters from a uniquely black perspective. *JET* was there all along, informing black Americans about the actions our government was taking and what it meant to them. We have grown with the black community and as such have become a leading source of information to the community. Today, as the largest and most widely read black newsmagazine, we continue to play that vital role.[32]

Encouraging readers and telling them that all things are possible was another critical task that the magazines were designed to do. By being excluded within the media in stories, this sent a resounding message that their lives were not important or that they are unable to accomplish what other races could achieve. Johnson sought to change this through words and actions.

Blacks were believed to be inferior so they were ignored. *EBONY* was used as a vehicle to offer hope for its readers. When all else fails, it is important to have something to carry you through. The messages propelled a movement of self-pride. Johnson articulated, "We believe then—and we believe now—that you have to change images before you can change acts and institutions."[33]

Readers valued and appreciated the publications because they were unique and relatable. The articles easily resonated with its audience because stories covered and addressed every walk of life and profession. Readers came to know the magazines, which sat on coffee tables across the country in black households for decades, as if they were a family member. Johnson said:

> With *EBONY* in particular, I'm trying to give readers something they can't get anywhere else. I'm giving them a positive approach to race relations. I'm not preoccupied with discrimination. Any black person who's been discriminated against doesn't need me to point it out. I need to tell people how to overcome that discrimination—how to succeed.[34]

Seeing people who have made it and have become successful was an important element in the magazine. Inspiring readers through words and images was pivotal and defining for Johnson because *EBONY* was a magazine of success and of achievement. He wanted it to mirror the lives of successful people but to also show the other side of life as well. "It deals with unsuccessful people, and it should, but our main thrust is to show that despite the difficulty, despite all the problems, it's possible for some people to break through, and you, whoever is reading the magazine just might be the person to do just that."[35]

People featured in the magazines were reflective of what Johnson wanted readers to see so that they believed they could do the same. He said, "Black people, in particular, need role models, people like themselves who overcame difficulties similar to what they themselves are experiencing. That's why we ask every successful person we interview just what they did to succeed."[36]

Johnson also desired that readers would find his own story inspirational and look to him as a living testament of what he hoped the magazine accomplished. "I see myself as representing what I'm trying to sell in *EBONY*...I'm one of the models. There are a lot of them now, but I'm one of them. I'm one of the people who says you can succeed against the odds."[37]

After subconsciously being told and shown the opposite of what Johnson set out to do, this re-education process launched a movement that came from the messages and intents fostered through Johnson's publications. He explained:

> We are telling black people that we have a great past, that we have a great heritage, that we have much to draw on, much to move forward on. And once we understand who we are, once we know we are important, that we have an identity, once we know there once lived people like us who succeeded against the odds, that will help us to have confidence in ourselves. That is what *EBONY* tries to do.[38]

For as much as Johnson worked to publish positive stories, he often maintained that serious issues, not always addressing the finer things, were dealt with in *EBONY* as well. Some readers and critics alike believed Johnson's take on the happier side of black life was taking the easy way out through soft journalism.

In the fifth anniversary issue, this growing concern was addressed in an editorial that read the following: "There are some who have accused *EBONY* of fence sitting. If being a middle-of-the-roader who refuses to carry either a chip on the shoulder or a hat in hand is fence sitting, we plead guilty. Frankly we are firm believers in carrying both a big stick and soft glove when approaching white folks on the race question."[39]

Johnson often let it be known how *EBONY* was not taking up a cause for action but showing readers another side of life. There was more than doom and gloom. There were people making history and accomplishing feats never done before. Why not place the spotlight on those occasions instead of the darker side of life, which blacks were already all too familiar with. That was Johnson's mind set. He told the Christian Science Monitor, "We try to emphasize and play up points on which Negroes and whites can agree rather than stress points on which they disagree. We try to avoid too much pressure. We're not the NAACP. We're a business."[40]

The magazine was destined to be a monument—even from the

beginning. Its first issue was casually placed on newsstands in black neighborhoods with no promotion or advertising. It still managed to sell out the first issue, selling out the 25,000 copies printed. Ben Burns, *EBONY*'s founding editor, said, "What was most innovative in *EBONY* magazine in its early years was its daring (for the period) editorial approach. For the first time a national black periodical openly rejected negativism and advocacy of a cause: the persistent theme of the Negro press from the start. Black journalism had always been synonymous with racial militancy, and newspapers bore such names as Whip and Defender. In contrast, *EBONY* in its opening editorial proclaimed: '*EBONY* will try to mirror the happier side of Negro life—the positive, everyday accomplishments from Harlem to Hollywood.'"[41]

Aimed to education and entertain, the main goal was to foster black pride in an effort to raise the self-esteem and self confidence in its readers. There really was a mis-educative approach that took place before the arrival of Johnson's publications. Blacks did not see themselves in a positive light. They were constantly being shown what they did wrong or they were ignored altogether. Johnson filled a void and showed people what they hadn't seen. The magazine was a form of escapism, a way for his race to see that the glass is half full instead of half empty.

Early on and even after Johnson's death, *EBONY* has been criticized for not reporting more stories about social justice and hard news. Herbert Nipson, executive editor of *EBONY*, said in 1980 the purpose of the magazines were not to tear down people in their own race. "We would sooner not do a story," he said. "In *JET* it would be a news story. But we wouldn't do a feature in *EBONY*."[42] In 1978 when Detroit's first black Congressman, Charles Diggs, was indicted on charges of taking payroll kickbacks from members of his staff, he became the first lawmaker of his race ever to be indicted for a crime by a federal grand jury.[43] Johnson said about the misfortune, "We don't rush to print critical things about black leaders—even if it's true. We've deliberately avoided doing anything on Charles Diggs in *EBONY*. We don't want to add to his humiliation—or to blacks' humiliation."[44]

Shirley Chisholm, the first black woman elected to Congress and the first black to seek a major party's nomination for the U.S. presidency, agreed with the stance Johnson took in not tearing down others of the same race in the media. She said, "I guess in a very real sense, white folks do that for us. *EBONY* is trying to reach out and cultivate positive images we desperately need."[45]

Sociologist E. Franklin Frazier's 1957 study "Black Bourgeoisie" attacked the publication for promoting stories of wealth and material possessions over articles that addressed difficult realities of life for blacks. Johnson's looking on the happier and brighter side of life was considered soft news and even "Uncle Tomming" by some.[46] Still, Johnson never backed down from his publication's goals because instead of selling out blacks, Johnson was steadfast in his notion of selling the race its own identity.

In 2000, Johnson said people like Frazier "had all made it, and I was talking and preaching to the people who didn't think they could make it. I was trying to show them by example that if all these black people could make it, they could make it."[47] Johnson went on to say he believed there were many avenues to deliver a message and that the choice he made was not through protest but promoting positivity about one's race. Johnson stated his beliefs by saying:

> There are many ways to fight. And I believe that mine is more effective than theirs. I think we brought about more changes than Franklin Frazier or some of the other people. I think we have to choose what road we take...Without soft pedaling or ignoring continuing problems, we wanted to highlight breakthroughs and to tell black Americans that there is no defense against an excellence that meets a pressing public need.[48]

Johnson was bold and confident in saying he represented what he was hoping to convey to his readers as a positive role model. He wanted to show them success as a person who came from nothing and made the most of his life. Johnson never gave up and said:

> I'm one of the people who says you can succeed against the odds. I'm not saying the odds aren't there. Many people assume *EBONY* is saying everything is just great, but we're not saying that. We're saying we have to deal with the world as we find it. And within the context of what we find, these are the ways we think you can succeed within the system.[49]

During *EBONY*'s inception, Burns' Communist and *The Chicago Defender* training made him long to report more about the harsh realities that blacks faced on a daily basis. Burns wanted to use the magazine as a vehicle to show the worst of racism on a larger scale. Johnson, as usual, saw otherwise. His formula, stories of success and the "brighter side" of life, worked by showing aspects of black life that few in the mainstream media seemed to talk about or had any interest in exploring. "It is why we are telling people what they can do rather than what they can not do. Enough people are out there giving examples of what you can't do. Whenever there is a black person doing a successful job in a unique situation, there is an *EBONY* story."[50] When Johnson bumped heads with Burns about what was best to write for the race, he'd sarcastically tell Burns, "I've been a Negro all my life and you're still new at it."[51]

Burns, who had free reigns to handle editorial as he so pleased, said that some of the early, sensational stories and images written under his leadership were to attract readers. This was during a time when advertisers didn't have African-American magazines on their radar for revenue. Ninety percent of the sales in 1945 when *EBONY* was founded came from newsstand sales. But once Johnson learned about subscriptions from Les Suhler, the Des Moines, Iowa-based subscription director of Cowles Publications' *Look* magazine, and recognized a middle class of African-American families, Johnson wanted to find a niche market. Thus, he made *EBONY* lean more toward being a family magazine.[52]

In 1949 Era Bell Thompson was promoted to managing editor of *EBONY*. Herbert Nipson, with an MFA in hand from State University of Iowa, was co-managing editor. Nipson later became executive editor. Nipson, skilled in layout and also photography, along with Bell, turned the magazine around so that its focus was considered a bit more insightful about controversial issues given the times. Lerone Bennett Jr., who came from the *Atlanta Daily World* and headed the magazine after Nipson, adjusted it during the 1960s to include serious political and social commentary and stories about civil rights.[53]

A book division was started and published Bennett's books that chronicled black history, including *Before the Mayflower* and *Pioneers in Protest.* The scholar's stories in *EBONY* ranged from articles like 1961's "The White Problem in America," to 1968's "Was Abraham Lincoln a White Supremacist?" The August 1979 special issue of *EBONY* was titled "Black on Black Crime: The Causes, The Consequences, The Cures."[54] "I expected criticism. I got nothing but accolades. It was the most courageous thing we have done in the last two or three years,"[55] Johnson said. With this change came topics that covered middle and working-class blacks on a national level.

Still, the criticism remained. A staple in the publication at one point was doing at home stories with notables. Readers got to see the homes of high-profile figures in sports and in entertainment. These kinds of up close and personal feature stories were a way to attract a new audience and even younger readers. "We're looking for people [for the covers] with instant recognition. And most of those people, among blacks, unfortunately, are entertainers and sports figures."[56] In 1980, Johnson expressed a concern about the advancement of blacks in positions of power. He said he felt more optimistic a decade earlier but his thoughts had since changed. "I sit on a lot of corporate boards. Blacks are not on corporate tracks to take over. There aren't even enough in training programs. Ten years from now, people are going to need inspirational stories as much as they do now."[57]

While this was of interest to audiences at large, the soft news label most associated with *EBONY* hung over the publication like a dark cloud. It even received criticism from Chicago native Bryant Gumbel, one of the high-profile personalities the publication recognized during the magazine's fifty fifth anniversary issue in an article titled "The 55 Most Intriguing Blacks of 2000."[58]

A year later, in 2001, Gumbel, at the time a co-host of CBS's "Early Show," delivered the 133rd commencement speech to the graduates of Howard University, where he told students how "it's not enough" for people to applaud athletes and entertainers, but they should question why so many blacks look to them for answers when it comes to changing the plight of blacks. Gumbel then told the graduates how they're "entitled to live a rich life" but "if all you're going to seek is a superficial *EBONY* magazine view of life…one that accentuates only your cars, and your clothes, then some guy's going to be standing here another 36 years from now once again bemoaning the plight of people of color in these United States of America."[59]

Johnson's daughter, Linda, who was CEO of *EBONY*'s parent company, took offense to the claim that the magazine promoted materialism. She wrote a letter to Gumbel, making it public and telling him, "We're glad that you found time to visit black America, but we regret that you were not better informed...We don't visit black America, we live here." Her letter also mentioned how "He's obviously misinformed and probably has not picked up a copy of *EBONY* in some time...We have chronicled every important historical event in the African-American community over the past 56 years." In a response to Johnson Rice's statement, Gumbel called her letter "foolish." He also suggested to her that "instead of complaining about the truth, maybe Ms. Rice should be more worried about the fact that everyone totally understood the reference I made and applauded it loudly."[60]

Johnson, in a 1985 interview with *The New York Times*, responded to criticism of *EBONY*'s focus by insisting that it has covered just about every major "assault on discrimination."[61] For him the movement was in the magazine's singular message, which was to primarily show blacks that no matter how large the obstacles, anything was possible.

And to those who complained the most about the publication's soft focus, Johnson didn't bite his tongue when he asked, "If all these other issues were crying out for someone to deal with, why hasn't someone put out a magazine to deal with them?"[62]

*EBONY* magazine fulfilled African Americans' yearning to be recognized and respected through the use of inclusion. They no longer felt invisible or ignored. A wave of pride in one's self is what it developed. The movement was in the message for all the world to see. Black is beautiful. Black is powerful. Black is mighty. Black is intelligent. Black is noble. Black is present.

## CHAPTER 6

# A DECISION THAT CHANGED HISTORY

***"There was a saying at JET and EBONY that, 'If Mr. Johnson is afraid to do it, that means it's a good story.' I was afraid to do it, but you have to do things that you're afraid to do."***

***John H. Johnson***

It was one of the most challenging decisions Johnson ever had to make, but it ended up helping him to change the course of history. Making history and writing about it were what Johnson did, but this time it was different. This was the moment when the daring publisher decided to show on the pages of a 1955 *JET* magazine the battered face and horribly bloated body of Chicago teen Emmett Louis Till, who was murdered by two white men, J.W. Milam and his half-brother, Roy Bryant, for allegedly whistling at a white woman, Carolyn Bryant, the wife of Roy, in Money, Mississippi.[1]

The killers, who beat and shot the fourteen-year-old before dumping his lifeless body into the Tallahatchie River, were acquitted. Four months later they admitted their guilt in a *Look* magazine article where Milam and Roy Bryant received $3,000 for their story.[2]

*The Chicago Defender* first ran the unretouched pictures of Till in a casket in its newspaper. Johnson then published them in his magazine after the teen's mother, Mamie Bradley Mobley, personally reached out to Johnson, asking that he run the images in his national weekly *JET*, because she would have his casket open to show the world what happened to her son. The newspapers and magazines sold out.[3] Johnson admitted to being downright afraid when it came time to run that photograph. Despite trepidation, he did so anyway.

People heard about lynchings and read about lynchings, but few had ever seen its ugly impact in person or in a picture. Johnson boldly revealed a few images in the September 15, 1955 issue, to give the world a glimpse of the evil hand of racism—face to face! During weekly *JET* editorial meetings, Johnson recounted that moment and its impact decades later. He recounted how people rushed to the newsstand and complained about the horrific photograph of the deceased teen, yet they still managed to leave the store with several copies of the magazine. But how and where did this painful moment in history all begin?

Just as Johnson used images in *JET* and in *EBONY* to highlight the beautiful aspects of America, he used images to show the harsh realities as well. Johnson used his magazines to display the good and the bad. Pictures can be more powerful than words because images are seared into one's memory.

African Americans were being hanged, burned alive and beaten to death by racist whites who used the horrible assaults to oppress blacks with fear. No one can deny that one of black America's most memorable, yet darkest moments in history, took place in August 1955 when Till was beaten to death. When the horribly mangled body of Till was returned to Chicago for burial, his school teacher mother, Mamie, asked photographers to shoot pictures, saying: "I want the world to see what they did to my boy."[4] She requested pictures taken of her son in the casket because she wanted the world to see what happened to her only child as an example of what African Americans, especially in the South, encountered at the hands of racist white people.

Johnson recalled there were "people on the staff who were squeamish about the photographs." He admittedly had reservations, too, but decided finally that if it happened, it was his publication's responsibility to print it and "let the world experience man's inhumanity to man."[5] The other rationale Johnson used to run the photos was because Till's mother wanted him to do it. Because of Johnson's great respect for his own mother, the request was something he had to grant no matter how worried he was about the decision. He said, "If she's not ashamed of it, I'm not ashamed of it. I was afraid to do it. There was a saying at *JET* and *EBONY* that, 'If Mr. Johnson is afraid to do it, that means it's a good story.' I was afraid to do it, but you have to do things that you're afraid to do."[6]

Johnson cited a time earlier when he made the decision to do something that made him a bit uncomfortable. The editorial team decided to do a story on the white problem in America for *EBONY*.

Ira Bell Thompson, then a co-managing editor, addressed Johnson about the article. She asked, "'Boss, do you know what you're doing? Do you know how many white people you're going to anger and all the things they can do to you?'" Johnson replied to her, "'Ira Bell, I don't know what I'm doing, but I'm going to do it anyway.' You have to dare to do things you're afraid to do."[7]

Stepping into unchartered territory was nothing new for him. Mainstream media refused to run Till's picture, and Johnson had his fair share of doubts, but because he was a steady advocate for his race, he dared to show the world. Johnson said he was uncomfortable showing the picture, but Johnson's unwavering courage in African-American history and the importance of documenting it accurately and completely took precedence. He was apprehensive about illustrating such a terrifying picture, but Johnson had respect for the teachable moment Till's mother wanted to give by showing the world what racial hatred looked like. As mentioned before, people had heard about lynchings and beatings, but this was the first time people got a chance to see this up close and personal on the pages of *JET*.

Till's photograph would be a painful and eye-opening reminder of the poisonous hate that racism spews. The images were called, "probably one of the greatest media products in the last 40 or 50 years, because that picture stimulated a lot of anger on the part of blacks all over the country," according to Charles Diggs, a former Detroit congressman.[8] The picture inspired people to want to take a stand and fight for civil rights. Timing is everything because Rosa Parks, often called the "Mother of the Civil Rights Movement," once said she didn't refuse to give up her seat because her feet hurt as legend once had it. The truth, she said, was that she thought about Till and the image she saw in *JET*. "I thought about Emmett Till and I just couldn't go back," she said about that fateful day.[9]

Using this picture in his magazine is often credited with igniting the Civil Rights Movement, because 100 days after Till's murder, Parks refused to give up her seat in the "colored" section on a crowded Montgomery bus so that a white man could have her place. Like many others who violated Alabama's bus segregation laws, Parks was arrested. A then unknown twenty-six-year-old minister named Rev. Dr. Martin Luther King, Jr. was asked to help with a citywide bus boycott in Montgomery. King called his Morehouse classmate and Alpha Phi Alpha Fraternity, Inc. brother, Robert E. Johnson, who was the executive editor of *JET* magazine.

King asked Robert E. Johnson for coverage of what he was doing in Montgomery. This was during a time when TV networks, newspapers, and magazines weren't covering the news and/or activities of black activists on a daily, weekly, or monthly basis. Their work was pretty much ignored by mainstream media. But it was Johnson, also the fraternity brother to King and Robert E. Johnson, who agreed to publish the stories. The image of Till is a powerful example that photographs carry dominance and influence either positively or negatively. Johnson explained this about his decision to show the Till pictures and what this meant historically:

> We printed them for the same reasons that the Jews show the Holocaust every year. They want young people to know about the atrocities. They want them to know how cruel some people can be in the world and how much we have to fight to improve. It's very important that we do that. That's consistent with the whole concept of freedom of the press. You're supposed to let people know what's going on and then let them judge me.[11]

Till's picture was pivotal in changing the world and altering how African Americans saw themselves when it came to the brutal realizations of racial hatred. Chris Metress edited the book *The Lynching of Emmett Till.* He said people, particularly African Americans, talked about the images' impact on their life. Metress said:

> You get testimony from white people coming of age at the time about how the case affected them, but you don't get them testifying, like countless blacks, that the *JET* photo had this transformative effect on them, altering the way they felt about themselves and their vulnerabilities and the dangers they would be facing in the Civil Rights Movement. Because white people didn't read *JET*.[12]

When Johnson died in 2005, Chicago Mayor Richard M. Daley told the packed audience at the funeral service how Johnson created more than a statement with his magazine. Daley said: "John Johnson had the courage of his convictions; his difficult decision to print the shocking photos of Emmett Till in his casket shamed America and helped spark the Civil Rights Movement. That wasn't a business decision—that was a cause."[13]

Johnson said the Rev. Jesse Jackson became so successful because he was surrounded by people who succeeded against the odds, namely himself. When Johnson, in 1977, was named the most outstanding African-American publisher in history by the National Newspaper Publishers Association,[14] Jackson acknowledged how Johnson used *JET* to educate his race but most importantly the world. Jackson said the following:

> *JET* is the only authentic national connection for the black community. The table of contents express the breadth of concern for the black community, and the regularity of the publication gives us a national rhythm. If that publication ceased, it would be like a giant chain lost all of its critical links. The publisher must be congratulated for his business acumen and his service. His is one of the outstanding services that our race has ever acquired. It does not depend on who is mayor, or who is president. It is a legitimate expression of self-reliance.[15]

This statement by Jackson about *JET* is an example of Johnson's use of his magazine to meet the cultural and sociocultural needs of the race. Jackson's reflection also showed the importance of history and why it must be documented correctly and accurately. Inclusion of African-American history leads to racial pride and self-esteem. In pointing out the pitfalls if this publication ended, Jackson articulated how the African-American community would be without critical links. This showed how he understood that Johnson used *JET* to document history as a means to teach the race and to show the historical contributions and accomplishments of African Americans and those in the African Diaspora.

In 2014, *JET* ceased publication and went online. This platform has not had the impact of the actual magazines. But, in 2017, a year after *EBONY* and *JET* were purchased by CVG Group, it was announced that *JET* would return as a quarterly publication, dedicated solely to millennials.[16] At the time of this book's publishing, this idea had not come to fruition.

*JET* was small in stature but it carried a heavy load, because the magazine was packed with hard-hitting weekly news stories about current events that happened to African Americans around the country. Just as Johnson used the images to highlight the beautiful aspects of America, he also used images and words to remind the world of darkness as well.

Till's mother, Mobley Bradley, died January 6, 2003, at the age of eighty-one, in the midst of penning her memoir *Death of Innocence*. The book was released a year later.[17]

In January 2017, it was revealed that Carolyn Bryant, the woman who accused Till of making physical and verbal advances at her, told *The Blood of Emmett Till* author Timothy Tyson during a 2007 interview, when she was seventy-two, that she lied on the Chicago teen. A manuscript about Bryant's life is in the Southern Historical Collection at the University of North Carolina Chapel Hill library archives. According to Tyson, the public will not be allowed to see it until 2036.[18]

# CHAPTER 7

# THE GOSPEL TRUTH

***"We have maintained that excellence knows no boundary and that the man or woman who builds a better mousetrap or sings a better song or preaches a better sermon cannot be ignored or denied."***

***John H. Johnson***

*JET* magazine was tiny in size but it carried much weight with information and pictures that chronicled the life of African Americans. Black people—even whites—turned to the newsweekly, and its monthly sister publication *EBONY*, to get a better understanding about how this race lives. What mattered. Who mattered. What was happening.

*EBONY* was known as a magazine of record with rich images and text, while *JET*'s short, quick news format was treasured as the law. If a person or an event in African-American history was noteworthy as being the first, being the best, or being the biggest, one could surely believe that both magazines would document those moments. It didn't matter if the subject or the occasion was celebrity driven, landmark times were to be celebrated for the African-American race. Johnson also used moments to educate people about those who weren't black yet contributed to African-American history.

A 1946 issue of *EBONY* shows this when Johnson introduced the world to the first white man to pledge the African-American Alpha Phi Alpha Fraternity Inc., in which Johnson was an active and life member.[1] Bernard Levin, who was twenty-two and a student studying dentistry at the University of Chicago, where Johnson briefly attended, was initiated in June 1946 through the same chapter that Johnson became a member, Theta Chapter. *EBONY* showed pictures of Levin and his line brothers doing things such as polishing the shoes of their big brothers, polishing trophies won by the Theta Chapter and cleaning the front of the fraternity house. Johnson, during this time, didn't have any problems with his printer attempting to censor his images in *EBONY* of a white man in servitude to African-American men. Interesting because four years later when a white woman, married to a shoe shiner, was shown in the same magazine polishing her black husband's shoes, the printer wanted Johnson to remove it. A former professor of dentistry at the University of Southern California, Levin died in 2008 at the age of eighty-four.[2]

Johnson was a visionary in words, actions, and deeds. He helped to break in careers of those who would go on to make their own history. He predicted one-of-a-kind feats and claimed successes when the artists themselves probably didn't have a clue about their career's lifespan. This was the case involving five brown-skinned brothers with big afros, hailing from Gary, Indiana, known as the Jackson 5.

Armed with a father, Joseph Jackson, who had a steadfast belief in them, and a praying Jehovah's Witness mom, Katherine Jackson, the talented young singers, dancers, and musicians also had the Midas touch with their young lead singer, Michael, who was just ten at the time. The group was only performing for a few years, mainly in local shows, before signing to a label, Steeltown Records, being dropped by that label and then signing to a new one, Motown Records, in 1969.

Funny how life works and there is much truth to the term six degrees of separation. When Johnson took a couples trip with his wife and Burns and his wife on the English ship S.S. Caronia in May 1950, they were placed at a side dinner table with a woman from New York, traveling to Paris with her three-year-old daughter.[3 4] It turns out that little girl grew up to be an artist developer for Motown. Her name was Suzanne de Passe and a group she worked with at Motown was the Jackson 5.[5]

Most impressed with the showmanship of little Michael and pleased with the full circle moment with de Passe, it wasn't difficult for Johnson to put them on the cover of *EBONY* though they were so new that they were only known in Indiana. Johnson didn't care. He made the executive decision to place them on the most sought-after piece of real estate on a magazine and even hailed them with the title "Hottest Young Group in History." Michael, who didn't say much in the story, did admit that he didn't know what he was doing. No one could tell otherwise because the kid had the "it" factor with a magnificent voice, dynamic dance moves and a cute face. The September 1970 issue became the Jacksons' first-ever national magazine cover for any publication.[6]

Johnson took a liking to the family and as Michael and his siblings grew up, they considered the Johnson Publishing Company headquarters home. They virtually grew up visiting 820 S. Michigan when they were newcomers to the industry and as they got older. Noted for the private luncheons at his company, Johnson had the delicious meals frequently for the Jacksons, turning it into a family affair with Joseph and Katherine's grandchildren later coming to break bread. Few were allowed on the 11th floor penthouse but the Jacksons were offered full range.

A 1972 visit to the company showed pictures of young Michael and Randy, lifting weights in Johnson's private gym on the eleventh floor.[7] Two years later a December 1974 issue featured the entire Jackson clan, all eleven members, on the cover. Three year earlier *Life* magazine's September 24 issue had the Jackson parents and the five boys gracing the cover. What set the *EBONY* cover apart and made it monumental was that it was the first time any national publication included all six brothers and three sisters with their parents.[8]

Michael and Johnson developed a special bond. Johnson knew of Michael's adoration for gospel legend Mahalia Jackson and took the time to send him a collection of her VHS tapes. Michael considered Mahalia to be one of his favorite singers because he said he could "feel her soul" when she sang.

Johnson Publishing Company is where Michael's artistic abilities were first known nationally with a drawing shown in the August/September 1975 issue of *EBONY Jr.*, with copies selling seventy-five cents and a one-year subscription of ten issues selling for ten dollars. The story, titled "The Jackson Family Has An Artist: Michael," includes a cartoon of an African-American mother and son with big curly afro. The mother, wearing a dress and fishnet pantyhose, complains to her son about inflation while expressing her desire to see something go down. The little boy, with full lips and wearing glasses, hands his mother a report card with the talk bubble saying, "Then my report card is just what you need, mom. All my grades went down."[9] Prior to this time, Michael revealed how much he liked "to do oil paintings and abstracts." He added how he liked "things that are very colorful."[10]

Michael came to respect and trust Johnson so much that as he got older, Michael turned to him for advice about business. One day Johnson recalled how Michael called him for counsel because "he didn't want to end up broke like so many athletes and entertainers."[11] In fact, Michael set up a financial committee, which included Johnson, accountant Marshall Gelfand, attorney John Branca, and producer David Geffen, who, like Johnson, were the only two outsiders on the team and were not paid.[12] Johnson said during one meeting at his Palm Springs home, he encouraged Michael "to look for investments that could serve as an annuity, such as the Beatles catalog." Though Johnson shared his opinions, Michael "firmly makes his own decision."[13] At an early point in Michael's career, he came under scrutiny "about his lifestyle" and spending habits. Johnson suggested he let people see "the real Michael…by giving back some of the good fortune he has enjoyed." Johnson said he discussed with Michael his commitment to the United Negro College Fund as well as his plans to hire other Blacks in his operation.[14] In a December 1984 issue, a story titled "The Michael Jackson Nobody Knows," the group, by now simply calling themselves The Jacksons, were preparing for their Victory Tour and "expected to gross over $70 million." Michael announced that his portion of the earnings would go toward charity, including the United Negro College Fund.[15]

When Michael got into trouble with sexual molestation allegations and struggled with pain killers, Johnson often lived by the motto and said, "We don't dance on people's graves." He maintained how *EBONY* and *JET* did not do what mainstream outlets did by working to assassinate people's character, especially black figures, before they were ever found guilty of anything. One article featured Michael on the cover with the title, "Michael Jackson Tries to Keep Career From Crumbling As He Fights Addiction to Painkiller Drugs and Charges of Child Molestation," and addressed rumors and charges levied against the superstar performer. In the story, it discussed his addiction to painkillers after suffering a head burn when his hair caught fire while filming a Pepsi commercial.[16] Another story had Michael saying, "Lies run sprints, but the truth runs marathons. The truth will run this marathon in court."[17] While not jumping to conclusions and outright accusing Michael of anything, *JET* ran several stories that allowed Michael to share his side. Johnson did not shy away from the news, but he did not try him in the pages of the magazine prematurely either.

Though Michael was leery of the media, he grew to trust *EBONY* and *JET* because of his history with Johnson and with *JET* Associate Publisher and Executive Editor Robert E. Johnson, who usually wrote all of his *EBONY* and *JET* cover stories. The 2003 documentary, *Living With Michael Jackson,* with an interview conducted by Martin Brashir was a setback for the performer who made it no secret that he felt betrayed about Brashir's depiction of him after opening himself up to eight months of interviewing, spending time and introducing Bashir to his children. A press statement said the British TV programme was "a gross distortion of the truth and a tawdry attempt to misrepresent his life and his abilities as a father."[18]

So when *JET* magazine Senior Editor Sylvia P. Flanagan approached Michael for an *EBONY* cover in 2006, he had resolved not to do interviews with any media—not even *EBONY*—since Robert E. Johnson, the man he entrusted with doing a great deal of his interviews, died in 1996.[19] But Flanagan, who would pick the brothers up in Indiana and drive them to Johnson Publishing Company when they were just getting started, was patiently persistent because she had history on her side. Michael knew Flanagan so there was a longstanding relationship in place. And the best way to earn someone's trust after it's been violated is by having someone there who has known a person in his youth.

For a year Flanagan called Raymone Bain, Michael's publicist, and personally spoke to Michael, fervently working to get him to agree to do a cover. In the meantime, a *JET* story was being written in September 2006 that recognized the twenty fifth anniversary of MTV and why it took so long for the network to play black music videos. Since Michael is the man credited for having his videos remove the barrier, a quote for the story was requested of him. He declined but agreed to make certain the story was accurate after Flanagan read a portion of it to him and subsequently received the King of Pop's approval.[20]

That was a start. Slowly but surely he began to let down his guard. Finally, after a little more than a year, he agreed to do the cover story. He requested that *EBONY* Senior Editor Joy Bennett write the story. Little did anyone know, especially Michael, that the December 2007 *EBONY* cover would be his last interview and photo shoot not only with the magazine but ever. He would make covers of *EBONY* and *JET* two years later because of his death from acute Propofol intoxication in June 2009. It is interesting how the beginning of Michael Joseph Jackson's career was documented in print on a national level with *EBONY* and ended with the same magazine.

The Jackson family spent so much time visiting the Johnson Publishing Company headquarters that they practically grew up on the pages of all the company magazines, including *EBONY, JET, EBONY Jr!* and *Black Stars*. When Johnson died in August 2005, Michael was unable to attend the funeral because he had just gone to Bahrain. The Jacksons sent a family representative, Randy, on behalf of them to show reverence.[21] The Jackson family might have gone Hollywood to onlookers but those on the inside knew they never forgot their roots or what Johnson did for them as a family.

Major stories about music weren't the only things covered in the glossy monthly. The September 1975 issue of *EBONY* featured the cast of the popular TV show "Good Times." The cover story, titled "Bad Times on the Good Times Set," included unrestrained interviews with the stars of the show and how many were disappointed with its direction. They wanted the show, centered around the Evans family who resided in Chicago's Cabrini-Green housing project, to have more depth with the plots and characters. The nine-page article also shined a light on salary concerns and problems from some cast members about Jimmie Walker's J.J. character doing too much "shuckin' and jivin.'" Esther Rolle, the show's matriarch, didn't like that "he's 18 and he doesn't work. He can't read and write. He doesn't think." The show's younger son, Michael, played by Ralph Carter, was bright and ambitious yet his role was reduced while the producers made J.J. "more stupid and enlarged the role," she said in the story.[22]

Just as Johnson worked to erase negative stereotypes for his race, Rolle and John Amos, the show's patriarch known as James Evans Sr., did the same as Rolle realized that negative images were "quietly slipped in on us through the oldest child."[23] Rolle and Walker had a contentious relationship because of it. When she died in 1998, all of the cast members who comprised the Evans family along with two other pivotal cast members from "Good Times" attended Rolle's memorial service except Walker.[24]

TV icon Norman Lear, the man who developed "Good Times," reportedly was troubled after reading the article because he thought the cast members were well taken care of and happy. Some even alleged that Lear's disapproval of the powerfully candid *EBONY* story caused Amos' role as James Evans Sr., one of television's few strong African-American fathers, to be killed off and written out of the show; however, during an interview with *JET* magazine in 2008, Amos set the record straight, saying, "The truth is we reached a point where we were at an impasse that we could no longer dialogue civilly about the character and I wasn't the most diplomatic guy in those days. The writers got tired of having their lives threatened about the script and I got tired of threatening."[25]

And while entertainment was a large part of Johnson's publications, it wasn't the only thing highlighted in the pages. As indicated earlier, people might not realize that it was because of Johnson that the Rev. Dr. Martin Luther King, Jr. received press coverage during the 1950s and 1960s in both *JET* and *EBONY* on a regular basis, because TV networks were not following his work, but Johnson was. This is how the world came to know and keep up with Dr. King's endeavors through the Civil Rights Movement. When Dr. King died, it was the only time in *EBONY* history that the magazine's red banner turned black.[26]

The magazine has had an impact across oceans as well. When South African Archbishop Desmond Tutu spoke during a fundraiser on behalf of Nelson Mandela in the 1980s, Tutu personally told Johnson how seeing *EBONY* magazine changed his life. Johnson recalled Tutu approaching him at the event, saying, "I've always wanted to meet you. When I was a little boy, *EBONY* was barred from South Africa. I remember people used to get a copy illegally and hide it."[27] Tutu explained how, at the age of nine years old, he saw his first copy of the magazine on the streets in the ghetto townships. Tutu told Johnson, "For the first time in my life, I saw black people like me who were doing things, making a success of their lives. For the first time, it changed my whole life. It made me believe that I could do what these people have done. And I have been doing that ever since."[28]

Another moment worth noting about *EBONY*'s impact was when Congressman Louis Stokes once presented on the Congress floor about what *EBONY* meant to people and how it educated the world. He explained, "When our black soldiers came home battle-worn from World War II to a hostile America, *EBONY* was there. When Rosa Parks stood up to the racist southern establishment and refused to move from her bus seat, *EBONY* was there. When the Supreme Court blasted the doctrine of 'separate but equal' and allowed Linda Brown to enter the school door, *EBONY* walked with her. *EBONY* followed the steps of our great leaders, Martin Luther King and Malcolm X, both on the road to freedom and the road to the grave."[29]

Johnson recognized what Stokes said about how he used the magazine to document history. He also acknowledged that it wasn't always easy making decisions to write about certain things. Johnson said, "As Congressman Stokes said—and I'm proud that he said it—there has not been a single burning issue or a single major event that *EBONY* has not touched. I must confess that I was afraid to deal with some of them, but—the record shows—I dealt with them."[30]

Nothing stays the same and Johnson adapted to the times with the role that *EBONY* played, changing since it was first published in 1945. Movement in the times and different needs from readers called for an innovative way of examining the publication's position. Evaluating the magazine's stance on what was considered prosperity was the first area examined. Johnson said this happened by redefining achievement from a different lens. Johnson said:

> We have, for example, redefined success. In the very beginning, we sometimes equated success with material things. We certainly don't believe that any more, nor do we say it any more. We think now that success is any accomplishment made by a person who sets out to do something. In other words, anyone who raises a successful family is a success. Two people who stay married for a long time are successes. Any positive goal that is set and met is success.[31]

It isn't uncommon for people to associate achievement by virtue of one's belongings and wealth. Johnson explained how at first labeling success with material possessions was necessary. "There was perhaps a need for that then. We needed to know then that some blacks were living as well as some whites. But as the magazine matured and blacks changed, we broadened the formula for success."[32]

His publications were used to educate people about issues that few others dared to touch in the 1950s. In the thirtieth anniversary issue, which sold for a dollar, the November 1975 issue featured an *EBONY* reprinted October 1951 shocking story about a Sanford, Florida, man who secretly lived as a woman. Titled "The Man Who Lived Thirty Years As A Woman," the article profiled the late Georgia Black, who was married twice and adopted a son. It wasn't until Georgia, born George Cantey, was on her deathbed and examined by a physician that her true identity was revealed.

George was fifteen years old when he ran away from Galeyville, South Carolina, because working as a slave in the fields was too much for him. Once relocating to Charleston, the illiterate and insecure teen landed a job in a mansion where he was trained and taught to take on the role of a female for a "male retainer." Georgia, the leader of the Women's Missionary Society, was photographed on her deathbed and spoke to *EBONY* about her life. According to the story, had it not been for the county physician slipping up and revealing what he discovered, people would not have learned of her secret until after her transition. Georgia's final words were "I never done nuthin' wrong in my life."[33]

A young sports sensation had the spotlight in the November 1982 issue of *EBONY*, which featured a little kid named Eldrick Woods. Lovingly known as Tiger by his family, the golf phenom was first introduced to the world in this story titled "A Golfing Champion At Six: Tiny Tiger Woods has done it all, including a hole-in-one."[34] Ten years later, he was featured in *EBONY* and in *JET* after becoming the youngest player ever to compete in a PGA Tour event.[35]

One *EBONY* article that rubbed someone the wrong way was titled, "Why Negroes Don't Like Eartha Kitt." Needless to say, the subject of the story, performer Eartha Kitt, was not pleased. She was already having a difficult time winning the affections of black fans so a story with this kind of title by the top African-American publication certainly did not ingratiate her with her community. But, as it turns out, the title was misleading because the story was actually favorable. In it there was a discussion of how Kitt's African-American fans might have gathered that she was "snubbing" her race mainly because she performed for mostly white audiences and preferred mingling with them away from the spotlight as well. Still, the cover's headline attracted readers but further contributed to her race alienating her. Nevertheless, throughout the years, she appeared on countless *EBONY* and *JET* covers. A January 1963 issue featured her on the cover with infant daughter, Kitt. The story was titled, "My Baby Travels With Me," and it was penned by Kitt herself. During a private luncheon and tour at Johnson Publishing Company in the late 1990s, Kitt was introduced to all the editors invited. However, when Johnson entered the room and asked, "How are you, Eartha?" She purred, "I was fine, John, until I saw you."[36]

In August 1999, Johnson hosted a different kind of private luncheon at his headquarters. This one was for rap sensation Sean Combs, then calling himself Puff Daddy, who was taking the world by storm since the release of his 1997 award-winning debut album *No Way Out.* At twenty-nine years old, the innovative performer made the cover of just about every major mainstream publication but he had yet to nab an *EBONY* cover. So in order to win over editors, namely Lerone Bennett Jr. and Johnson, who wasn't fond of rappers, Combs agreed to breaking bread with them in Chicago. The luncheon, attended by high-ranking *EBONY* and *JET* editors, included a soul food luncheon requested by Combs. In addition to fried chicken, peach cobbler was served for dessert.

On this day, however, the rest of the company's employees were not allowed to eat in the company's tenth floor cafeteria as Combs did not want to be disturbed during his visit. Because he was the biggest and hottest star in the country at the time, surprisingly, Johnson agreed to his request. Always looking to take care of his employees, since they were being asked to leave the building during lunch time, Johnson saw to it that every employee was given a crisp new ten dollar bill to eat out. Combs appeared on the cover of *JET* after the visit.[37] He sent thank you gifts to top *JET* and *EBONY* editors involved. For Johnson, a plant the size of a small tree was delivered. To the *JET* editor who wrote the story and had written his first *JET* cover story, her gift came a few weeks later than the others. Combs sent her, the author of this book, a special, personalized plaque to commemorate RIAA certified multi-platinum sales of more than six million copies of *No Way Out* by Puff Daddy and The Family. At the start of the new year, it got off to a bang with Puff Daddy finally gracing the January 2000 *EBONY* cover with the title, "The Puff Daddy Nobody Knows."[38 39]

Everyone wanted to be on the cover of *JET.* People were entertained but more often than not they were being educated. *JET* provided the gospel truth in a variety of ways. From medicine to sports to entertainment, there was something to learn each week. In the April 1, 1976 issue, readers were introduced to Henrietta Lacks, a woman who died of cervical cancer in 1951. But just because she died did not mean she was gone forever. *JET* readers learned that Lacks' cancer cells became the first immortalized cell line, but the only problem was that they were being used without her family's permission. Today, HeLa cells, as they are known, are one of the most important cell lines in medical research.[40]

The gruesome pictures of Till earned *JET* the reputation of having coffin and death images. Providing these kinds of photographs continued for the small magazine with the large impact. Shocking 1967 pictures of soul singer Otis Redding showed him being pulled from the icy waters of Lake Monona near Madison, Wisconsin, after a plane crash. The twenty-six-year-old singer was still buckled in his airplane seat.[41] Another image shows Redding just as he's being lifted from the water.[42] His young life was cut short and his widow wanted to make certain to see him every day so she had him buried in front of the house.[43]

An April 25, 1968, cover story, featuring Coretta Scott King and her four children, was titled "King's Widow: Bereavement to Battlefield." Written by Simeon Booker, the article showed Rev. Dr. Martin Luther King, Jr.'s four children and widow, viewing an open casket of the thirty-nine-year-old slain civil rights leader.[44]

*JET* conducted an interview with Stanley "Tookie" Williams, the co-founder of the Crips street gang who was sentenced to die in 1981 for the 1979 murder of four people in Los Angeles. Williams granted his last ever interview, to the author of this book, only five days before his scheduled lethal injection. His final image, in a coffin, would be included in the story. Williams, who renounced his gang affiliation and became an anti-gang activist, winning the 2005 President's Call to Service Award for good deeds on death row, expressed his innocence for twenty-six years. He said few reporters bothered to ask if he was guilty. "No, not culpable of those crimes. I've done many things, but that isn't one of them, and I believe that's why I'm here because of karma, the things I got away with many moons ago."[45]

*EBONY*'s pictorial history showed the infamous 1930 photo of a public lynching with two black men, Thomas Shipp, eighteen, and Abram Smith, nineteen, hanging from a tree in Marion, Indiana, as white residents below looked, smiled, and pointed. In 2005, *JET* interviewed James Cameron, ninety-one, who was sixteen years old in 1930 and with the two teens, barely escaping being lynched and the third person in the well-known image.[46]

*JET* had also earned a reputation for stories about oddities. The weekly brought attention to the story of Celestine Tate, whose teen mother tried to abort her with a coat hanger. Surviving the botched abortion, she was born with a rare birth defect, arthrogryposis multiplex, rendering her arms and legs useless. Known for her feisty personality, Tate made headlines in 1976 after going to court to win the right to keep her infant daughter. Tate changed the baby's diaper with her mouth and teeth. As a result, the judge granted her "full and free custody" of the child.[47]

Determined not to get on welfare after the death of her daughter's father, Tate enrolled in a Philadelphia-based piano course with a special handicapped music program where she mastered the keyboard in six months. A favorite on the early talk show circuit, she made a living on the Atlantic City Boardwalk by playing the portable organ with her tongue, churning out crowd-favorite classics like "Amazing Grace" and "Stormy Weather." She self-published her memoir, *Some Crawl And Never Walk* in 1995, typing the entire manuscript on a typewriter with her tongue. Boxing great Evander Holyfield put up $15,000 for her to complete it through Dorrance Publishing Company, a pioneering self-publishing company based in Pittsburgh.[48] In 1986, she was taken to court for being in violation of Atlantic City's anti-begging ordinance, but after wowing over the courtroom and the officers who testified against her, she was exempted from the begging ordinance. Tate, who had two healthy daughters and an adopted son, married Roy Harrington in 1991. She died in 1998 after her gurney was struck by a cab.[49]

Another story *JET* audiences discovered was about San Fernando, California, Siamese twins Mary Yvette and Gladys Yvonne Jones McCarter, who were joined at the head.[50] Known by their middle names, Yvette and Yvonne were gospel singers and in 1974, at the age of twenty-five, were considered the oldest living Siamese twins. The sisters, who earned an associate's degree from Compton Community College and eventually moved into a one-bedroom apartment of their own, died in 1993 of natural causes at the age of forty-three years old. They were buried together in a specially-made double casket.[51]

*JET* introduced its readers to a rare genetic disorder known as progeria, which causes a person to age rapidly. Shomari "Peedie" Snipes, one of only twelve people in the country and the only black in 1983 known with the disorder, graced the cover of *JET* with his mother, Susan.[52] The Gibsonville, North Carolina, native underwent triple bypass surgery a few days before succumbing to heart failure at fourteen years old in 1992. Two weeks before his passing, his lifelong dream of meeting basketball great Michael Jordan came true. Peedie met the basketball icon who presented him with a pair of autographed size thirteen Air Jordan sneakers.[53]

A new section was being introduced in *JET* by 2003 called In the Spotlight where fresh talent was showcased. Playwright Tyler Perry, who at this time was quietly a millionaire because of his sold-out urban stage plays starring him dressed as a feisty grandmother character named Madea, was initially pitched during a *JET* meeting for the section. After recognizing his power in the African-American community with this type of theatre, Johnson acknowledged Perry's value and wanted the world to know as well. In December, the Atlanta native received his first-ever national cover on a major magazine.[54]

Putting Perry on the cover did call for one concern by Johnson. Audiences knew the Madea character more than the man who brought her to life, so Johnson wondered how advertisers would respond to putting a man on the cover of *JET* dressed like a woman. Johnson did not let that short-lived worry concern him for long. He continued to let fear steer him toward the right decision because for him this became an indicator that he was doing something correct. So that Perry wasn't on the cover dressed as Madea solo, it was suggested that he do a split as Madea and as himself. This would give readers the opportunity to recognize and learn more about the thirty-four-year-old playwright behind the popular Madea character.

The cover, designed by Perry who graciously created the image layout, initially had the pistol-packing granny holding a purse in her right hand and a gun in the left. Because Johnson was very much concerned about his advertisers, he requested that the gun be removed. Perry placed an image of himself, dressed as a man, in front of the weapon. The magazine ended up being the highest-selling issue in 2003 out of fifty-two issues.

## CHAPTER 8

# GIVING VOICE TO BLACK CONSUMERS

***"I had to look for black men not afraid to disagree with white people."***
***John H. Johnson***

On the sixth floor of the Johnson Publishing Company building, where the advertising department was located, were framed posters that served as reminders. The images of the ads displayed how *EBONY* pushed to show that its readers were an untapped market. "If these men and women have rhythm, they've put it to work on marketing cycles or computer electronics or fabric patterns...*EBONY* is where forty-nine million people do their shopping," Johnson said.[1]

First and foremost, Johnson was a businessman. He is known for his work in publishing but it was because of his business acumen that he achieved such notoriety and went down in history as one of the greatest American publishers.

He is credited as one of the first to acknowledge the size of the black consumer market in the 1950s by showing how black people had disposable incomes and purchased brand name products. Though their skin was various shades of brown, their money was always green, and, for this reason, if advertisers appealed to them, they could rake in more money. He wondered if advertisers on Madison Avenue knew "that Negro buying power this year (1950) is $11 billion, and what are you doing about it?" By 1974, that buying power was a whopping $60 billion.[2] Johnson was a man of action. His boldness made the white advertising gatekeepers take notice like he made mainstream publishers take notice, but the process started slowly.

Ads were not solicited until six months after starting *EBONY*. Most ads in Negro weeklies were for skin bleaching and hair straightening, ways to attain the European standards of beauty. Johnson wanted to steer clear of these types of ads but eventually he succumbed because those helped to pay bills. This shouldn't have been a shocker that early ads in *EBONY* included lots of small ones about sex books, skin bleach, wig advertisements and ways to grow hair. Then there were ads for whiskey, cigarettes and feminine products. By 1946, gross ad revenue was only $27,000.[3]

The skin and hair ads were offensive to *EBONY* readers and at one time Johnson canceled them in the magazine. But always one to capitalize on what people seemed to demand, he observed that for all of their objections, everyone seemed to strive for longer hair and a lighter complexion.

He started a beauty company, first known as Beauty Star, to sell skin bleach and hair products like Satene.[4] There was Raveen "for the thrilling beauty of lovelier, more lustrous hair" and Star Glow "for lighter, brighter skin appearance."[5] By the time Johnson founded Fashion Fair Cosmetics in 1973, Vantex was part of the line. A skin bleach, Vantex was a top seller for the pioneering cosmetic company.

When Johnson initially tried to sell Madison Avenue on black consumers, he was met with opposition. Numbers and figures always spoke louder than any person ever could and Johnson saw an opportunity to pioneer in the advertising arena when the 1950 census showed that the "Negro" population at that time was about 15 million, with the "Negro" family income tripling since 1940.[6] It also showed that this population was growing faster than the white population. The data displayed that "Negroes" outspent the rest of the market, proportionately, in ten of sixteen categories such as clothing, food at home, personal care, tobacco and liquor. Quickly consumed products were where this race spent the most money since discrimination prevented many from dining out, joining country clubs or taking trips. "Hell," Johnson once told one Madison Avenue heavyweight, "we got figures to show you Negroes buy half the Scotch whisky in America!"[7]

The 1973–1974 bear market lasted between January 1973 and December 1974. Affecting all the major stock markets in the world, particularly the United Kingdom, it was one of the worst stock market downturns in modern history.[8] When it crashed, Johnson wasn't affected much because most of his investments were in companies he owned or controlled.[9]

Johnson was fifty-five years old when he made history once more by acknowledging the historic neglect of African-American women and creating yet another solution to address the problem. Cosmetic lines were producing make-up that wasn't made with African-American women or their complexion in mind. Oftentimes women of color had to mix shades, while darker-skinned ladies couldn't wear any makeup or if they did, it was always several shades lighter than their true tone.[10]

In 1973, Johnson created the largest black-owned cosmetics company in the world with Fashion Fair. Because of his steadfast belief that in every disadvantage there was an advantage, he didn't set out to start a cosmetic company, but out of necessity and as the true businessman that he was, he did so.[11] The models in his pioneering *EBONY* Fashion Show, the first and largest African-American traveling fashion show, conceived in 1956 and started in 1958, often mixed cosmetics designed for white women in the hopes they'd find a match for their darker skin.[12] Naysayers told him that he couldn't bypass mass distribution outlets and concentrate on high-line stores like Neiman Marcus and Marshall Field's to sell his cosmetics. Like many times before, he proved them wrong but not without risks. For five years he lost $1 million a year before turning things around.[13] Eventually, Fashion Fair became the largest black cosmetics line in the world. It was no longer considered simply a black line but a line as the company made more money.

Before *EBONY* and *JET*, advertisers saw no need to reach out to black consumers. In their minds, African Americans were nonexistent. Johnson had to convince Madison Avenue that black dollars were worthy of being included in the money pool, so Johnson is credited with creating the "black consumer" by opening the eyes of Madison Avenue to the multibillion-dollar influence of the African-American consumer market.[14] His hard work and determination were the underlying reasons that he was able to show how there was profit in using black models and campaigns with black themes that appealed to those consumers who would shape the way companies market their products to African Americans.

Johnson's rationale was quite simple. He believed that before a solution could be given, one must first identify the problem. The lifeblood of magazines relies upon more than subscribers because advertising dollars keep magazines afloat. Though Johnson's publications were pioneering, there was the problem with the lack of advertising as it related to African Americans. Like Ralph Ellison's

1952 book *Invisible Man*, it was as if people of color were not considered consumers because they did not exist to those doing the marketing.[15] Just as the mainstream media ignored African-American stories, so did the advertising industry when it came to seeing their money as viable. Corporations and advertising executives refused to acknowledge people of color. Ads did not include African-American models. Essentially, the black consumer was an untouched, untapped market.

*EBONY* couldn't get advertising. It was unheard of to place in black publications and no one was willing to be the first. He thought that if he had white salesmen, they could talk to people on the golf course. But that didn't work because they didn't sell anything. Black salesmen also didn't sell anything.[16]

Johnson, who obviously had a clear background in journalism, paved a new path once more and instead of waiting for others to do something, he started selling ads himself. Johnson recalled that moment and said:

> Here again it was do or die. I either had to sell advertising or go out of business. Circulation would not carry a magazine of that size. My mother and most of her friends owned Zenith products. I felt I could confidently say I knew lots of blacks who owned Zenith. If advertised, they could sell more. I knew I had to go to the top.[17]

He had no choice but to think outside of the box and to find a creative way to sell ads. "I tried white salesmen, black salesmen. I tried advertising in trade magazines. I couldn't sell ads. I was ready to go out of business. I thought I've got to rely on myself."[18]

Growing up as a kid too poor for toys forced him to rely on his imagination when playing. Having kids in Chicago make fun of his heavy Southern drawl from Arkansas forced him to work on his speech. Those moments in his life prepared him as an adult. Those disadvantages proved to be advantages to help him get ahead, because he used his ability to speak well and to think outside of the box as a way to enable himself and his magazine to break through the ad barrier.

And again, using an untraditional approach made this possible. First, Johnson thought of a target company. He used his mother and her friends to figure out that Zenith Radio Company would be his pick because all of them, and most African Americans, had Zenith televisions and radios. "I picked Zenith as my first goal because my mother had a Zenith radio for ten years and it worked," he said during a 1975 interview.[19]

Johnson set up an appointment with Commander Eugene F. McDonald, head of Zenith, who immediately let Johnson know he wasn't interested in advertising. Johnson, always seeking a way to get ahead and knowing how to utilize his skills at winning people over, drew upon something he understood to work. He knew that the most important person in the office is the secretary, because if a person could convince the secretary about what she/he wanted to say then that person could convince the boss. By convincing the secretary of something important, Johnson knew she would convince the person with the power to make decisions.[20] This strategy worked. Because Johnson was so persistent with wanting to meet with him, McDonald eventually conceded. Always careful to plan and prepare well in advance, Johnson did research on not only the company but on McDonald. Johnson learned that McDonald was an arctic explorer, and since Johnson had written a story about Matthew Henson, the first African American to explore the North Pole, Johnson figured that would be another way to connect with McDonald.[21]

This human touch and unique strategy worked because McDonald was able to see the July 1947 issue of *EBONY*, which featured Henson's story. McDonald was so impressed that not only did he end up taking out ads, but before Johnson left his office, McDonald "called the chairmen of Swift Packing Company, Elgin Watch Company, Armour Food Company and Quaker Oats."[22] Johnson, using creativity to connect with McDonald, opened the doors for Johnson and his companies. This method additionally helped to pioneer the way for those to come.

A year after *EBONY* was founded, Johnson sold his first national advertising to Zenith Corporation. "A magazine of the size and quality of *EBONY* must have advertising to survive," he said.[23] Salesmen and advertising executives were later added by Johnson. Of his encounter with McDonald, Johnson recalled in 2004: "He was intrigued. He didn't know such a market existed…I sold him so well that we put out a video on the secret of selling the Negro market. I had to look for black men not afraid to disagree with white people. You can't agree with somebody and sell 'em. You've got to disagree with them."[24]

Zenith ads were a mainstay in *EBONY* after that fateful meeting.

In 1974, Johnson was elected to Zenith's board of directors. By 1975, there were about thirty-nine Zenith televisions and countless radios at Johnson Publishing Company. At his home he had another ten Zenith televisions. In a press release, Zenith chairman Joseph S. Wright said this about his appointment:

> The long association between Zenith and Mr. Johnson makes his election to the Zenith board particularly appropriate. In 1946 the late Eugene F. McDonald, Jr., Zenith's founder-president, became interested in the then fledgling *EBONY* as a result of a meeting with Mr. Johnson. Zenith became *EBONY*'s first national advertiser. This association has continued during the growth of both of these Chicago-based companies over the past 28 years.[25]

During his pitch to Quaker Oats, Johnson was confronted with one concern and that was placing ads in the magazine of Aunt Jemima, an overweight black mammy who was wearing a handkerchief. Blacks at one time fiercely protested the image. Johnson decided to run the ads anyway, saying, "After all, Negroes are buying plenty of Aunt Jemima flour no matter how much they protest."[26] By the 1960s, the image of Aunt Jemima began to change with the handkerchief eventually being removed and the skin lightened a bit.

*EBONY*'s revenue topped $1 million annually, by 1952, making it the highest attained by a black publication.[27] Johnson's drive was the foundation for most things in his life. He knew persistence would pay off, and when he saw a void, Johnson was eager to fill it. The best businessmen were able to identify a need and satisfy it in markets that were untouched. He said, "We made our own experts. A key responsibility, the best manager is a good teacher."[28] The early lessons his mother taught him, which hinged upon believing in a higher power, carried him through moments when his back was against the wall. "That's been the story of my life, at every critical turning point in my life, people, black and white, always told me no at first. And I almost always turned the nos into yeses."[29]

In being persistent, something else Johnson did was send an advertising salesman to Detroit every week for ten years before the company broke its first automobile account. Because this was before routine air travel, his account exec traveled by train. William P.

Grayson, who also finally broke an advertising account with Campbell Soup in the East, headed the New York office.[30] "Grayson said he spent 15 years, six months, five days, two hours and 30 minutes working on that account," Johnson said in 1985. "It was difficult because we had to persuade people. We couldn't do it then by marching, and we couldn't do it by threatening. We had to persuade people that it was in their best interest to reach out to black consumers in a positive way."[31]

Johnson also explained how he and Grayson worked with an agency, Redmond, Marcus and Schure, to design ads in the major media to raise awareness about the black consumer as well as *EBONY*. Some critics, according to Johnson, called their advertising campaign "one of the most brilliant" of the sixties. One said, "*EBONY* is running the biggest black market operation in the U.S.A." Another stated, "When was the last time you saw a cotton-pickin negro?" Then there was this one, "All headaches are created equal." Finally, another said, "We think that white is beautiful, too."[32]

During an interview, Johnson recalled how he spent nearly a decade trying to sign Detroit automakers. Through persistence and a will of steel, Johnson was patient; Chrysler finally bought an ad. He said:

> When a man is in trouble, he'll try anything. It was just time and persistence. We just wouldn't go away. I'm not sure their reluctance was racial. The only way I can succeed is to assume that everything is not racial. We've got to assume that people are decent and that one of the reasons they won't do business with us is because they think it's not to their advantage. That's how I must think in business. We're not talking race relations here because that's a different posture. I never sold anything based on saying, 'Help me because I'm black.' I always said, 'Help me because I can help you.'[33]

Many unfounded notions were held regarding blacks and their purchasing power. For instance, once an advertising executive for Johnson went to sell to a major flour company. The company refused to purchase any advertisement because it believed African Americans did not like, of all things, chocolate cake or chocolate frosting. Johnson had his executive conduct a survey, which not only proved that African Americans eat large quantities of chocolate cake and frosting, but they also enjoyed eating chocolate ice cream.[34]

Johnson's simple strategy of using research studies helped to disprove many myths about people of color. He even pioneered ways to help others tap into the "Negro" market by producing two sales movies. One was called *There's Gold in Your Backyard*. The other was titled *The Secret of Selling the Negro*; this one cost $20,000 to make. This color film instructed salesmen representing *EBONY* advertisers. A staff of fourteen *EBONY* "field men" showed it to more than five hundred major advertising executives.[35]

Johnson used the films to speak on behalf of his people. He knew while representing himself, he was ultimately representing others. He demonstrated this value by showing African Americans that not only must they be conscious of the content when selling to their race, but it is critical to pay close attention to the objective. Johnson took it upon himself to be in charge of the black agenda with a goal and future in mind. He was purposeful in the rationale for each tip he suggested to white advertisers, for he knew whites marginalized people of color. In doing this, so many whites played into the stereotypes noted during this time. For others, they marginalized African Americans so much that they didn't see black people as three dimensional, meaning complex or intelligent beings. Basic pointers about treating the African American as human when selling was most prominent amongst the plan. Here's what Johnson remembered in the manual:

> Instruct salesman to be friendly. Don't use first names unless the Negro customer or retailer indicates a willingness to 'trade' first names. 2) Treat every black as an individual. 3) Talk to blacks on the same level that you use in talking to other customers. 4) In conversation, don't use the term 'nigger,' 'Negress' 'darky' or 'boy.' 5) Avoid perpetuating the stereotype of the happy-go-lucky menial, the stupid, ghost frightened or 'Uncle Tom' servant, or the fat, over jovial 'mammy.'[36]

Johnson was a proud man and he resented having to demean himself early to get ahead, especially when it came to selling advertising. He once recalled how he had a meeting with the executive of a shampoo company who questioned the cleanliness of black people. Johnson, while clearly offended by this notion, "swallowed his pride and laughingly informed the white businessman, 'I take a shower every day and wash my hair with shampoo.'"[37]

The use of having African Americans appear in ads when marketing to people of color was a major selling point for Johnson. As simple and as logical as it would have appeared, it wasn't, because white companies did not want to show African-American models. Even with this countries' history of African Americans cooking, washing, and cleaning for whites as maids, advertising companies refused to use African-American models doing the very things they had been doing since the beginning of time.

Research and comparison strategies were used to prove Johnson's point that blacks would purchase products if they saw themselves being represented in ads instead of only whites. "These things are accepted today, but they were new in the '40s. There were no major black models before *EBONY* and there were few black salesmen for major companies before *EBONY*. I don't think we are completely responsible, but I don't know anyone else who is more responsible," Johnson said in 1985.[38]

Johnson's agency and dedication toward helping his people to not be singled out through marginalization helped to pioneer cooperative economics, where African Americans could profit with others. He said:

> We broke the back of this prejudice by proving that black people, like other people, respond more positively to ads featuring men and women they can identify with…Little by little, ad inch by ad inch, there dawned a realization that it was more believable and more effective to appeal to black consumers in advertisements featuring black models that looked like black Americans.[39]

Within ten years after the birth of *EBONY*, the magazine was known for trailblazing and introducing hundreds of major advertisers to a "$16 billion Negro market that had virtually gone untapped."[40] "Today, largely because of *EBONY* stories which picture the Negro as a person who works, who is professional, who is respectable—merchants who sell the finest products are convinced that Negroes are worth seeking out. In *EBONY* alone, a total of 1,569 of them have spent nearly $10 million in the past 10 years in reaching this Negro audience."[41]

By 1952, advertising revenue exceeded $1 million and that same year Johnson was recognized by Commerce magazine for being "more responsible than anyone else for educating mainstream corporate America regarding the African American consumer market."[42] Johnson helped pave the way for new jobs for African Americans in advertising. In 1955, "hundreds of models and sales promotion men, dozens of Negro public relations firms and market consultants are now employed by some of the nation's top advertisers."[43] Top trade publications recognized *EBONY*'s leadership in selling to African Americans. The following was once mentioned: "Advertising growth from 18 to 20 pages per issue in 1946 to an average of 60 pages per issue in 1955. Today, *EBONY* can boast of having attracted more than half of the 100 top advertisers listed by Advertising Age, as well as an average of 700 advertising pages yearly, with nearly 150 in color."[44]

The year 1955 also marked a time where Johnson was concerned about angering advertisers but felt the need to print the controversial Emmett Till images anyway despite the possible loss of advertising dollars he waited so long to receive. Walking in his convictions worked to Johnson's advantage. "The Emmett Till thing never lost us any circulation. And let me say something now. Every year the media focuses on Emmett Till. He is now a hero. And where do you think they come for all the photographs."[45]

In his autobiography, Johnson stated how in 1964 *EBONY* "grossed a record $5.5 million from the sale of advertising space alone." The following year he observed how ads in the publication were "comparable to many general market magazines."[46]

When Johnson was named Publisher of the Year in 1972 by the Magazine Publishers Association, it noted how *EBONY* "soon began outselling top white publications in black areas fourteen and fifteen to one. *EBONY* now has a circulation of more than 1.2 million copies a month."[47] It also stated, "Johnson Publications are distributed throughout the United States and in forty foreign countries, including many of the newly independent African nations."[48]

Johnson delivered a speech titled "The Call for Greater Commitment in Minority Enterprise" during the Interracial Council for Business Opportunity at New York's Americana Hotel in 1974. He discussed essential ingredients for minority owners. He said:

> What I believe was present in our early black business—and is needed now—is a total commitment to succeed by the minority entrepreneur. This must be an individual commitment. It is the consuming passion to succeed— 'to lose and start again at one's beginning' that makes for success in business. There was a time when certain goods and services were not produced for the black consumer. I am referring to personal beauty care products and services, restaurants, funeral services, insurance, newspaper and yes—even magazines. During this time, the all pervasiveness of racism was such that more than one-tenth of our population was neglected by the major providers of goods and services. Fortunately, there were men and women around who were bold and daring enough to accept the challenge of an overlooked marketplace. Otherwise, these critical human needs would not have been met. These were our first black entrepreneurs. Guts, common sense, business savvy, confidence and the flaming desire to succeed, were their main stock in trade. Our early black entrepreneurs typify a unique determination toward survival. And their determination holds a valuable lesson for us today.[49]

Four decades after starting his Johnson Publishing Company, Johnson said, "I don't think there is any such thing as a black business or a white business–there is just good business and I consider myself a good businessman. It just so happens that my business is looking after the interests of black people."[50] While his interest was in African Americans, he didn't necessarily believe it was wise to stay separate from white organizations for financial reasons. He explained:

> You have to understand that I don't believe in black capitalism. Black people ought to have the right to become capitalists, but black capitalism presupposes that you're only going to sell to black people. If I sold only to black people, I would not have a very successful company. Most of my subscriptions and newsstand sales are made to blacks, but 90 percent of my advertising is made to whites. So I don't believe that we ought to limit our sales to the black community. I think a black businessman ought to strive to be a businessman and to sell to

> any customers who will buy from him. If Kentucky Fried Chicken can sell chicken to blacks, we ought to be able to sell something to whites.[51]

Being a risk taker also allowed Johnson to succeed against the odds. His ability to lead the way, sight unseen, allowed him to venture into territories considered off limits by others. Johnson said:

> It's true. You have to dare to do things that you're afraid of. As a matter of fact, my editors often identify a hot story, one that will sell in *EBONY*, as one that I'm afraid to publish. Some of our best articles have been ones that I had a certain amount of fear about publishing. For example, I was fearful of the one called, 'Was Abraham Lincoln a Segregationist.' But it succeeded. Then we devoted a whole issue to the 'white problem' in America; I was afraid of that. But in each case, after thinking about it and weighing all the circumstances, I'd say, 'I've got to go forward with this.'[52]

He proved successful in selling national advertising. A new trend even developed where African-American models were used in ads. National brands also began to employ African American salesmen as well. Upon the death of Johnson in 2005, Earl G. Graves, publisher of the pioneering Black financial magazine *Black Enterprise*, wrote: "It's safe to say that there would be no Black Enterprise magazine without the vision and tenacity of John Johnson. And his vision lives on-- stronger than ever. Here it is, the year 2005, and *Look* and *Life* are history. *EBONY* is still making history!"[53]

Johnson made history throughout his life. He received thirty-one honorary doctorates during his lifetime. An honorary doctor of laws degree was presented by Harvard University during a commencement in 1998.[54] Prior to this day, Johnson made history, in 1975, by becoming the first leading black businessman to be honored with his own day. Later he was named to the board of directors of the associates of the Harvard Business School.[55] He said being on the board entailed the following: "You tell them if the business school is preparing people for the outside world. They give us cases to read and you give them a little money."[56]

Harvard Business School's Steven S. Rogers, an MBA Class of 1957 Senior Lecturer of Business Administration who teaches entrepreneurial finance, developed a new course in 2017 titled Black Business Leaders and Entrepreneurship with fourteen new cases using black protagonists. One of those focused on the work of Johnson. Rogers was inspired to include the pioneering publisher because he observed how Harvard Business School had 10,000 cases but less than 100 had black protagonists. The first-year students read approximately three hundred cases, but in 2016 only two of the cases had a black protagonist with students not knowing they were black until the end of the class.[57] The segregated curriculum at Harvard Business School, like most universities and colleges other than Historically Black Colleges and Universities in this country, foster a miseducation by denying black students the opportunity to see black role models. As a result, black brilliance is denied once more in the academy and the world in general.

During an interview with the podcast show "Cold Call" in February 2017 to recognize Black History Month, Rogers recalled how hearing Johnson speak at the university changed his life and now he's working to change lives by introducing Johnson's legacy at the university since Harvard provides the curriculum to other business schools around the world.

Rogers said this about Johnson during the "Cold Call" interview:

> Thirty years ago when I was a student here I heard him speak. He came to our African-American Student Union conference. That's when I found my purpose in life, when I heard him speak, because what he said at that time was, 'All of you in this audience, you have the opportunity to matriculate at the best business school in the world.' He said, 'The question that I have of you is: what are you going to do with it?' He said, 'Here's your answer.' He said, 'You take that education and you make a lot of money. Then with that money, you uplift your community.' Ever since then I knew my purpose in life, and that was to use business and the benefits and all the rewards of business to help uplift my community and help people who are less fortunate than I am, specifically the African-American community. So he's a special man in our country's history and a special man to Harvard Business School.[58]

Johnson had simple advice for young people wanting to start out in business. He made it no secret how he had never known anyone to fire a person who was making money for a company. The advice he delivered was this:

> I would tell them to get rid of the idea of wanting to start at the top in everything. I would tell them to prepare themselves, to take any kind of job to get their feet in the door of their chosen field, and then do their job, whatever the job is, so well that they make themselves indispensable to their employers.[59]

A great number of strides were made in advertising because of Johnson's persistence and efforts to give voice to black consumers, but no matter how hard he tried, ads for fashion, fragrance and designer clothes continued to elude him. He said, "Blacks wear them, but so far we haven't been able to convince advertisers that we do."[60] His backing behind the *EBONY* Fashion Fair world's largest traveling fashion show didn't seem to matter with his wife, Eunice, traveling the world over, purchasing one-of-a-kind creations from the top designer houses. Eventually, Fashion Fair cosmetics started its own fragrance line, Mr. J, described as worn by the "distinctive man" who is "loved by discriminating women," and Eunece, described as "bewitching" for ladies who "can stand the attention" because the "memory lingers."

To combat the lack of ads in fashion and fragrance, Johnson created his own in house ads, placed in both *EBONY* and *JET*, to promote Fashion Fair cosmetics. During the season when the fashion show was on the road, five-page spreads would be included in the weekly *JET* to showcase the jaw-dropping designs paraded down the runway on the models.

Johnson's creative mind and adept business sense always looked for new opportunities. He was not one to rest on his laurels or previous successes. He was forever marching onward and upward, seeking his next venture. If there was a need for an untapped service, Johnson was open to figuring it out not because he was trying to make history. He was trying to make money.

# CHAPTER 9

## THE RISE OF THE EMPIRE

***"When people laugh at me, that's when I get creative."***
***John H. Johnson***

The stretch of John H. Johnson Way takes up several blocks on the prestigious Michigan Avenue, encompassing the area where Johnson erected the building that housed his company on Tuesday, December 5, 1971. Before then, he planted seeds at two other locations, 5619 S. State Street in 1943 and 1820 S. Michigan Avenue in 1955.

In historic headquarters, Johnson presided over his empire from his penthouse office that overlooked Lake Michigan. Most company meetings were held on the ninth floor conference room where Johnson sat at the head of the table that faced the door of the boat shaped, glass wall enclosed conference room, often referred to as the "fishbowl," as he described it.[1] There were no board of directors. It was only his mother, Gertrude Johnson Williams, and his wife, Eunice, a graduate of Selma, Alabama's Talladega College with a degree in sociology and a master's degree in social work from Chicago's Loyola University.

Johnson always did things his way and managed to make history in the process, but he would always be the first to tell anyone, "I wasn't trying to make history. I was trying to make money."[2] *Negro Digest,* which began with no advertising, eventually reached a circulation of 150,000.[3] It is considered "the first magazine in the history of Negro journalism to attain full self-supporting status and economic success through sheer popularity with readers."[4]

When *EBONY* was founded in November 1945, there were other black publications around. There were many that failed. Johnson's big competition, however, was *Our World*, which promoted black progress. Founded in 1946, Johnson said *Our World* had "a lot of white money behind it" and a smart black Harvard University-educated lawyer, John P. Davis, as publisher.[5][6] While many magazines like *Our World* were run by committees or groups of people "who couldn't make up their minds," Johnson took pride in knowing that he "was accountable only" to himself for his mistakes.[7] The initial copy of *EBONY* sold out its 25,000 copies in 1945. Five decades later, circulation topped 1.5 million monthly. As the largest selling black-owned magazine in the world, by 1990 *EBONY* had more than 9 million American readers.[8]

When *Our World* ended in 1955, the sale of its assets were up for grabs along with the title. White Texas publisher George Levitan hoped to purchase it since it was competition for *EBONY*; however, after putting down $14,000, Johnson outbid Levitan so that *Our World* would be forever gone. He got their photo files and even one of the magazine's photographers, a man by the name of Moneta Sleet Jr., who would go on to make history in 1969 as the first black photographer and first black male to win a Pulitzer Prize.[9]

Heading a privately-owned company was the ideal situation for Johnson. He cited an early instance where had he had a board, he might have possibly lost his company. Countless people often said he should have had a board to ensure the company's infinite existence; however, he felt he knew best and never took his hands off the company he founded and nurtured. He was patient. He was persistent. He kept trying and realized that though he did many things before he succeeded, he understood the importance of trusting the process because it wasn't one thing that worked. It was the process.

Johnson said, "When I was trying to push *EBONY* up to the million mark, I tried fourteen different circulation-boosting plans. If a board were my boss, I would have been fired after the fourth because they were expensive. I knew all this cost too much, but I was the boss."[10] Having complete ownership and say in how his company ran was the good luck charm to remain on his side until his death.

Johnson was a proud man but he wasn't too proud to reach out to others in an effort to figure things out about publishing. At the time of Johnson's death, he was considered one of the greatest publishers alongside Time, Inc. president and chief editor Henry Luce. But several decades before Johnson earned his stripes, he phoned Luce, telling him how much he admired him and how he wanted to learn how Time Inc.

was operated. It turns out that Luce was equally interested in what Johnson was doing and invited him to New York. Johnson said, "He showed me around his building, had me meet with editors and people in circulation and advertising. I learned an awful lot. And here I was with *EBONY*, which took its format from Luce's then biggest publication, *Life*."[11]

Johnson didn't just stop with Luce. He was preparing to build his own empire and wanted to learn from the best. Sure, he studied the model from Luce's publication but he made it a point to find out more than simply editorial matters. Johnson reached out to other publishers and magazine owners for counsel. For questions about circulation, Johnson contacted a man named Gardner Cowles Jr., president of Cowles Publications, the publisher behind the monthly picture magazine *Look* and a pocket-sized news digest called *Quick*.[12] Cowles said in 1975:

> I always liked John Johnson and the nerve he showed. In the early days, he would ask me all kinds of questions about *Look*. His problem was the cost of getting subscribers, so I sent him to Des Moines to see Les Suhler, our subscription director. He saw Les off and on for several years and got results. Johnson has good instincts.[13]

Taking Cowles' advice, Johnson reached out to Suhler, who thoroughly explained how *Look* got subscribers through direct mail and the kinds of letters that worked the best. "He showed me the colors in the letters which got the biggest response," Johnson recalled. "It turned out that blacks and whites responded the same to the colors. Now isn't that interesting?"[14] Johnson would later have an entire floor, the sixth, in his headquarters that was dedicated to his in-house subscription department and circulation.

During the fifth anniversary of *EBONY* in 1950, to celebrate "easing close to the half million mark" with circulation and having "coved blue-chip advertisements," full page ads were taken out in the *New York Times* and in the *Chicago Tribune*.[15] This marked the first time that a black publication had ever taken out ads in major white dailies. This move was one of many that clearly set Johnson's publications apart from the rest.[16]

He was constantly seeking to grow his publications and attract loyal readers. While *JET* was established in 1951, a staple came in 1952 when Johnson introduced the Beauty of the Week, a full-page image of a beautiful bathing suit-clad woman with an hourglass figure.

The magazine was all black and white but introduced full color with the December 27, 1999, issue that featured singer/songwriter/producer Kenneth "Babyface" Edmonds and then wife Tracey along with their young son, Brandon, on the cover. It was also a double issue. Prior to becoming all color, a few issues in previous years would have Week's Best Photos in color to test the waters and provide something new for the readers.

Along the way, other publications Johnson created included *Tan Confessions*, founded in 1950 to compete with a white magazine *True Confessions*, and *Copper Romance*, both featured true-to-life, confessional stories. *Negro Digest* ended in 1951 and *JET*, the pocket-sized newsweekly, started the same year since Johnson observed that *Look* magazine's sister publication was a small, pocket-sized newsmagazine called *Quick*. Since Johnson was striking the coal while it was hot, he published another small magazine called *Hue* in 1953. Its focus was feature stories. This was a pocket sized, ad less monthly with pictures and short stories. He said in 1953, "We have reached a point where our magazines are in direct competition with each other."[17] *Copper Romance* and *Hue* had short runs and eventually ended. *JET* outlasted them all, including *Quick,* just as *EBONY* outlived *Life* and *Look*.[18] *Tan Confessions*, which also offered advice written by white writers, chronicled the life of African-American women but eventually went on to do features on celebrities, hoping to appeal "to the mushrooming teen-age market," so by 1971 the name was changed to *Black Stars.* In 1975 it had a young readership of 200,000 but ended in 1981. Things were also going a bit rough financially in 1981 because that's when "75 of the 325" people employed at his company were laid off.[19]

However, the company saw impressive growth in the early sixties. The circulation continued to soar for Johnson's publications, particularly *EBONY* and *JET*. There came a time when even other races couldn't help but to take notice. "I must have been doing something right, for my leading magazines reached all-time highs in the sixties, and we received unprecedented acclaim in the black and white communities. When we celebrated the twentieth anniversary of *EBONY* in November 1965, *EBONY* was selling 900,000 copies a month, and its three sister magazines, *JET, Tan* and *Negro Digest*, were selling a total of 2.3 million copies a month."[20]

Negro Digest returned in 1970 with a new name, *Black World.* Its rebirth, with former *EBONY* editor Hoyt W. Fuller at the helm, was a way for new writers to have their voices heard. "The magazine made a major contribution to the cultural transformation of that period, discovering and developing scores of new poets and short-story writers," Johnson said.[21] But when the Freedom Movement began to wane, the circulation took a sharp turn and dropped tremendously. For a second time *Negro Digest* ended.[22] He said in 1985:

> *Black World* was discontinued because readers stopped supporting it. *Black World* at one time had a circulation of more than 100,000. When I discontinued it, it had a circulation of 15,000. I think we should bring it back one day, and I think we need to find a way to make cultural and literary articles exciting. That's got to be one of our objectives, and I think we ought to bring the magazine back before too long.[23]

A book division was started in 1963 and launched by Doris Saunders. Lerone Bennett Jr.'s *Before the Mayflower* and *Burn, Killer, Burn,* written by death row convict Paul Crump, were the first books published that year.

By 1973 at least forty-two books had already been published in the book division by the company. Bennett's book was a best seller along with *The EBONY Cookbook, The EBONY Book of Black Achievement* and *Pioneers in Protest,* also written by Bennett. Other top selling books included the six volume *EBONY Classics* and a three-volume pictorial history titled *Black America.* Saunders worked for eighteen years as a librarian before leaving the company but returned to continue working as the head of the book division in 1973. Renowned historian and then *EBONY* Senior Editor Bennett had at least seven books under the division this year and even had his own ads in *EBONY* and in *JET* to sell all of them. One of the early ads recommended Bennett's books for "Black history and Afro-American studies."[24] By this time the *EBONY* Book Club was founded where readers could purchase two books for four dollars and ninety-five cents. The regular price of the books ranged from three dollars and fifty cents to nine dollars and ninety-five cents and consisted of other titles such as *Unbought and*

*Unbossed* by Shirley Chisholm, *Die Nigger Die* by H. Rap Brown, *The Rise and Fall of a Proper Negro* by Leslie Alexander Lacy, *Black Power, Confessions of a White Racist* by Larry L. King, *Seize the Time* by Bobby Seale and the *American Myth* by C.T. Vivian, to name a few.[25] An *EBONY* Jr! line of books for youth was also added. Described as the "ideal gift for the young reader," titles included *Color Me Brown* by Lucille Giles, *What Color Are You?* by Darwin Walton, *Lil Tuffy and His ABC's* by Jean Pajot Smith, *The EBONY Book of Black Achievement* by Margaret Peters and *The Legend of Africania* by Dorothy W. Robinson, to name a few. Prices ranged from one dollar and fifty cents to five dollars and fifty cents. Nearly fifty titles at one time were under the division.

Expressing an interest in Africa, Johnson started yet another magazine, *EBONY Africa*, which was founded in 1964. Its first issue was published in March to address African readers and issues in the country. Emperor Haille Selassie, ruler of Ethiopia, was on the cover and a story titled Selassie's Message to the Negro explained how "the ties that bind Ethiopians to Negro Americans are historic and strong.[25] The magazine was short lived because it "foundered on the hard realities of national and linguistic barriers."[26]

A travel service, *EBONY*-Jetours, was later established. A one-page ad in an April 1973 issue promoted a trip to Las Vegas for "round-the-clock action" at $249.00. Readers could select from four possible dates with flights departing from Chicago's O'Hare International Airport. For four days and three "unforgettable nights," travelers could stay at the Las Vegas Hilton Hotel. Entertainment in the hotel's showroom was provided by either Bill Cosby or Tony Bennett.[27]

Also in 1973, Johnson bought a radio station for $1.8 million and called it WJPC (AM/FM 950). He became the first black owner of a Chicago station. WJPC, which had an urban contemporary format, was where Tom Joyner got his start as a deejay. In 1985, Johnson purchased the radio station WLNR (106.3), which had a soft contemporary urban format. It was sold to Broadcast Partners in 1994. [28]

Johnson recalled one of his proudest moments was when he bought his first radio station and First National Bank, as the signator, loaned him—the same colored boy they denied—the more than million dollars. Johnson said this full circle moment showed him that nothing is impossible. He said he learned from it not to make enemies or burn bridges behind you. "Always hold out the likelihood someone will change his/her mind."[29] Johnson remained with First National Bank for more than four decades. It was the same bank that turned him down in 1942 when he needed money to start his magazine, because they didn't do business with "Negroes."[30]

Johnson wasn't the only person in his empire who was making money and history. *EBONY* Fashion Fair was renowned as the world's largest traveling fashion show. It was founded in 1958 and directed by his wife, Eunice. Not only did the show present fashions from the world's top fashion houses and have models strutting down the runway in haute couture, but the extravaganza raised more than $55 million for charities and scholarship funds. Most of the money went to the College Fund/United Negro College Fund to assist students in higher education.[31] Purchasing a ticket to the show also helped to boost subscriptions as every person attending had a choice of either a free one-year subscription to *EBONY* or a six-month subscription to *JET*. Major national organizations, including groups like sororities and the Urban League, sponsored the shows in various cities. The person heading each group would have his/her picture published in *EBONY* along with the schedule for the show's season. Delta Sigma Theta Sorority, Inc., in which Eunice was a lifetime member, always sponsored the kick-off show in Matteson, Illinois, located in the south suburbs of Chicago.

The models were hand selected by Eunice. Female models for the fashion extravaganza were required to be at least 5'10" or taller without shoes and had to wear an American dress size of 6-8. A full figure model was always selected and she needed the same height measurements but had to wear a size 16-18. Only two male models, usually one dark and one light in complexion, were selected each season. To be considered, male applicants needed to be 6'2" to 6'4" without shoes and could fit a suit size 44L to 46L. Although the models were undeniably beautiful and the fellas attractive, they weren't usually selected for their looks. They were chosen based on who fit the requirements and could wear the clothes, as models were often trained how to strut the catwalk since most never modeled a day in their life.

Creations by designers like Yves Saint Laurent, Christian Lacroix, Laura Biagotti, Halston, Oscar de la Renta, Givenchy, Sarli, Issey Miyaki, Roberto Cavalli, Bob Mackie, and Marc Bouwer were featured. Fewer black designers had their creations showcased, including B. Michael, Patrick Kelley, Quinton de Alexander and Stephen Burrows.

The show was criticized for its lack of more black designers, but it was recognized for helping notables launch their high-profile careers. Actors Richard Roundtree, noted for his role as *Shaft*, and Judy Pace, known for her roles in films like *Brian's Song* and *Cotton Comes to Harlem*, were among those who started as models with the show. Pioneering model Pat Cleveland, one of the first supermodels before the term was formally used, and Janet Langhart Cohen, a former syndicated Good Day host who went on to marry former Defense Secretary William S. Cohen, were two others renowned for getting their start with *EBONY* Fashion Fair.[32]

Andre Leon Talley, Vogue magazine's editor-at-large, got his start in 1982 after Eunice hired him to be fashion editor of *EBONY*. For a year he worked under her leadership and accompanied her on the Concorde on buying trips to Paris and Milan. Make-up artist Reggie Wells, who would go on to become Oprah Winfrey's personal makeup artist, also got his start working with Eunice's models.

Being a pioneer always posed its fair share of problems along the way. This proved true with the fashion show. Models were selected from a range of women with various skin tones, which became problematic when it came to applying make-up. When Johnson noticed the women mixing foundations in order to find the right match for their complexions, he took action. Johnson was disappointed that black women learned to settle for, as he called them, "hand-me-down products made for the white market."[33] He decided to do something about it by approaching major cosmetic distributors in an effort to have them produce a line for women with darker complexions. His pleas fell on deaf ears because distributors didn't want to "alienate white women customers" or they simply didn't feel there was a need for "black-oriented products."[34] That's when Johnson and his wife visited a private lab with mixtures in hand that were created by models. From this they developed their own product, The Capsule Collection, in 1969 that started as a mail-order package.[35]

In 1973, Fashion Fair cosmetics, borrowing its name from the *EBONY* Fashion Fair, was started by his wife. Fashion Fair became one of the only full-line of cosmetics in major stores. "We learned there were thirty-five skin shades among blacks and that cosmetics made for white women weren't right for black women, so we developed our own shades. We had been sending the *EBONY* Fashion Fair into many cities with black models showing the latest fashions, so we had them use the new cosmetics."[36] Model Judy Pace, who later married baseball legend Curt Flood, along with music legend Aretha Franklin were among the first models for Fashion Fair ads. Franklin, known as the Queen of Soul, was the first celebrity spokesperson for the cosmetic line.[37]

During a 1989 speech at the Illinois Business Hall of Fame Award, where Johnson was being honored, the publisher said the cosmetics line was then sold in nearly 2,000 department stores in the U.S., Europe, Africa, Canada, and West Indies. It was doing roughly $9 million since 1973, he said.[38]

Fashion and beauty were two markets Johnson had cornered. He started Supreme Beauty in 1960 with a hair relaxer called Raveen for ladies and a hair wave kit called Duke for men.[39] Supreme Beauty was born from Johnson's first non-publishing venture, Beauty Star Cosmetics, which started as a mail-order firm in 1946.[40] Beauty Star had hair care products, including Satene.[41] Johnson even had a mail-order business named Linda Fashions, which sold dresses. Vitamins, books through the *Negro Digest* Book Shop, and Star Glow wigs were also sold.[42] A cheaper cosmetic line called Ebone was later sold in department stores. And, *EBONY* and Spiegel joined forces in 1991 to launch a catalog line called E Style, geared toward African-American consumers. Spiegel Inc. was once the nation's largest in-home catalog company.[43] The partnership marked the first licensing agreement Johnson had ever done. That same year the company also completed its first joint venture, with Conrad and Associates, for the *EBONY/JET* Guide to Black Excellence.[44] A 12" by 12" calendar series was later launched for six dollars and ninety-five cents; it was called Great Black Americans and featured people like Rev. Dr. Martin Luther King, Jr., Maynard Jackson, Zora Neale Hurston, Marian Anderson, and Ralph Ellison.

With so many publications and business ventures, Johnson transitioned to larger locations for his flourishing company. First, he spotted a building at 1820 S. Michigan Avenue. But by 1960, Johnson was ready to move again. He saw a vacant lot at 820 S. Michigan Avenue. that overlooked Grant Park and had a two-mile view of skyscrapers, museums, and Lake Michigan. The only problem was that this was during a time when a great deal of whites still were not willing to take African-American money. He explained by saying the following:

> Again, even in 1960, we had to find a white lawyer to purchase that land in trust so the owners didn't know who would eventually get it. We minority people have to find subtle ways to solve our problems. It took me eleven years before I got a building on that lot. I didn't construct that building for any sophisticated financial reasons. I did it to increase my own feeling of accomplishment and to dedicate it to the pride of the black race.[45]

The eleven-story building, with a dedication service held on May 16, 1972, cost $11 million.[46] It had Travertine marble and wide glass windows. Visitors were greeted in the lobby by Richard Hunt's dramatic sculpture, Expansive Construction, with custom-built furniture and a Travertine floor. The 18 ½ foot walls were made of bronze and Mozambique wood. Each floor had its own personalities, characterized by vibrant colors, patterns, and designs. The seventh floor, which housed the library and *JET* editorial offices, had an African feel with animal skin patterned carpet, extending on the elevator bank wall. Hale Woodruff's painting, Red Landscape, was on a brown leather wall in the reception area along with matching brown leather chairs and a sofa. Even the specially designed and woven carpets were different and so were the bathrooms on each floor. The elevators had removable panels that were changed every three months to showcase the themes reflective of each season. The carpets also changed to complement the elevator walls. This was done frequently when the empire was first built. The fish bowl conference rooms were on two floors and included electrically controlled draperies and retractable projection screens that were concealed in the ceiling. The building included its own photography studio on the first floor and a photo lab on the eighth floor.

A million dollars' worth of one of the largest private-owned collections of African and African-American art, including pieces by Jacob Lawrence, Charles White, and Romare Bearden, was on the wall. On its seventh floor, the company was renowned for having one of the largest African-American book collections. On the shelves were many first editions, autographed by the greats, ranging from Richard Wright to Alex Haley. Johnson's penthouse suite was on the eleventh floor. It included an eleven-foot buried wood desk, edged with silver leaves, painted gold. A panel concealed in the desk controlled the lighting, music system, doors, and draperies. A picture phone was built in it as well. An office wall concealed a bar and a television, which sat on hand-set raw suede. There was an exercise room, sauna, and special barber's chair.[47]

Because Johnson wanted convenience, on the tenth floor, he had private dining rooms and a cafeteria, offering employees a full buffet, including desserts, all for a dollar.[48] Word had it there was a time when he considered raising the price to two dollars so employees could have more steak lunches, but employees complained so much that he conceded. It remained that price until his death.

FIGURE 12: Princess Grace of Monaco spends time with Johnson in his executive suite at Johnson Publishing Company during a meeting he hosted for board members of Twentieth Century Fox Film Corporation in 1976. She made history as the first woman on the board and he made history in 1971 as the first black. Courtesy Johnson Publishing Company, LLC. All rights reserved.

Johnson's empire was equipped with other conveniences, too. As the first black to hold a position on the board of directors for Twentieth Century Fox in 1971, it wasn't always easy for the busy Johnson to make time for movie going so he had the movies come to him. The building had its own theater room where top films were privately screened for Johnson and company employees months before nationwide release. *JET* magazine had a "Movies to See" section each week that made it logical for advance viewings. Johnson had his own special seat and though microwave popcorn later became popular, he preferred doing things the old-fashioned way by bringing his own skillet popped corn in a small brown bag. When screening movies, it wasn't unusual to have directors and celebs sit in on the flicks. *Training Day* director Antoine Fuqua brought an early version of the movie in 2001 when he was still trying to decide upon the ending. The film earned Denzel Washington his second Oscar, making him the second African-American man after Sidney Poitier to ever win for Best Actor.

In 1972, Johnson continued to make more history. This time he became the first black publisher to receive the magazine industry's most prestigious honor by earning the Henry Johnson Fisher Award for Publisher of the Year. "Responsible daring" is how Johnson described the business tactics he employed during his acceptance speech. He said:

> It is scarcely necessary to remind publishers that magazines must entertain as well as inform. But the danger here is that the publisher will blunder into the sin of dullness by mistaking his own limitations for the limitations of the public. We have to anticipate what the reader will want tomorrow by walking a step ahead of him. In fact, we have to anticipate the reader's desires and wishes by leading him, step by step, to what he really wants.[49]

While *JET* magazine was being purchased by more than half a million readers each week, in April 1973 a magazine for kids was started called *EBONY* Jr!, which sold for seventy-five cents. Michael Jackson had original drawings that appeared in the publication, known for cartoons like Sunny and Honey and a gallery on the back cover that allowed children to have their drawings featured. The August/September 1975 issue of *EBONY* Jr! was the first national publication to mention Jackson's artistic abilities and even had cartoons that he drew.[50]

By 1975 *EBONY* Jr! had a circulation of 300,000.[51] With so many magazines under his belt, some on the editorial staff were concerned that he was casting too wide a net. But one thing Johnson learned from his past is that even when others don't believe in you, if you believe in yourself, that's more than enough. "Mr. Johnson can't be talked out of an idea," *EBONY* executive editor Herbert Nipson said. "He makes a decision and he's a smart enough businessman to pick the right time."[52] And just as he impulsively knew when to start a new venture, he was not afraid to end one when he felt the tides had changed. *EBONY* Jr. ended in October 1985 because it was not profitable.

The 1974 issue of *Black Enterprise* featured a list of the top 100 African-American owned businesses in the nation. Johnson Publishing Company had $27.8 million in sales and 245 employees. It ranked No. 1 as the top Black business in the city and No. 2 in the entire country.[53] Eight years later Johnson would make history as the first Black to make Forbes' list of 400 wealthiest Americans. Some dubbed him the "Negro Hugh Hefner" because Johnson's empire rivaled that of Hefner's empire. But Johnson stood alone. In fact in 1982 when he made the Forbes 400, Hefner was not on the list.[54] By 1980 the company's worth was $61 million, second in sales only to Motown Industries, the record and entertainment company.[55] By 1985 he had an estimated worth of $50 million. Because his company was private and family owned, its worth was not publicly known.[56]

Johnson won a reputation for his staunch policy about simple things ranging from attendance and tardiness. There was the phrase CPT (colored people time) but that did not apply to JPC for he made certain to have employees sign in if they were even a minute late. A security guard sat at the front desk to make certain the sheet was signed.[57] On some days, he would even sit in the lobby to see those making their way into the building beyond the start time. He was known to fire people for saying things he disagreed with. Remember the employee he got rid of because the gentleman used the word failure? "Nothing personal, but I'm too insecure myself to have people around me who believe that failure is a possibility. Failure is a word that I don't accept."[58]

He was always making history, positively and negatively. While he made Forbes' list, two years later he was voted as one of *Fortune* magazine's 10 Toughest Bosses in 1984. By then his worth was well over $100 million with Johnson Publishing Company as the only private company and the only black owned to make the infamous roll. Qualifications for those to make the survey's list included "being autocratic, ruthless, grueling and intimidating." Candidates were culled from interviews with management consultants, executive recruiters, investors, corporate chairmen, and other professionals who specialized in treating executive stress. Present and former employees at the time were interviewed to find out how the ten were actually regarded as the toughest.[59]

Terms like "standout callousness" and being a "brutally honest" boss known to go off in "wild temper tantrums" is how Johnson was described in the article. Employees past and those working for him at the time of the story most often summed up the experience of working at his company like that of a "plantation." One employee communicated, "He runs his business like a plantation." Another employee said, "Just like on a plantation, he is lord and master." Others used the term "slave master" because with so few places for black journalists to work, they were paid low salaries though the pay was improving by 1984 when the article was written.[60] Another former employee mentioned how Johnson would frequently ask those who questioned his decision, "If you're so smart, why aren't you rich?"[61]

The story began by using a narrative of how Johnson fired EBONY Senior Editor Alex Poinsett after twenty-six years of loyal service. "He threatens to fire his top people every other week," is what a former employee said. One who worked at the company at the time the story was written said, "It's like a crescendo with Johnson. First he puts you down with words. Then when you're down, he flattens you out. Then he walks on your face."[62]

Those who met Johnson or ever heard him speak in public knew that he was witty and charming. There was nothing pretentious about this millionaire. Behind closed doors, Johnson took his business seriously and was considered by some to have ruled by fear. One thing about Johnson, for anyone who knew the man, was that if he could dish it out, he could take it and own it. He cussed like a sailor and would pound a fist on the table to drive a point home, especially before preparing to say something by loudly exclaiming, "Goddammit!" He told the Harvard Business Review in 1976 that he dealt with anger by letting it flow through words. "If I'm mad at somebody, I just go in a room, close the door and cuss him or her out where nobody can hear me. Sometimes I write a letter that I don't mail. I've done a lot of that. I think we have to let the steam off." [63]

With that said, Johnson didn't deny any of the claims made in the *Fortune* story but stated the involuntary servitude was baseless. Fully loaded Cadillacs were given to some executives and low-level managers had Zenith televisions and stereos in their offices. Everyone enjoyed the best lunch in town for only $1 at the company's private cafeteria. There was a salad and dessert bar, beverages, and hot, home-cooked delicious meals resembling a dinner buffet prepared by a full kitchen staff. Employees could eat as much as they liked with no questions asked.

"Nobody is in slavery here," Johnson told the reporter of the article. "Anybody who is unhappy can always leave. And all my top execs have company cars and they aren't small cars. I've been on a plantation and it was never like that."[64] When the publication asked why so many employees used the term "plantation," to describe Johnson Publishing Company, he said, "I am a private company. Hell, Time Inc. (the publisher of *Fortune*) was a plantation when Henry Luce was there. I am like Henry Luce."[65]

An image of Johnson, sitting on an exercise bike in his private fitness room on his eleventh floor penthouse suite at the company headquarters, accompanied the story. Fit and more than capable of going the distance, Johnson firmly added, "I am tough. I make no apologies...I gotta be doing something right."[66] Johnson acknowledged that his landmark eleven-story building had become the go-to place in Chicago. Teachers took groups of school children to see the Johnson Publishing Company building and notables, ranging from Hollywood elite to dignitaries, made it a point to visit the house that John H. Johnson built. "People from all over the world have come here to see...the miracle of Johnson Publishing. It is something of a shrine. In the days of Alexander the Great and Napoleon...I am trying to be that kind of leader, riding ahead of the other horses. I am considered a legend in my time."[67]

He wasn't oblivious to the fact that he ran his company with an ironclad fist, but Johnson believed that he was a person who was compassionate. He explained:

> Some people say I'm tough and I guess maybe I am, but always, always I think, whether people perceive it or not, I try to be fair. At the end of every day, I go into a room by myself, and I review the day, and the one question I always ask myself is: 'Was I fair? Did I do the right thing?' And there have been times when I didn't do the right thing, and I have apologized for it, and I have corrected it. I guess I'm proud of the fact that I'm able to do that.[68]

Grayson Mitchell, a former journalist at Johnson Publishing Company, told the Washington Post in 1980, "Very few people love him. But they respect him. All he cares about is money. That's what made Mobil Oil great. That's what made all the great businesses of America."[69]

Ben Burns, the founding editor of *Negro Digest*, *EBONY* and *JET*, was fired in 1954. It turns out that Burns' "never-ending arguments for balance to report some of the worst of racism" along with his "Communist and Defender training in protest proved a source of continual acrimony" between the two "for almost all the years" Burns worked for him.[70]

Johnson said how Burns' constant opposition to stories where there "must be achievement" and have more than "sex" as the "only redeeming feature" were the final nail in the coffin for their work relationship. Johnson said this in his autobiography, "Burns continued to oppose the policy, and we kind of had a running battle. In fact, he literally defied me. We would agree on an approach to a story, and he'd go to the plant and insert a sensational story and claim afterward that the story came in at the last minute and that he couldn't reach me or change it."[71]

Burns vehemently denied the claim and wrote a letter to *Fortune* magazine when Johnson explained that Burns was behind all "the sex and sensationalism in *EBONY*." Burns said he would not be the "white scapegoat." He continued by saying:

> Mr. Johnson, and no one else, as any of his employees over the years will testify, always set and retained close to his vest the editorial policies of the magazine. It was his appetite for quick circulation gains that brought about the policy of sensationalism—and it was my assignment as editor to find yet another sex, mixed marriage, passing or scandal story that fitted the formula he set.[72]

In 1957, Burns went on to do PR with Al Golin, where an early client of theirs was Ray Kroc, a former salesman of malted milk machines who founded a new franchise-type drive-in chain restaurant called McDonald's.[73] The same year that Johnson made history as the first African American named on the Forbes 400, Kroc was included as well.

When *JET* magazine was founded in 1942, its size was 5 ¾" by 4" and sold for fifteen cents.[74] The newsweekly was small enough to fit into a back pocket with the size 4" by 5 ¾" and had 68 pages.[75] By 1972, the magazine increased in size slightly by becoming 5" by 7 ½".[76] By 1989 it was 7 ⅜" by 5 ¼" and was selling for one dollar and twenty-five cents.[77] When the print version ended in 2014, it was 5 ⅛" by 7 ⅜".[78]

On the other hand, *EBONY*, its sister publication, was noted for its large size like *Life* magazine, which it patterned itself with a size of 13 ¾" by 9 ¾" size and sold for twenty-five cents.[79] By the March 1982 issue, the size changed to 8 ½" by 11" like the standard dimensions of other magazines at the time. Muhammad Ali and then-wife Veronica graced the cover of the one dollar and seventy-five cents issue.[80] The cover story was titled "Muhammad Ali's Multi-Million Dollar 'Retirement' Home."

Johnson, a man of tradition, reluctantly changed the size though it cost much less to have a smaller publication. After losing ads because of *EBONY*'s large format, Johnson was open to reducing the size when major advertisement from Ford, Campbell Soup, and General Motors ended.[81] He liked the dominance of the larger magazine and how it allowed for bigger pictures and more space for stories.[82] The February issue with singer/actress Stephanie Mills on the cover with the title "The Painful Education of a Young Superstar" marked the last large *EBONY* magazine.

A spring poll in Advertising Age showed that *EBONY* and *JET* were the most-read magazines in the country by black men and women. *EBONY*'s circulation was 1.3 million in 1979. Six hundred thousand black women were his "closest competitor" by reading *Essence*, a publication geared toward black women, while *Sports Illustrated* came in second as one favored by black men. Few know this but Johnson even allowed *Essence* to put subscription cards in *EBONY*. "And I've never let any other magazine do that," Johnson said in 1980.[83] By 1989 he had bought 20 percent of the outstanding stock of *Essence*.[84] In 1980, as previously mentioned in this chapter, Johnson's company was one of the most successful black businesses in America. During this time he also owned a small $50,000 portion of the Chicago White Sox, making him the only black with any money in the team. This was a move he made when he was trying to keep the team in the city.[85]

By 1984, *Black Enterprise* reported that as one of the nation's three largest black-owned businesses for more than twenty years, the company had revenues of $138.9 million that year. In November 1984 former PR executive George Pryce published the first issue of *MBM*, subtitled Modern Black Man, magazine. Aimed at upwardly mobile black men in an effort to show that men of color weren't all on "welfare" or "out mugging someone," the bimonthly magazine, published and edited by Pryce, was based in New York. But it had a lavish debut party in January 1985 at Chicago's Oak Street Hippo Bistro.[86]

One thing about Johnson was that he was always trying to reinvent himself by starting new ventures just to prove he could capture lightning in a bottle once more. Pryce maintained he was not trying to be in competition with Johnson. Johnson, on the other hand, was not one who had any previous interest in starting a men's magazine, but he had a change of heart after seeing the success of GQ (Gentleman's Quarterly); MBM was the added fuel he needed to rise for a good challenge and found *EM* (*EBONY* Man), a magazine geared toward men, in 1985. Some say he started *EM* with the goal of putting MBM out of business, because it was Johnson's first new magazine in a dozen years. Johnson promoted internally at Johnson Publishing with former *JET* editor Willie Wofford taking the helm of *EM*. Anticipating he would have to sink a million dollars into unchartered territory with the venture, Johnson made a five-year commitment to *EM*.[87] Johnson believed the key to success was "to stay out there long enough for people to realize that you're out there." *EM* lasted longer than five years—outliving the demise of *MBM*—but ended thirteen years later in 1998.

Though the empire had expanded by 1985, starting a new magazine came at an odd time for the privately held company when after twelve years, *EBONY Jr!* had just ended in October. Sales for *JET* were down due to "declining liquor advertising" and WLOU, the AM station Johnson bought in 1982 for $16 million, was no longer holding its own in first place but had fallen to sixth place since that time.[88] The Fashion Fair cosmetics line was always the saving grace for the company, many times having revenues higher than *EBONY*'s. Interestingly enough, as stated earlier, Johnson also had a 20 percent stake in Essence Communications Inc., which at one time published *Essence*.[89]

By 1985 the empire included Supreme Life Insurance Company where he got his start as an office boy fresh out of high school, but at this point, he was now its chairman and chief executive officer.[90] The empire also housed Fashion Fair Cosmetics, three radio stations, three magazines, a book publishing company, and a TV production company, which hosted the *EBONY-JET* Showcase and the American Black Achievement Awards (ABAA), which first broadcast on December 10, 1978, and was a tribute to black excellence.

The ABAA celebrated its tenth anniversary in 1989. The celebration took place at Transamerica Celebrity Theater in Hollywood and was seen on a major network, CBS. At that time, it was the first national TV production to provide public recognition to top people of color in diverse fields, ranging from entertainment to sports to business to religion. The two major awards included the Jackie Robinson Award, given to an individual thirty years old or younger who made the overall or singular greatest achievement for the year. Another major award was the Martin Luther King Jr. Award, given to an individual older than thirty, who made the overall or singular greatest achievement for the year. Andrew Young was the recipient of the first Martin Luther King Jr. Award while Stevie Wonder received the first Jackie Robinson Award. Not one to forget how his life was changed because of how Harry H. Pace touched it, Johnson saw to it that two $5,000 awards were also given to high school seniors who showed academic excellence.

In 1982 Tom Joyner hosted the *EBONY / JET* Celebrity Showcase, which premiered in Chicago, Atlanta, and D.C. because of their large black populations "to test the show before sending it all over the country."[91] Joyner was also the producer of the half-hour series. No stranger to the company, Joyner was noted for his work as on-air personality and program director of the Johnson Publishing Company WJPC-AM radio. In Joyner's 2005 memoir, *I'm Just a DJ But...It Makes Sense to Me*, he explained how Johnson hired him as a radio personality with the promise that if he could boost ratings for the radio's poor ratings, at least bringing it to a No. 2 status in the Chicago market, Johnson would put him on television. Joyner brought the ratings up.[92]

*EBONY / JET* Celebrity Showcase only lasted a year, with Joyner completing twenty-six episodes. Johnson said that in addition to it not having "the quality we wanted it to have," the exorbitant cost to produce it was also a problem.[93] But two years later, the show was resurrected with a slightly new name called *EBONY /JET* Showcase in 1984. By September of that year, Bill Cosby kicked off the first episode for Showcase, which was a weekly hour, nationally-syndicated interview show. Linda Johnson Rice served as the show's executive producer, while Beverly A. Price, served as the producer, with both helping to line up the guests. Shot on location, the two co-hosts were Deborah Crable and Greg Gumbel. Later, in 1987, Darryl Dennard became a co-host. That year the show continued to make history by being the only black syndicated program to reach 92 percent of the black U.S. households and 73 percent of U.S. households.[94] By 1991 a new co-host team was in place with Sherri Paysinger and Elliott Francis.

Johnson revealed in 1985 that he was surprised by how far the company had come because given the times when JPC was first born in the 1940s, the challenges of rising above racism seemed a difficult obstacle to cast away. He wasn't sure if, or how much, progress would be made but he knew that he would survive in some way. He said the following:

> If you are talking about 1945, I would not have believed that we would have come as far as we have. But if you are talking about the Supreme Court decision of 1954, I would have believed that we would have made even more progress. My position now is that we have made a lot of progress, but that it is going to be slower in the future. I think our biggest task in the future is not going to be making new progress but holding on to and maintaining the progress we've made.[95]

In 1987, Johnson's daughter earned an MBA from Northwestern University's J.L. Kellogg Graduate School of Management. As vice president and assistant to the publisher at JPC and director of *EBONY* Fashion Fair, she was promptly promoted to president and chief operating officer of her father's company. He had a belief that any employee had to do more than one thing at a time and work his/her way up the ladder at his company. A person couldn't just graduate with an MBA and run his company. Johnson said:

> I don't employ MBAs because they are taught to run things. I don't plan on letting them run my company. You have to come

> in at a lower level and work your way up...I did make one exception. My daughter graduated...on Saturday and I made her president on Monday. But she was my daughter.[96]

*EBONY*'s fiftieth anniversary was celebrated with the creation of *EBONY* South Africa in 1995. A November/December premiere issue stated how the mission was to be "a continuation of a dynamic that helped free both African Americans and South Africans, and it reminds us that Africans and African Americans are bound together by history and hope."[97] A year earlier, after Nelson Mandela made history as South Africa's first black head of state and the first elected in a fully representative democratic election, Johnson dedicated an issue to South Africa in August 1994. The magazine featured Nelson Mandela on the cover with the title, "Nelson Mandela and The New South Africa: South Africa Free At Last!" Looking to capitalize and document the country's history after triumphing over apartheid, Johnson desired to bring a glossy monthly like the one he started in the United States some fifty years earlier to coffee tables in living rooms in South Africa. However, the post-Apartheid bandwagon was not what he hoped it would be because people could not buy into the levels of success he showcased in the magazine. South Africans could not conceive of the type of success they were being force fed to believe they could achieve when millions of them were unemployed and too poor to think about purchasing a magazine.

Fraser Mtshali, who was editor in chief of the country's biggest-selling lifestyle magazine targeted for blacks, believed that though *EBONY* South Africa's intentions might have been well meaning, they were sorely misplaced. He said the publication was "seeing South African through American eyes" by producing "an American *EBONY* with a touch of South Africa rather than a South African *EBONY* with a touch of America." Advertising was always a problem even when circulation numbers soared. According to the Audit Bureau Circulations South Africa, during the first half of 1999, circulation numbers were high at 23,880 but by the year's end, they declined to 22,477. The magazine ended in 2000.[98]

At its peak—and while Johnson was alive—the empire Johnson built had bureaus in Los Angeles, New York, Washington, London, Paris. There was even a location in Johannesburg, post-Apartheid.

But hard times also would hit *EBONY* in the U.S. eventually.

Crain's 2008 list of Chicago's largest minority-owned companies listed Johnson Publishing as No. 1, with a revenue of $453.3 million in 2007, beating out Oprah Winfrey's Harpo Inc. [99] However, the magazines struggled financially with a decline in print advertising sales throughout the media industry amid a rough and tumbled economy. Sales for *EBONY* ads, according to Publishers Information Bureau Data, dropped 12 percent to $56.7 million in 2008. *JET* advertising revenue declined 19 percent to $26.6 million in 2008 with the magazines combining some issues and calling them special double issues. [100] *JET*, once the No. 1 African-American newsweekly in the U.S. and the world, was said to have reached more than 9.7 million readers each week, according to media market research conducted in Spring 2004. By 2005, its weekly circulation claimed a weekly figure of 956,909, according to the Association of Magazine Media.

FIGURE 13: Johnson receives the Presidential Medal of Freedom from President Bill Clinton during White House ceremonies in 1996. The honor is the nation's highest bestowed on civilians. Courtesy Johnson Publishing Company, LLC. 

# CHAPTER 10

## END OF A DYNASTY

***"Retirement is not in this company's vocabulary. If you are well and able to work, you can stay at the company."***
***John H. Johnson***

John H. Johnson loved Johnson Publishing Company as much as life itself. He said he would "push a 10-story building on a baby if it meant stopping a threat to his business." He had a way with words, especially when he was trying to get his point across about the importance of having a thriving business. Though he admitted that the statement "was a joke, an in-house joke," and he said "it in jest," those who knew Johnson knew that nothing would stand between him and his company.[1]

It was literally his world and the air he breathed; even after "working" hours and on weekends, he spent much of his time on the 11th floor in his penthouse suite. He hardly ever went to the condo that he shared with his wife in the Carlyle on Chicago's Lake Shore Drive. Johnson considered work his form of relaxation and it was evident that the headquarters was his home.

In his autobiography he discussed never selling and the importance of complete and total ownership. "Well, it's very simple. You just don't sell any stock to anybody and you don't try to merge. I'm not for sale. I'm not for sale."[2] He spoke of how other black businessmen, particularly an organization of publishers, wanted him to join forces with them, but he refused because it wasn't sound business for him. "They were talking about all of us going in to sell an advertiser together. I don't believe in group selling," he said.[3] This wasn't done in an effort to "pit" himself against the others; Johnson was hell-bent on doing things his way. He said, "I do not want to put the destiny of my company in the hands of anyone else—particularly if they haven't done as well as I have."[4]

The building, however, was eventually sold. By November 2017 it was purchased for $11 million by a developer, 3L Real Estate, who planned to convert it into one hundred and fifty rental apartments.[5] The iconic EBONY/JET sign that sat on top of the building still remains.

Also that same year, a portion of Johnson's company would be sold, no longer bearing his name. It was located for a short time in WeWork, a co-working facility, before editorial offices planned a move from its birthplace of Chicago to Los Angeles. The relocation never happened but the editorial departments of the company and Fashion Fair Cosmetics severed ties.

Throughout the years, some argued it was because of the economy that things crumbled for the Johnson Publishing Company empire. Magazines and newspapers were folding and laying off employees across the country in record numbers by 2014. Many others believed that mismanagement and poor leadership rerouted the company's course. The following timeline illustrates the changes that have occurred at the house that John H. Johnson built since his death:

**2005**

**August 8**

John H. Johnson, eighty-seven, dies of heart failure at Chicago's Northwestern Memorial Hospital.

**August 14**

Hundreds of people line up along South Michigan Avenue to view Johnson's body and to pay their respects at the visitation. The viewing lasts from 2:00 p.m. to 7:45 p.m. in the Johnson Publishing Company lobby at 820 S. Michigan Avenue.[6]

**August 15**

Johnson Publishing Company is closed in honor of its chairman and founder. The funeral takes place at 11:00 a.m. at Chicago's Rockefeller Memorial Chapel on campus of the University of Chicago.[7]

**November**

The dedication of Honorary John H. Johnson Ave. takes place on the corner of where Johnson's headquarters is located. John H. Johnson Ave. stretches from 8th Street and South Michigan Avenue to 12th Street and South Michigan Avenue. "I believe my father is smiling at us today as we witness his favorite place in the world having its address changed to 820 John H. Johnson Avenue," said Johnson's daughter, Linda Johnson Rice, President and CEO of Johnson Publishing Company.[8]

**2006**

**July**

Bryan Monroe, a former president of the National Association of Black Journalists and assistant vice president/news for Knight Ridder, is named Vice President and Editorial Director of *EBONY* and *JET*. Monroe becomes the first person in the company's history since Johnson's death to simultaneously run both publications.[9]

Employees are no longer required to sit at "assigned tables" in the tenth floor cafeteria at the headquarters. Assigned seating started several decades earlier, reportedly after a scuffle broke out between employees when one person sat in another's chair during lunch.

**2007**

**August**

Johnson Rice, a University of Southern California (USC graduate and former trustee, gives $2.5 million to Annenberg School for Communications to establish the Johnson Communication Leadership Center, which provides undergraduate scholarships and hosts seminars focused specifically on issues relating to African Americans in the media. "Johnson Publishing Company is excited to fund this new initiative at USC," said Johnson Rice in a statement. "The scholarships as well as the extensive exposure to mentorship, research, and travel are innovative ways to support the African-American perspective in the journalism and communication fields."[10 11]

**September**
Anne Sempowski Ward, a former assistant vice president of African-American marketing for the Coca-Cola Company, is appointed President and Chief Operating Officer of Fashion Fair Cosmetics, which is described as "the world's largest cosmetic and skin care company for women of color."[12]

<u>2008</u>
**October**
Johnson Rice additionally appoints Sempowski Ward as Johnson Publishing Company's Chief Operating Officer. Johnson Rice said in a statement, "Anne has a proven track record of successful leadership. She is a visionary with a strategic focus on growth for Johnson Publishing Company. I look forward to the energy and tenacity she will bring to this position as she has so evidently done with Fashion Fair Cosmetics."[13]

<u>2009</u>
**January**
Employees receive news of reorganization three days after the presidential inauguration. The move is reportedly made to steer the company out of its financial woes. Monroe's position of Editorial Director for *EBONY* and *JET* is eliminated. Jobs are created for Editor in Chief of *EBONY* and for Editor in Chief of *JET* for which anyone interested would have to apply. A Senior Vice President, Publishing, position also is created. Johnson Rice said in a statement, "I am deeply committed to maintaining our presence and long-standing legacy in the African-American community. Reshaping our organizational design will help ensure that we continue to evolve with the ever-changing media landscape."[14]

**February**
Half of the company's staffers receive calls at their desks, stating that their positions are eliminated and are told to reapply for new jobs. The other half of the company's staffers, with long-standing tenure (combination of years and age), either opt for buyout offers or wait it out before finally being terminated.

**April**
The first appointment under the *EBONY/JET* reorganization is with Mira Lowe, who makes history when she is named *JET* magazine's first female Editor in Chief. Harriette Cole, a former *Essence* editor who was serving as *EBONY*'s creative director, is named interim Editor in Chief for the monthly.

**May**
Johnson Publishing Company has trouble paying its printing bill to R.R. Donnelley & Sons Co., who take out mortgages for about $12 million on the Johnson-owned properties.[15]

**June**
Crain's Chicago Business reports by Eddie Baeb and Ann Saphir reveal: "*EBONY* owner Johnson Publishing Company is under siege, battered by sharp drops in advertising and circulation amid the severe downturn in its 67-year history. In the past three months, Johnson has been hit with contractors' liens claiming the company failed to pay for work worth nearly $500,000. In May, Johnson mortgaged its South Michigan Avenue headquarters building and parking garage to its printer, R.R. Donnelley & Sons Co. Loan documents say the deal secured previous debts to Donnelley totaling $12.7 million—another sign of financial distress for the nation's largest Black-owned publishing company."[16]

*EBONY* Fashion Fair, the historic traveling fashion show, suspends its fall production.[17]

**2010**

**January**
Eunice W. Johnson, wife of Johnson who was secretary-treasurer and director of *EBONY* Fashion Fair, dies at ninety-three. *EBONY* Fashion Fair, the world's largest traveling fashion show, formally ends after more than five decades.[18]

**February**

Retired basketball legend Earvin "Magic" Johnson is in talks to purchase Johnson Publishing Company. "There have been discussions. There's no definitive agreement," said Eric Holoman, president of Los Angeles-based Magic Johnson Enterprises. The NBA star reportedly would fold the publishing company into Magic Johnson Enterprises. The company's historic headquarters would be included in the sale, with a purchase possibly satisfying liens placed on the building by a creditor.[19]

**June**

Desiree Rogers, longtime best friend of Johnson Rice, starts consulting work by assisting with various aspects of corporate strategy as it relates to the company's core brands, *EBONY, JET*, and Fashion Fair. Reportedly, her initial contract was for two months. In November 2009, Rogers made national headlines when she resigned from her position in the Obama Administration under the cloud of the Salahis gatecrasher fiasco at Obama's first White House state dinner for India's prime minister.[20] Rogers made history that same year as the first black White House social secretary.[21]

**June**

Amy DuBois Barnett is named Editor in Chief of *EBONY*. The slot was filled on an interim basis for fourteen months by Cole. Barnett was a writer and editor for women's magazines, including *Honey, Harper's Bazaar* and *Essence*. "She understands the richness of *EBONY* and she's not afraid to push the envelope. She brings an interesting background of experience," Johnson Rice said in a statement.[22]

**July**

Sempowski Ward resigns as president and Chief Operating Officer while she is on maternity leave. The announcement comes six weeks after Rogers' arrival. A publicist at Johnson Publishing Company ruled out Rogers as Ward's successor, saying in a statement, "She is not being considered for president and Chief Operating Officer." Rice said in a statement about Ward, "Anne has been a significant asset to our company and led key, corporate-wide initiatives for *EBONY, JET,* and Fashion Fair. During Anne's tenure, we underwent significant restructuring and reorganization of the company. Her contributions have helped to position the company for the future." Ward made history as the first person outside of the Johnson family to serve as president and Chief Operating Officer of both the publishing and cosmetic divisions for Johnson Publishing Company.[23]

**August**

Rogers is named Chief Executive Officer at Johnson Publishing Company. "Desiree has a proven track record of successful business leadership. She is a long-standing confidant and a savvy businesswoman who is committed to the strategic growth of Johnson Publishing Co.," Johnson Rice, chairman and Chief Executive Officer, said in a statement. The move replaces Johnson Rice in the position of CEO with Johnson Rice remaining as chairman. In a 2011 interview with the *Chicago Tribune*, Rogers believed there to be a different vision for *EBONY*, confidently telling the newspaper, "The magazine is really Vanity Fair plus O (the Oprah Winfrey magazine plus soul."[24]

Johnson College Prep, named in honor of John H. Johnson and wife, Eunice, opens on Chicago's South Side. The school is a campus of the Noble Network of Charter Schools, the highest-performing network of open enrollment high schools in the city of Chicago. A Fresno, California, school, Fresno Colony Elementary School, was first renamed to John H. Johnson Elementary School on July 1, 1977.[25]

**November**

In Johnson's autobiography, he wrote, "I am not for sale." But Johnson Rice, desperate to dig the company out of a financial slump, sells her father's historic 820 S. Michigan Avenue headquarters building to Chicago's Columbia College. "The sale of 820 S. Michigan is part of the continuing evolution of the company that my father and mother started in early 1942. Just as when JPC moved to this location in 1972, my father would be the first to say it makes good business sense to relocate to space that serves the current needs of the company," Johnson Rice said in a statement.[26] The 11-story, 110,00 square-foot historic building was designed by an African American, John W. Moutoussamy. It was the first owned by an African-American in the Loop. The building reportedly sold for $8 million.

The college planned to use the building for a library and other institution-related functions. Johnson Publishing Company moves from ownership to leasing two floors with smaller quarters at 200 S. Michigan. Staff continues to be cut.

**November**

Johnson's name is quietly dropped from Howard University's School of Communications. He visited the campus of Howard University in 2003 and presented a check for $4 million that would someday be used for a down payment toward the construction of a new building that would house the communications school that had been renamed that year in his honor.[27] In 2008, Johnson Rice cited economic reasons for the change of plans. In October 2016, Howard University renames it the Cathy Hughes School of Communications.[28]

**2011**

**January**

Mira Lowe resigns as Editor in Chief of *JET*.[29]

**April**

Mitzi Miller, a writer and editor at women's magazines, including *Honey*, is named Editor in Chief of *JET*.[30]

First major redesign of *EBONY* takes place with the April issue, featuring comedians-actors Chris Rock, Steve Harvey, and Mo'Nique on the cover. The redesign, hoping to distance the magazine's image from older readers and the reputation of being "your grandmother's magazine," is aimed at appealing to "goal oriented, engaged, stylish" readers between the ages of 29 and 35.[31]

**July**

Johnson Publishing Company announces that JP Morgan Chase & Co.'s special investments group will become an investor and part owner of the company, which also produces Fashion Fair Cosmetics. It is the first time in the company's nearly 70-year history that it will not be fully family owned. JP Morgan Chase & Co. acquires a "substantial" minority stake in the company. The special investments group is a private equity unit within JP Morgan Chase. Johnson Rice said in a statement, "JP Morgan Chase's investment in our firm is a logical outgrowth of our longstanding relationship. It positions Johnson Publishing for continued growth as a family-owned publisher of the black community's most-trusted media brands by providing financial resources to take our iconic *EBONY* and *JET* magazines to the next level and accelerate our growth strategy for Fashion Fair Cosmetics."[32]

**2012**

**January**

The United States Postal Service (USPS presents one of the nation's highest honors to Johnson by posthumously commemorating him with a Black Heritage Forever Stamp during a dedication ceremony in the lobby of the historic Johnson Publishing Company building at 820 S. Michigan Ave. Johnson is the 35th honoree in the Black Heritage stamp series. "John Johnson's unyielding commitment to journalistic excellence and his unparalleled reporting on African- American culture have distinguished him as one of America's greatest publishers," said USPS Chicago Senior Plant Manager Anthony Vaughan.[33] This memorable occasion marks the last event held at the historic headquarters.

*JET* goes from being published weekly to bi-weekly and promises advertisers a circulation of 700,000 instead of 800,000.[34]

**June**

The final day of the move from the historic Johnson Publishing headquarters takes place.

The company relocates to 200 S. Michigan where they lease the twentieth and twenty first floor. Johnson Publishing Company has more than fifty percent fewer employees than it had in 2005; yet, it continues to eliminate positions and struggle financially.

**2013**

**January**

Cheryl Mayberry McKissack, founder, president and CEO of Nia Enterprises, LLC, a Chicago-based online research, marketing and digital consulting firm, is appointed Chief Operating Officer. "She has a proven track record in transforming companies through strategic innovation and in using technology to help create growth opportunities," Rogers said in a statement.[35]

**September**

Johnson Publishing Company arranges new financing through Gibraltar Business Capital LLC, a firm that specializes in "alternative" lending, or loans that traditional banks don't provide because they're too risky. In a news release, Johnson Rice said the new financing will allow the company to "execute our strategic goals, strengthen our brands and lead to future growth."[36]

## 2014

**April**

DuBois Barnett, having completed the June *EBONY* music issue, resigns. Mitzi Miller is named the new *EBONY* Editor in Chief (EIC) on the same day, becoming the first woman in company history to have held EIC titles for both *JET* and *EBONY*.[37]

**May**

*JET* announces its end with print editions after sixty-three years. *JET* transitions to a digital-only magazine app in late June.[38]

*EBONY* and *JET* staffs merge under Mitzi Miller's leadership on May 30, 2014, with four people from *EBONY*—one from *JET* —having their positions eliminated. Miller retains all her staff with the exception of one person. Author is among four *EBONY* staffers to have position eliminated. Her departure signals being the last editor who remained at the company to have worked under the direct leadership of the company's pioneering founder. She was also the only person in the company's history to have written for *EBONY*, *JET*, *EBONY* Man, *EBONY* South Africa, *EBONY* Fashion Fair and *EBONY*.com.[39]

**June**

The last print edition of *JET* is the June 23 issue, which hit newsstands on June 2. Final issues never reached some shelves because Source Interlink Distribution, the nation's second largest magazine distributor, suddenly went out of business.[40]

## 2015

### January

The historic Johnson Publishing Company archives are up for sale at $40 million, including the Pulitzer Prize-winning photograph of a grieving Rev. Dr. Martin Luther King, Jr's widow, Coretta Scott King, holding their young daughter, Bernice, at her husband's funeral in 1968. Rogers told the *Chicago Tribune* of the archives that documented the history of African Americans, "It's just sitting here. We really need to monetize that in order to ensure growth in our core businesses."[41]

### February

Miller resigns as Editor in Chief of *EBONY*.[42]

### June

Kierna Mayo, vice president of digital content for *EBONY*.com, is named Editor in Chief of *EBONY*. Kyra Kyles, editorial director of *JET*mag.com, is named head of digital editorial.[43]

## 2016

### June

*EBONY*, *JET*, *EBONY*.com and *JET*mag.com are sold to Austin, Texas-based firm, CVG Group, after being run as part of Johnson Publishing Company. The print and web titles are now under a new name, *EBONY* Media Operations. Johnson Publishing Company continues to handle the archives and Fashion Fair Cosmetics. The details of sale remain private with new owners agreeing to take on any debt incurred by JPC. It is announced that Rogers will lead Fashion Fair Cosmetics. Mayberry McKissack is named Chief Executive Officer of *EBONY* Media Operations, and Johnson Rice remains in the company as chairman emeritus of Johnson Publishing Company. "This is the next chapter in retaining the legacy that my father, John H. Johnson, built to ensure the celebration of African Americans," Johnson Rice said in a statement.[44]

Mayo resigns as Editor in Chief of *EBONY*; Kyles is named Editor in Chief of the magazine.[45]

Columbia College makes plans to sell the historic Johnson Publishing Company building, which has been vacant since the business moved out in 2012. Johnson's eleventh floor penthouse office, once initially considered to be used for a museum by the college, is cleaned out.[46]

**November**

Howard University launches a John H. Johnson Entrepreneurship Speaker Series with Johnson Rice as the first speaker. The John H. Johnson Endowed Chair for Entrepreneurship was established by Johnson Publishing Company and Johnson Rice in 2016. According to a statement by Johnson Rice at its creation, the Chair was launched "to strengthen a culture of entrepreneurial activity across the University among students, faculty, staff, alumni and community business owners." Johnson Rice added, "We are very proud of the longstanding relationship we have with Howard University and value the sincere ties we have with the historical institution. Howard University graduates have worked with Johnson Publishing Company in both the past and present, and the skills and talents they possess have helped to build the company to what it is today."[47]

**2017**

**February**

Chicago Mayor Rahm Emanuel announces that Johnson Publishing Company is being considered for landmark status. "As we celebrate Black History Month, it is the perfect time to honor this building that stands tall as a decades-long epicenter of black history and culture," Mayor Emanuel said. "This designation will cement this building's status as a landmark that is not just part of the legacy of the city of Chicago, but the history of our nation." The landmark designation process started with a preliminary recommendation at the February 2, 2017, meeting of the Commission on Chicago Landmarks.[48]

It is confirmed that there are plans for *JET* to return after ending print editions in 2014. There will be four issues a year and the magazine will be based in Los Angeles. Repositioning the magazine toward millennials, Tracey Ferguson is named Editor in Chief for the magazine and for *JET*.com. Ferguson is the founder of a women's fashion magazine titled *Jones*.[49]

**March**
Johnson Rice is named CEO of *EBONY* Media once again with Mayberry McKissack leaving to pursue "other business ventures."[50]

**April**
Fashion Fair remains at 200 S. Michigan but moves to a lower floor on nine. Johnson Rice has an office at this location.

*EBONY* Media, which houses *EBONY* editorial, moves out of the 200 S. Michigan building and temporarily relocates into WeWork, a co-working space facility, located at 125 S. Clark Street. A few months later, it eventually moves to 800 West Huron.

For the first time in history what was once *EBONY* editorial and *EBONY* Fashion Fair cosmetics are not housed in the same location.

**May**
The William Morris Endeavor (WME signs *EBONY* and *JET* magazines, which operates under *EBONY* Media Operations, as clients. The longest-running talent agency "will work with EMO to expand its current print and digital footprint, enhance the brand and utilize the magazines' over 70 years of archival content," according to a press statement.[51] Johnson Rice said, "We signed both brands with William Morris to represent us in broadcast opportunities and media opportunities and events like The Power 100. They're going to handle both brands across multiple platforms."[52]

A third of the company is let go, including Kyles, Editor in Chief of *EBONY*. Ferguson is additionally named Editor in Chief of *EBONY*, *EBONY*.com and *JET*mag.com. There is mention that the company will move to Los Angeles.[53]

Johnson Rice denies that there were "extensive layoffs" or that the company is leaving Chicago. "We will still have a big presence in Chicago, because our sales and marketing team is there, our production is in Chicago. So I want to be real clear on that—we're not leaving Chicago," Johnson Rice said. Editorial staff will be in Chicago and in New York. *JET* editorial will be based in Los Angeles.[54]

**June**

Desiree Rogers leaves *EBONY* Fashion Fair. Johnson Rice becomes Chief Executive Officer of Johnson Publishing Company, which has Fashion Fair Cosmetics, regaining both positions at a company founded by her late father. "We are well-positioned to continue my father's legacy and move these businesses forward in the future...I am delighted to resume the leadership of both companies," Johnson Rice said in a statement.[55]

**July**

Johnson Rice is named to Tesla's Board of Directors, becoming the first African-American and second woman to join the board.[56] [57]

**September**

Ferguson leaves the company.[58]

**October**

Shirley Henderson, whose *EBONY* position was eliminated in May 2014, returns to serve in the role of *EBONY*'s Contributing Editorial Director. Under her leadership, author is asked to contribute as freelancer.

**2018**

**July**

Johnson Rice resigns as CEO of *EBONY* Media Operations. "For the past year I was CEO of both EMO and Johnson Publishing Company. I transitioned out of the CEO role at EMO to focus on JPC," she told Journal-isms.[59]

# FINAL THOUGHTS

## The Man in the Mirror Theory

Mirrors offer a reflection of self. It is unfortunate that sometimes people don't always like the image they see staring back. If someone or something has its own identity of an established history and rich legacy, then what's the mystery? Let it be the best that it knows how to be. But you see, some aren't for the people because they don't know the people, can't relate to the people, and don't like those whom they serve. In an effort to assimilate, these misguided souls will take something with its own identity, history, and legacy, and, out of ignorance, wipe it out. They will distance themselves from the past by removing any reminders of it. This includes artifacts and people who know the truth. What's known then becomes HIS story. The question is now Who am I? To know thyself is to love thyself. They will start over by imitating others. Remember, they no longer know themselves. They no longer care to know either. They sit closed mouthed when people say, "That's racist," or "you're racist," for they lack enough knowledge to defend this charge levied against them. Too damn foolish to realize marginalization was the reason this thing became necessary in the first place. So who is really racist? Instead of doing for self and leading the way, they will go from being leaders to followers. They will become awful imitators of the originator. Oh, but when it's convenient, they will use the history in blackface to pretend to care about those whom they serve. They really don't. Don't believe the hype. They only care about elevating self at the expense of stepping on and over their people. Self-hatred is the worst hatred. Imitation isn't always the highest form of flattery. It is often an indication of an identity crisis. They'll go from uplifting to putting down their own. They'll go from lauding to laughing at their people. The Man in the Mirror Theory then re-introduces the mis-education that some men spent blood, sweat, and tears to eradicate. So what becomes of a history that loses score? It becomes the Mis-Education of the Negro once more.

# EPILOGUE

I did not understand it then but I certainly do now.

On Monday, August 15, 2005, the day of the funeral, Staci R. Collins Jackson, Assistant Vice President of Johnson Publishing Company (JPC) Corporate Communications, and I greeted VIP upon their arrival at the headquarters. Jackson and I were the last to leave the building that day before the final limousine with VIPs exited en route to the church, Rockefeller Memorial Chapel, on the campus of the University of Chicago, for the 11:00 a.m. service.

Santita Jackson, the daughter of the Rev. Jesse L. Jackson Sr., sang a heartfelt rendition of Mahalia Jackson's classic tune "Trouble of the World."[1] Vickie Winans had mourners on their feet with "We Shall Behold Him."[2] When it ended, the packed church listened to the rousing recessional tune "Take The 'A' Train" by Billy Strayhorn that was one of Edward "Duke" Kennedy Ellington's signature pieces. Johnson's longtime friend and fellow Arkansas native, former President Bill Clinton, who remained by the side of Johnson's widow, led the family processional behind the casket.

The *JET* editorial staff headed back to the offices and worked feverishly into the wee hours of the morning on the tribute issue to our late pioneering boss. Burning the midnight oil was nothing new for the *JET* editorial team, but it was bittersweet not having to wait on the phone to ring just to hear Mr. Johnson's final approval after having read each page before closing an issue and being allowed to head home. This chapter of the story was signing off permanently. We witnessed how he made history and we helped him to write it, for the *JET* editorial team was unlike any other. We met with Mr. Johnson every day for meetings about contents for the weekly. Our dealings with him were much more intimate.

A day earlier approximately forty-six JPC employees, along with myself, were selected at the request of "the John H. Johnson family" to stand in pairs near Mr. Johnson's casket at either end, serving as an honor bearer, for the viewing. During fifteen-minute shifts between the hours of 2:00 p.m. and 7:00 p.m. at the offices during the lobby public visitation on Sunday, August 14, those chosen, ranging from editors to executives, stood inside of a red velvet rope that separated his coffin from the hundreds of people who filed into JPC, lining the sidewalk on Michigan Avenue down the street and around the corner, to view his body. So many people came that the five-hour visitation was extended an extra forty-five minutes.

FIGURE 14: Christian stands in the lobby as honor bearer during 2005 public visitation for John H. Johnson at the Johnson Publishing Company headquarters. Margena A. Christian's personal photo. 

Upon entrance into the house that John H. Johnson built, perched prominently on the building's two-story marble wall in the lobby, was an 8-foot-tall portrait of the publisher (the same one that appeared on the cover of his autobiography) that overlooked his polished mahogany casket, which lay in a bed of red roses.

A fellow *JET* editor and I stood during a 5:45 p.m. to 6:00 p.m. rotation where it was determined by my colleague that I should stand at his casket's feet. After my journey at JPC that began in August 1995 and ended May 2014, I later realized why I had to stand at his feet during the public viewing at 820 S. Michigan, the one place on this earth he loved being more than any other. I was the lone person in all of editorial, *JET* and *EBONY*, left to carry the torch. I marveled that I was the last editor standing who worked directly under John H.

Johnson's tutelage to have remained at his empire before my position as Senior Editor for *EBONY* was eliminated.

I was the one editor who seemed touched by some good fortune. I'm more than certain that most colleagues would have loved to stay at JPC for a while longer but they did not have that option. A great majority made their exit in 2010 just before the company moved from 820 S. Michigan Avenue into the new office up the street on the twenty-first floor at 200 S. Michigan Avenue. I can say that for whatever reason I was chosen to be the one left as a foot soldier and reminder of his legacy.

It was not an easy journey and I dealt with my fair share of bumps and bruises along the way, including put downs and being viewed as lesser than by some to arrive at the company following his death simply because I chose to start my career at a pioneering black publishing company instead of going the mainstream route like they did. What they didn't realize is that I may have been small in stature, standing at a mere 5'2," but I loomed large when it came to holding my own and standing my ground around that place. "You certainly have fire!" is what I could often hear Mr. Johnson tell me as he chuckled through his whistle of a laugh during my first interview with him and Linda in her ninth floor, corner office at 820 S. Michigan, in 1995.

FIGURE 15: Linda Johnson Rice congratulates Christian, then *EBONY* senior writer, upon celebrating 15 years in editorial at Johnson Publishing Company in 2010. Margena A. Christian's personal photo. All rights reserved.

That fire kept me burning. That fire kept me determined. That fire fueled my passion. That fire showed me that I was "sick and tired of being sick and tired." That fire quelled my fear of always wondering would I be the next to be fired due to my longstanding connection with the company, which proved to be a blessing and a curse. That fire moved me to simultaneously work two part-time jobs as an adjunct professor at dual City Colleges of Chicago while working full time at JPC and attending graduate school in an accelerated three-year program to earn my doctorate.

I never missed a deadline and my work was always thoroughly researched and well sourced. I saw the light at the end of the tunnel. I saw the ship and the house that John H. Johnson built crumbling right before my very eyes. It hurt so much that during the final days at the headquarters, sometimes I would be one of the last persons in the building. I would walk from floor to floor, scanning each area, taking it all in, thinking and reminiscing with tear-stained eyes about the history being left behind and thrown away. I stood on the tenth floor in the dining area where the Jacksons practically grew up, breaking bread as a family, in the presence of Mr. Johnson, the first publisher of a national publication to take a chance on the little brown-skinned siblings from Indiana by putting them on *EBONY*'s cover. I wondered what Mr. Johnson would think of what was becoming of his empire. I already knew the answer. Denial can be dangerous and some people never seemed to understand this concept. Words and thoughts matter. They have profound meaning.

So, how did John H. Johnson want to be remembered? Did he ever really say? Without a doubt he most certainly did. Mr. Johnson always found a way to speak his mind and articulate his desires. If only more people had taken the time to listen.

Lerone Bennett Jr. was someone who did hear him clearly. During a 1985 interview in *EBONY*, Mr. Johnson told Bennett that he hopes future generations and historians remember the footprints in the sand that he made. Johnson chose the following words:

> I want them to say he had an idea and that he believed in it and that he refused to accept failure in pursuit of it. I have other magazines, but the flagship is still *EBONY*, and I hope future historians will say that we changed the negative image black people had of themselves. I hope they will say that we gave

> black people faith and confidence in themselves and that we told them about their great heritage. I hope they say, finally, that we brought to life, through the historical articles and the books we published, the great black leaders of the past, and that we gave young people the feeling that if our ancestors could do it, during those difficult times, then we can do it today.[3]

Perhaps it was appropriate that magazines like *EBONY* and *JET* were likened to family members. After all, there was a time when most black homes had glossy copies of both publications sprawled across the coffee table. From young to old, male and female, people in the U.S. and across oceans once read *EBONY* and *JET*. Sadly, simply put, but nothing lasts forever.

FIGURE 16: Lerone Bennett Jr. (3rd, l) and Christian share a moment with Three Mo' Tenors (Cook, Dixon & Young) (l-r) Victor Trent Cook, Thomas Young and Rodrick Dixon during an *EBONY* photo shoot in the photography studio at Johnson Publishing Company in 2002. Bennett died on February 14, 2018. His favorite song was "Make Them Hear You," which Dixon sang during Bennett's funeral.
Margena A. Christian's personal photo. 

People and things are in our lives for a reason, a season, or a lifetime. My season ended at the place I called home for nearly two decades. I understood the reason was for me to run the race and to promote what Johnson stood for through my writings. He encouraged stories that fostered hope, inspiration, and education. If Johnson could carry the world on his shoulders, surely I could carry his message and mission so that people never forget him.

History becomes His Story when not placed in the proper hands. The world must remember and never forget what Johnson accomplished, represented, and fought to achieve on behalf of African Americans. He only had a high school diploma and figured it out, building an empire that withstood the test of time for more than six decades when he made his transition.

John H. Johnson made a way out of no way by understanding the power of words and images. Failure was never an option for him. The boy from Arkansas, Johnny, succeeded against the odds, building an empire that spanned decades and changed black media forever.

# NOTES

## Preface

1. Christian, Margena A. "Decades of Fashion: EBONY Fashion Fair Then and Now." *JET* 17 Dec. 2001: 34-39.
2. Christian, Margena A. "The 51st Annual EBONY Fashion Fair Presents The Runway Report 2008-2009. *JET* Oct. 6, 2008: 19-22.
3. Ibid.
4. "The EBONY Family: Employee Excellence and Loyalty Help Make EBONY a 35-Year Success." *EBONY* Nov. 1980: 35-41.
5. "Remembering John H. Johnson (1918-2005)." *JET* 29 Aug. 2005: 12-43.
6. "The EBONY Family: Employee Excellence and Loyalty Help Make EBONY a 35-Year Success." *EBONY* Nov. 1980: 35-41.
7. Ibid.

## Prologue

1. Johnson, John H. *Succeeding Against the Odds*, 207.
2. Ibid., 206.
3. Rosenthal, Phil. "Johnson Publishing CEO Desiree Rogers Trying to Breathe New Life into EBONY, JET Magazines." *Chicago Tribune* 6 Mar. 2011.
4. Bennett Jr., Lerone. "EBONY Interview with John H. Johnson." *EBONY* Nov. 1985: 45.
5. "The Forbes Four Hundred." *Forbes* 13 Sept. 1982.
6. Johnson, John H. *Succeeding Against the Odds*, 311-312.
7. Raffin, Deborah. Sharing Christmas. Grand Central Publishing 1990: 89.

8. Ibid., 90.
9. Sweet, Neesa. "Leadership Profile Series on John H. Johnson: Publisher, Chairman & CEO Johnson Publishing Company." *Sky* 1988: 42.

**Introduction: In Remembrance**

1. "Thousands Gather to Remember John H. Johnson." Press Release. *The University of Chicago News Office.* 15 Aug. 2005: 4.
2. "Celebrating the Life and Legacy of John H. Johnson." *EBONY* Oct. 2005: 53-71.
3. "Thousands Join in Historic Farewell Celebration of Publisher John H. Johnson in Chicago." *JET* 29 Aug. 2005: 8.
4. "Harvard Law Review Gets First Black President." *JET* 26 Feb. 1990.
5. "Thousands Join in Historic Farewell Celebration of Publisher John H. Johnson in Chicago." *JET* 29 Aug. 2005: 7.
6. Ibid., 4.
7. Johnson, Erick. "End of an Era: How EBONY and JET Fell into the Hands of a Little Known Firm in a Deal Shrouded in Mystery." *Chicago Crusader* 16 June 2016.
8. Johnson, John H. and Lerone Bennett Jr. *Succeeding Against the Odds.* First Printing. Johnson Publishing Company, Inc., 1989: 172.
9. Oak Woods Cemetery; *The Cultural Landscape Foundation.*
10. The Cultural Landscape Foundation Oak Woods Cemetery.
11. Graveyards of Illinois Oak Woods Cemetery.
12. Oak Woods Cemetery.
13. U.S. Department of Veteran Affairs
14. "Remembering John H. Johnson (1918-2005)." *JET* 29 Aug. 2005: 42.
15. "John H. Johnson School of Communications; Mr. Johnson Contributes $4 Million to Howard University Capital Campaign." *JET* 17 Feb. 2003: 6-10.
16. "School of Communications Named to Honor Cathy Hughes." *Howard Magazine* Oct. 2016.

17. "Howard University Announces the Cathy Hughes School of Communications." Education. *HowardUniversity.edu.* 6 Oct. 2016.
18. Presidential Medal of Freedom." *The American Presidency Project.* 9 Sept. 1996.
19. Ibid.
20. "The Medal of Freedom Awards: Publisher John H. Johnson and 10 Others Receive Nation's Highest Civilian Honor." *EBONY* Nov. 1996: 34.
21. Bennett Jr., Lerone. "Homage to 'The Beginner.'" *EBONY* Oct. 2005: 81-94.
22. Kinnon, Joy Bennett. "EBONY October 2005: Celebrating the Life and Legacy of John H. Johnson 1918-2005." Oct. 2005: 60.
23. "Letters and Pictures to the Editor." *EBONY*. Dec. 1945. 51.
24. Burns, Ben. *Nitty Gritty: A White Editor in Black Journalism*. Mississippi: University Press of Mississippi, 1996: 98.
25. Johnson, John H. and Lerone Bennett Jr. *Succeeding Against the Odds*. First Printing. Johnson Publishing Company, Inc., 1989: 64.
26. "Photog Griff Davis Dies in Atlanta at 70." *JET* 16 Aug. 1993: 15.
27. "Doctoral Duo." *JET* 6 July 1972: 17.
28. Shipp, E.R. "After 40 Years, EBONY Drawing Praise, Criticism." *The New York Times* 21 Dec. 1985.
29. Ibid.
30. Ibid.
31. Berler, Ron. "EBONY Is 40: Publisher John Johnson Tells His Auspicious Story." *The Dallas Morning News* 1985: 2.
32. Ibid.
33. Ibid.
34. Ibid.
35. Ibid.
36. Ibid.
37. "Celebrities Pay Tribute to Publishing Titan John H. Johnson." *JET* 29 Aug. 2005: 44.
38. Ibid., 46.
39. Ibid., 54.

40. "Halle Berry, Denzel Washington Get Historic Wins at Oscars." *JET* 8 Apr. 2002: 14-18, 51-59.
41. Bennett Jr., Lerone. "Homage to 'The Beginner.'" *EBONY* Oct. 2005: 92.
42. Jackson Sr., Jesse. "The TV Networks Owe Us an Apology For Ignoring John H. Johnson." *Target Market News* 18 Aug. 2005.
43. Ibid.
44. Goodman, Amy. "Media Giant John H. Johnson Paved the Way for Black-Owned Press." *Democracy Now.* 16 Aug. 205AD.
45. Johnson, John H. and Lerone Bennett Jr. *Succeeding Against the Odds.* First Printing. Johnson Publishing Company, Inc., 1989: 9.
46. "JET Celebrates 45 Years of the Hottest Black Music, TV and Movie Stars." *JET* 3 Nov. 1997: 58-64.
47. "TV's Greatest Black Moms." *JET* 15 May 2006: 15-18.
48. Goodman, Amy. "Media Giant John H. Johnson Paved the Way for Black-Owned Press." *Democracy Now.* 16 Aug. 205AD.
49. Fitzgerald, Mark. "Oprah 'Furious' at 'Chicago Defender' Editor." *Editor & Publisher* 26 Aug. 2005.
50. Ibid.
51. Ibid.
52. Ibid.
53. Goodman, Amy. "Media Giant John H. Johnson Paved the Way for Black-Owned Press." *Democracy Now.* 16 Aug. 205AD.
54. Alpha Phi Alpha Fraternity.

**Chapter 1. Mother to Son**

1. *The John H. Johnson Interview.* Johnson Publishing Company: 2007.
2. Ibid.
3. Bennett Jr., Lerone. "In Memoriam: Mrs. Gertrude Johnson Williams (1891-1977)." *EBONY* July 1977: 124.
4. Ibid.
5. Johnson, John H. and Lerone Bennett Jr. *Succeeding Against the Odds.* First Printing. Johnson Publishing Company, Inc., 1989: 37.

6. *The John H. Johnson Interview.* Johnson Publishing Company: 2007.
7. Ibid.
8. Johnson, John H. and Lerone Bennett Jr. *Succeeding Against the Odds.* First Printing. Johnson Publishing Company, Inc., 1989: 36.
9. Ibid., 39.
10. Ibid., 39.
11. "Died: James Williams." *JET* 23 Nov. 1961: 23.
12. Bennett Jr., Lerone. "EBONY Interview with John H. Johnson." *EBONY* Nov. 1985: 45.
13. Johnson, John H. and Lerone Bennett Jr. *Succeeding Against the Odds.* First Printing. Johnson Publishing Company, Inc., 1989: 174.
14. Ibid.
15. Ibid., 27-28.
16. Ibid.
17. "Great Black Men in History: John H. Johnson/My Childhood." *ProjectBlackMan.com*: 2007.
18. Ibid.
19. Ibid.
20. Johnson, John H. and Lerone Bennett Jr. *Succeeding Against the Odds.* First Printing. Johnson Publishing Company, Inc., 1989: 42.
21. "Great Black Men in History: John H. Johnson/My Childhood." *ProjectBlackMan.com*: 2007.
22. Johnson, John H. and Lerone Bennett Jr. *Succeeding Against the Odds.* First Printing. Johnson Publishing Company, Inc., 1989: 42.
23. "Great Black Men in History: John H. Johnson/My Childhood." *ProjectBlackMan.com*: 2007.
24. Ibid.
25. Johnson, John H. and Lerone Bennett Jr. *Succeeding Against the Odds.* First Printing. Johnson Publishing Company, Inc., 1989: 42.
26. Ibid., 40.
27. Ibid.
28. "A $500 Loan Fueled EBONY's 30-Year Rise." *Detroit Free Press* 21 Nov. 1975: 2.

29. *The John H. Johnson Interview.* Johnson Publishing Company: 2007.
30. Johnson, John H. and Lerone Bennett Jr. *Succeeding Against the Odds.* First Printing. Johnson Publishing Company, Inc., 1989: 46.
31. Ibid.
32. Gilfoyle, Timothy J. "Chicago Fortunes: Interviews with Lester Crown and John H. Johnson." *Chicago History* Fall 2000: 59.
33. Johnson, John H. and Lerone Bennett Jr. *Succeeding Against the Odds.* First Printing. Johnson Publishing Company, Inc., 1989: 47.
34. Ibid.
35. Ibid., 52.
36. Johnson, John H. and Lerone Bennett Jr. *Succeeding Against the Odds.* First Printing. Johnson Publishing Company, Inc., 1989: 53.
37. "Illinois Business Hall of Fame." American National Business Hall of Fame Video Series Presents John Johnson. 1989.
38. Johnson, John H. and Lerone Bennett Jr. *Succeeding Against the Odds.* First Printing. Johnson Publishing Company, Inc., 1989: 53.
39. Thimmesch, Nick. "John H. Johnson: The Man Behind EBONY." *Saturday Evening Post* Oct. 1975: 94.
40. Johnson, John H. and Lerone Bennett Jr. *Succeeding Against the Odds.* First Printing. Johnson Publishing Company, Inc., 1989: 94.
41. Ibid., 53.
42. Ibid., 54.
43. Ibid., 59.
44. Ibid., 78.
45. Thimmesch, Nick. "John H. Johnson: The Man Behind EBONY." *Saturday Evening Post* Oct. 1975: 94.
46. Gilfoyle, Timothy J. "Chicago Fortunes: Interviews with Lester Crown and John H. Johnson." *Chicago History* Fall 2000: 58-72.
47. *The John H. Johnson Interview.* Johnson Publishing Company: 2007.
48. Johnson, John H. and Lerone Bennett Jr. *Succeeding Against the Odds.* First Printing. Johnson Publishing Company, Inc., 1989: 59.

49. Bennett Jr., Lerone. "EBONY Interview with John H. Johnson." *EBONY* Nov. 1985: 48.
50. Ibid.
51. *The John H. Johnson Interview.* Johnson Publishing Company: 2007.
52. Johnson, John H. and Lerone Bennett Jr. *Succeeding Against the Odds.* First Printing. Johnson Publishing Company, Inc., 1989: 175.
53. Ibid.
54. Sweet, Neesa. "Leadership Profile Series on John H. Johnson: Publisher, Chairman & CEO Johnson Publishing Company." *Sky* 1988: 42.
55. Johnson, John H. *Salute to Greatness Dinner Speech.* 1988. Unpublished. Atlanta Marriott Marquee Hotel in Atlanta, Ga.
56. Johnson, John H. and Lerone Bennett Jr. *Succeeding Against the Odds.* First Printing. Johnson Publishing Company, Inc., 1989: 174.
57. Ibid.
58. Marshall, Marilyn. "Publisher Defies Failure." *Houston Defender* 3 June 1990: 2.
59. Christian, Margena A., and Jesse Jackson Sr. "He Chronicled Our Struggles but Found the Good and Praised It." *EBONY* Nov. 2010: 104-107.
60. Christian, Margena A., and Jesse Jackson Sr. "He Chronicled Our Struggles but Found the Good and Praised It." *EBONY* Nov. 2010: 105.
61. Johnson, John H. and Lerone Bennett Jr. *Succeeding Against the Odds.* First Printing. Johnson Publishing Company, Inc., 1989: 17.
62. Christian, Margena A., and Jesse Jackson Sr. "He Chronicled Our Struggles but Found the Good and Praised It." *EBONY* Nov. 2010: 106.
63. Bennett Jr., Lerone. "EBONY Interview with John H. Johnson." *EBONY* Nov. 1985: 52.
64. Ibid., 54.
65. Johnson, John H. and Lerone Bennett Jr. *Succeeding Against the Odds.* First Printing. Johnson Publishing Company, Inc., 1989: 38.

66. Rowan, Carl T. "Words That Give Us Strength." *Reader's Digest* Apr. 1987: 49-58.
67. "In Memoriam: Mrs. Gertrude Johnson Williams (1891-1977)." *EBONY* July 1977: 124.
68. "The $5,000 Gertrude Johnson Williams Literary Award.'" *EBONY* March 1988: 96.
69. "*EBONY* Contest Winner Scores in Education and Art." *EBONY* May 1998: 126-130.
70. "What's Online in September: New Voices and Culture.'" *EBONY* Sept. 2008: 20.
71. Johnson, John H. and Lerone Bennett Jr. *Succeeding Against the Odds*. First Printing. Johnson Publishing Company, Inc., 1989: 322.

## Chapter 2. Building An Empire

1. Johnson, John H. and Lerone Bennett Jr. *Succeeding Against the Odds*. First Printing. Johnson Publishing Company, Inc., 1989: 36.
2. Ibid., 62.
3. Ibid., 64-65.
4. Ibid., 67.
5. Ibid.
6. "Mary J. Herrick Collection." 1970.
7. Thimmesch, Nick. "John H. Johnson: The Man Behind EBONY." *Saturday Evening Post* Oct. 1975: 94.
8. Johnson, John H. and Lerone Bennett Jr. *Succeeding Against the Odds*. First Printing. Johnson Publishing Company, Inc., 1989: 64.
9. Ibid.
10. Ibid.
11. Thimmesch, Nick. "John H. Johnson: The Man Behind EBONY." *Saturday Evening Post* Oct. 1975: 94.
12. Johnson, John H. and Lerone Bennett Jr. *Succeeding Against the Odds*. First Printing. Johnson Publishing Company, Inc., 1989: 64.
13. "Former Teacher Mary Herrick Feted By Her Well Known Students." *JET* 14 May 1984: 8.

14. "Mary J. Herrick Collection." 1970.
15. Thimmesch, Nick. "John H. Johnson: The Man Behind EBONY." *Saturday Evening Post* Oct. 1975: 94.
16. "Former Teacher Mary Herrick Feted By Her Well Known Students." *JET* 14 May 1984: 8.
17. Ibid.
18. Ibid.
19. Johnson, John H. and Lerone Bennett Jr. *Succeeding Against the Odds.* First Printing. Johnson Publishing Company, Inc., 1989: 64.
20. Johnson, John H. and Lerone Bennett Jr. *Succeeding Against the Odds.* First Printing. Johnson Publishing Company, Inc., 1989: 80.
21. Ibid.
22. Ibid., 87.
23. Gilfoyle, Timothy J. "Chicago Fortunes: Interviews with Lester Crown and John H. Johnson." *Chicago History* Fall 2000: 58-72.
24. Thimmesch, Nick. "John H. Johnson: The Man Behind EBONY." *Saturday Evening Post* Oct. 1975: 37.
25. Bennett Jr., Lerone. "EBONY Interview with John H. Johnson." *EBONY* Nov. 1985: 48-50.
26. Johnson, John H. and Lerone Bennett Jr. *Succeeding Against the Odds.* First Printing. Johnson Publishing Company, Inc., 1989: 82.
27. Ibid., 75.
28. Granger, Bill, and Lori Granger. *Lords of the Last Machine: The Story of Politics in Chicago.* Random House, 1987.
29. Johnson, John H. and Lerone Bennett Jr. *Succeeding Against the Odds.* First Printing. Johnson Publishing Company, Inc., 1989: 175.
30. Ibid., 10.
31. Ibid., 67.
32. Ibid., 68.
33. Ibid., 70.
34. Bennett Jr., Lerone. "EBONY Interview with John H. Johnson." *EBONY* Nov. 1985: 46.
35. Ibid.
36. Ibid.

37. Johnson, John H. and Lerone Bennett Jr. *Succeeding Against the Odds*. First Printing. Johnson Publishing Company, Inc., 1989: 49.
38. Ibid., 105.
39. Ibid.
40. Ibid.
41. Ibid.
42. *Delta Sigma Theta Sorority*.
43. "Remembering John H. Johnson (1918-2005)." *JET* 29 Aug. 2005: 42.
44. *Alpha Phi Alpha Fraternity*.
45. "Sphinx: 67th Anniversary Convention Issue." *Sphinx* May-June 1973.
46. Ibid.
47. "Celebrating the Life and Legacy of John H. Johnson." *EBONY* Oct. 2005: 71.
48. "Ninety-Second Annual Communication Proceedings: Most Worshipful Prince Hall Grand Lodge F. and A.M." 14 Oct. 1958.
49. Gilfoyle, Timothy J. "Chicago Fortunes: Interviews with Lester Crown and John H. Johnson." *Chicago History* Fall 2000: 68.
50. Bennett Jr., Lerone. "EBONY Interview with John H. Johnson." *EBONY* Nov. 1985: 58.
51. Johnson, John H. and Lerone Bennett Jr. *Succeeding Against the Odds*. First Printing. Johnson Publishing Company, Inc., 1989: 254-255.
52. Ibid 317.
53. "The Forbes Four Hundred." *Forbes* 13 Sept. 1982.
54. Johnson, John H. and Lerone Bennett Jr. *Succeeding Against the Odds*. First Printing. Johnson Publishing Company, Inc., 1989: 309.
55. Bennett Jr., Lerone. "EBONY Interview with John H. Johnson." *EBONY* Nov. 1985: 46.
56. Ibid.
57. Ibid.
58. Ibid.
59. Reardon, Patrick T. "Not Much on Their Plates: When It Comes to Influence, Owners of Low License Numbers Take a Back Seat To No One." *Chicago Tribune* 17 Jan. 1999.

60. Bennett Jr., Lerone. "EBONY Interview with John H. Johnson." *EBONY* Nov. 1985: 45.
61. Thimmesch, Nick. "John H. Johnson: The Man Behind EBONY." *Saturday Evening Post* Oct. 1975: 96.
62. Gilfoyle, Timothy J. "Chicago Fortunes: Interviews with Lester Crown and John H. Johnson." *Chicago History* Fall 2000: 72.
63. Johnson, John H. and Lerone Bennett Jr. *Succeeding Against the Odds*. First Printing. Johnson Publishing Company, Inc., 1989: 335; "Blacks Must Abandon Politics of Poverty, Philosophy of Despair." *Sphinx* May-June 1973: 29–34.
64. The University of Chicago press release Sept. 13, 1983; Johnson, John H. and Lerone Bennett Jr. *Succeeding Against the Odds*. First Printing. Johnson Publishing Company, Inc., 1989: 257.
65. Backstage. *EBONY* March 1982: 18.
66. Thimmesch, Nick. "John H. Johnson: The Man Behind EBONY." *Saturday Evening Post* Oct. 1975: 96; Treadway, Tyler. "Johnson Turns $500 Loan Into Publishing Powerhouse." *Arkansas Business* 13 Feb. 1995.
67. Ibid.
68. Ibid.
69. Ibid.
70. Ibid.
71. Ibid.
72. Johnson, John H. and Lerone Bennett Jr. *Succeeding Against the Odds*. First Printing. Johnson Publishing Company, Inc., 1989: 282.
73. Thimmesch, Nick. "John H. Johnson: The Man Behind EBONY." *Saturday Evening Post* Oct. 1975: 96.
74. Ibid.
75. Johnson, John H. and Lerone Bennett Jr. *Succeeding Against the Odds*. First Printing. Johnson Publishing Company, Inc., 1989: 272.
76. Michaeli, Ethan. *The Defender: How the Legendary Black Newspaper Changed America*. Boston New York: Houghton Mifflin Harcourt, 2016. 473-474.
77. Johnson, John H. and Lerone Bennett Jr. *Succeeding Against the Odds*. First Printing. Johnson Publishing Company, Inc., 1989: 13.

78. Burns, Ben. *Nitty Gritty: A White Editor in Black Journalism.* Mississippi: University Press of Mississippi, 1996: 25.
79. Ibid., 113.
80. Ibid., 139.
81. Ibid.
82. Ibid., 111.
83. Hall, Carla. "John H. Johnson: From Office Worker to Millionaire Publishing Mogul." *The Washington Post* 14 Sept. 1980.
84. Johnson, John H. and Lerone Bennett Jr. *Succeeding Against the Odds.* First Printing. Johnson Publishing Company, Inc. 1989: 179; Thimmesch, Nick. "John H. Johnson: The Man Behind EBONY." *Saturday Evening Post* Oct. 1975: 95.
85. Burns, Ben. *Nitty Gritty: A White Editor in Black Journalism.* Mississippi: University Press of Mississippi, 1996: 112.
86. Ibid.
87. Hall, Carla. "John H. Johnson: From Office Worker to Millionaire Publishing Mogul." *The Washington Post* 14 Sept. 1980.
88. Johnson, John H. and Lerone Bennett Jr. *Succeeding Against the Odds.* First Printing. Johnson Publishing Company, Inc. 1989: 199.
89. Thimmesch, Nick. "John H. Johnson: The Man Behind EBONY." *Saturday Evening Post* Oct. 1975: 95.
90. Laramie, Eddie. "Black Publisher Advises Young People to Learn." *People* 26 May, 1974.
91. Hall, Carla. "John H. Johnson: From Office Worker to Millionaire Publishing Mogul." *The Washington Post* 14 Sept. 1980.

## Chapter 3. Opportunity in Adversity

1. Johnson, John H. and Lerone Bennett Jr. *Succeeding Against the Odds.* First Printing. Johnson Publishing Company, Inc., 1989: 3.
2. Ibid., 6.
3. Ibid., 37.

4. Grossman, James R. *Land of Hope: Chicago, Black Southerners, and the Great Migration.* University of Chicago Press, 1991: 34.
5. Colin III, Scipio A. J., and Talmadge Guy. "An Africentric Interpretive Model of Curriculum Orientations for Course Development in Graduate Programs in Adult Education." *PAACE Journal of Lifelong Learning* 7 (1998): 46.
6. Johnson, John H. and Lerone Bennett Jr. *Succeeding Against the Odds.* First Printing. Johnson Publishing Company, Inc., 1989: 119.
7. Ibid., 121.
8. Ibid., 119.
9. Ibid., 114.
10. Ibid., 87.
11. Ibid.
12. Ibid.
13. Ibid., 111.
14. Ibid., 50.
15. Ibid., 92.
16. Burns, Ben. *Nitty Gritty: A White Editor in Black Journalism.* Mississippi: University Press of Mississippi, 1996: 27.
17. Johnson, John H. and Lerone Bennett Jr. *Succeeding Against the Odds.* First Printing. Johnson Publishing Company, Inc., 1989: 114.
18. Burns, Ben. *Nitty Gritty: A White Editor in Black Journalism.* Mississippi: University Press of Mississippi, 1996: 55, 57.
19. Ibid., 92.
20. Ibid., 4.
21. Free Northern Negroes 1833
22. Penn, I. Garland. *The Afro-American Press and Its Editors.* Springfield, Massachusetts: Wiley & Co., 1891: 117-118.
23. Burns, Ben. *Nitty Gritty: A White Editor in Black Journalism.* Mississippi: University Press of Mississippi, 1996: 29.
24. Ibid.
25. Ibid., 28-29.
26. Johnson, John H. and Lerone Bennett Jr. *Succeeding Against the Odds.* First Printing. Johnson Publishing Company, Inc., 1989: 121.
27. "The Press. Quick End." *Time.com.* 27 April 1953.

28. Brown, Dorothy Deloris. Personal interview. August 25, 1969. Chicago, Illinois.
29. Johnson, John H. and Lerone Bennett Jr. *Succeeding Against the Odds*. First Printing. Johnson Publishing Company, Inc., 1989: 114.
30. Burns, Ben. *Nitty Gritty: A White Editor in Black Journalism*. Mississippi: University Press of Mississippi, 1996: 28.
31. Johnson, John H. and Lerone Bennett Jr. *Succeeding Against the Odds*. First Printing. Johnson Publishing Company, Inc., 1989: 120, 152.
32. Burns, Ben. *Nitty Gritty: A White Editor in Black Journalism*. Mississippi: University Press of Mississippi, 1996: 29.
33. Ibid., 30.
34. Johnson, John H. and Lerone Bennett Jr. *Succeeding Against the Odds*. First Printing. Johnson Publishing Company, Inc., 1989: 117.
35. Johnson, John H. and Lerone Bennett Jr. *Succeeding Against the Odds*. First Printing. Johnson Publishing Company, Inc., 1989: 119.
36. U.S. History.org. The Red Scare.
37. Burns, Ben. *Nitty Gritty: A White Editor in Black Journalism*. Mississippi: University Press of Mississippi, 1996: 56.
38. Burns, Ben. *Nitty Gritty: A White Editor in Black Journalism*. Mississippi: University Press of Mississippi, 1996: 36.
39. Johnson, John H. and Lerone Bennett Jr. *Succeeding Against the Odds*. First Printing. Johnson Publishing Company, Inc., 1989: 74.
40. Johnson, John H. and Lerone Bennett Jr. *Succeeding Against the Odds*. First Printing. Johnson Publishing Company, Inc., 1989: 77.
41. Burns, Ben. *Nitty Gritty: A White Editor in Black Journalism*. Mississippi: University Press of Mississippi, 1996: 56.
42. Michaeli, Ethan. *The Defender: How the Legendary Black Newspaper Changed America*. Boston New York: Houghton Mifflin Harcourt, 2016: 257.
43. Burns, Ben. *Nitty Gritty: A White Editor in Black Journalism*. Mississippi: University Press of Mississippi, 1996: 45.

44. Johnson, John H. and Lerone Bennett Jr. *Succeeding Against the Odds*. First Printing. Johnson Publishing Company, Inc., 1989: 129.
45. Burns, Ben. *Nitty Gritty: A White Editor in Black Journalism*. Mississippi: University Press of Mississippi, 1996: 45.
46. Ibid., 46.
47. Ibid., 36.
48. Ibid., 112.
49. Ibid., ixx.
50. Johnson, John H. and Lerone Bennett Jr. *Succeeding Against the Odds*. First Printing. Johnson Publishing Company, Inc., 1989: 201.
51. Hall, Carla. "John H. Johnson: From Office Worker to Millionaire Publishing Mogul." *The Washington Post* 14 Sept. 1980.
52. Burns, Ben. *Nitty Gritty: A White Editor in Black Journalism*. Mississippi: University Press of Mississippi, 1996: 32.
53. Ibid.
54. Johnson, John H. and Lerone Bennett Jr. *Succeeding Against the Odds*. First Printing. Johnson Publishing Company, Inc., 1989: 120.
55. Burns, Ben. *Nitty Gritty: A White Editor in Black Journalism*. Mississippi: University Press of Mississippi, 1996: 31.
56. Ibid., 32.
57. Johnson, John H. and Lerone Bennett Jr. *Succeeding Against the Odds*. First Printing. Johnson Publishing Company, Inc., 1989: 123.
58. Gilfoyle, Timothy J. "Chicago Fortunes: Interviews with Lester Crown and John H. Johnson." *Chicago History* Fall 2000: 64.
59. Burns, Ben. *Nitty Gritty: A White Editor in Black Journalism*. Mississippi: University Press of Mississippi, 1996: 34.
60. Ibid., 36.
61. Ibid., 30.
62. Ibid., 36.
63. Ibid.
64. Johnson, John H. and Lerone Bennett Jr. *Succeeding Against the Odds*. First Printing. Johnson Publishing Company, Inc., 1989: 130.

65. Burns, Ben. *Nitty Gritty: A White Editor in Black Journalism.* Mississippi: University Press of Mississippi, 1996: 35.
66. Johnson, Paul Lindsey. "Interview: John H. Johnson." *The Crisis* Jan. 1987: 32-48.
67. Ibid 34.
68. Burns, Ben. *Nitty Gritty: A White Editor in Black Journalism.* Mississippi: University Press of Mississippi, 1996: 38.
69. Bennett Jr., Lerone. "EBONY Interview with John H. Johnson." *EBONY* Nov. 1985: 52.
70. Hall, Carla. "John H. Johnson: From Office Worker to Millionaire Publishing Mogul." *The Washington Post* 14 Sept. 1980.
71. Ibid.
72. Ibid.
73. Bennett Jr., Lerone. "EBONY Interview with John H. Johnson." *EBONY* Nov. 1985: 52.
74. Ibid.
75. Hall, Carla. "John H. Johnson: From Office Worker to Millionaire Publishing Mogul." *The Washington Post* 14 Sept. 1980.
76. Thimmesch, Nick. "John H. Johnson: The Man Behind EBONY." *Saturday Evening Post* Oct. 1975: 36.
77. Ibid., 94.
78. Ibid., 36.
79. "Color Success Black." *Time* 2 Aug. 1968: 32.
80. Johnson, John H. and Lerone Bennett Jr. *Succeeding Against the Odds.* First Printing. Johnson Publishing Company, Inc., 1989: 131.
81. "Illinois Business Hall of Fame." American National Business Hall of Fame Video Series Presents John Johnson. 1989.
82. Harvard Business School Global Alumni Conference. Unpublished speech. 1998.
83. "Illinois Business Hall of Fame." American National Business Hall of Fame Video Series Presents John Johnson. 1989.
84. *Alpha Kappa Alpha Sorority.*
85. *Alpha Phi Alpha Fraternity.*
86. *Alpha Kappa Alpha Sorority.*

87. Johnson, John H. and Lerone Bennett Jr. *Succeeding Against the Odds*. First Printing. Johnson Publishing Company, Inc., 1989: 146.
88. Ibid., 145.
89. Ibid., 146.
90. Ibid., 147.
91. Ibid., 149.
92. Ibid., 149-150.
93. Burns, Ben. *Nitty Gritty: A White Editor in Black Journalism*. Mississippi: University Press of Mississippi, 1996: 85.
94. Johnson, John H. and Lerone Bennett Jr. *Succeeding Against the Odds*. First Printing. Johnson Publishing Company, Inc., 1989: 164.
95. Flash Newspic Color.
96. Burns, Ben. *Nitty Gritty: A White Editor in Black Journalism*. Mississippi: University Press of Mississippi, 1996: 96.
97. Johnson, John H. and Lerone Bennett Jr. *Succeeding Against the Odds*. First Printing. Johnson Publishing Company, Inc., 1989: 164.
98. Burns, Ben. *Nitty Gritty: A White Editor in Black Journalism*. Mississippi: University Press of Mississippi, 1996: 87.
99. Ibid., 97.
100. Johnson, John H. and Lerone Bennett Jr. *Succeeding Against the Odds*. First Printing. Johnson Publishing Company, Inc., 1989: 165.
101. Ibid.
102. Burns, Ben. *Nitty Gritty: A White Editor in Black Journalism*. Mississippi: University Press of Mississippi, 1996: 98.
103. Ibid.
104. Ibid., 99.
105. Johnson, John H. and Lerone Bennett Jr. *Succeeding Against the Odds*. First Printing. Johnson Publishing Company, Inc., 1989: 213.
106. Burns, Ben. *Nitty Gritty: A White Editor in Black Journalism*. Mississippi: University Press of Mississippi, 1996: 98.
107. Ibid., 99.
108. Ibid., 100.
109. Booker, Simeon. "My JET Years 1953-2006: Simeon Booker, Washington, D.C., Bureau Chief." *JET* 13 Nov. 2006: 32-36.

110. Johnson, John H. and Lerone Bennett Jr. *Succeeding Against the Odds.* First Printing. Johnson Publishing Company, Inc., 1989: 191.
111. Burns, Ben. *Nitty Gritty: A White Editor in Black Journalism.* Mississippi: University Press of Mississippi, 1996: 94.
112. Ibid., 95.
113. Ibid.
114. Ibid., 94.
115. Johnson, John H. and Lerone Bennett Jr. *Succeeding Against the Odds.* First Printing. Johnson Publishing Company, Inc., 1989: 166.
116. Ibid.
117. Burns, Ben. *Nitty Gritty: A White Editor in Black Journalism.* Mississippi: University Press of Mississippi, 1996: 102.
118. Johnson, John H. and Lerone Bennett Jr. *Succeeding Against the Odds.* First Printing. Johnson Publishing Company, Inc., 1989: 167.
119. Burns, Ben. *Nitty Gritty: A White Editor in Black Journalism.* Mississippi: University Press of Mississippi, 1996: 102.
120. Johnson, John H. and Lerone Bennett Jr. *Succeeding Against the Odds.* First Printing. Johnson Publishing Company, Inc., 1989: 167.
121. Ibid., 166.
122. Burns, Ben. *Nitty Gritty: A White Editor in Black Journalism.* Mississippi: University Press of Mississippi, 1996: 103.
123. Ibid.
124. Ibid., 104.
125. Ibid.
126. Ibid., 105.
127. Ibid.
128. Ibid.
129. Hall, Carla. "John H. Johnson: From Office Worker to Millionaire Publishing Mogul." *The Washington Post* 14 Sept. 1980.
130. Johnson, John H. and Lerone Bennett Jr. *Succeeding Against the Odds.* First Printing. Johnson Publishing Company, Inc., 1989: 166.
131. Burns, Ben. *Nitty Gritty: A White Editor in Black Journalism.* Mississippi: University Press of Mississippi, 1996: 115.

132. Johnson, John H. and Lerone Bennett Jr. *Succeeding Against the Odds*. First Printing. Johnson Publishing Company, Inc., 1989: 78.
133. Burns, Ben. *Nitty Gritty: A White Editor in Black Journalism*. Mississippi: University Press of Mississippi, 1996: 115.
134. Ibid., 110.
135. Ibid.
136. "Chicago Gambler Buried in Cadillac-Style Coffin." *JET* 19 March 1984: 22-24.
137. Bennett Jr., Lerone. "EBONY Interview with John H. Johnson." *EBONY* Nov. 1985: 58.

## Chapter 4. Black Magazines Matter

1. Johnson, John H. and Lerone Bennett Jr. *Succeeding Against the Odds*. First Printing. Johnson Publishing Company, Inc., 1989: 311-312.
2. "EBONY Magazine's January 2009 Barack Obama Collector's Issue Breaks Sales Records." *EBONY*, John H. Johnson.
3. "Harvard Law Review Gets First Black President." *JET* 26 Feb. 1990.
4. "Failure Is a Word I Don't Accept: An Interview With John H. Johnson." *Harvard Business Review* (1976): 79–88.
5. Burns, Ben. *Nitty Gritty: A White Editor in Black Journalism*. Mississippi: University Press of Mississippi, 1996: 17.
6. Shipp, E.R. "After 40 Years, EBONY Drawing Praise, Criticism." *The New York Times* 21 Dec. 1985.
7. "Letters and Pictures to the Editor." *EBONY*. April 1946: 51.
8. Johnson, Paul Lindsey. "Interview: John H. Johnson." *The Crisis* Jan. 1987: 34.
9. Bennett Jr., Lerone. "EBONY Interview with John H. Johnson." *EBONY* Nov. 1985: 45.
10. Thimmesch, Nick. "John H. Johnson: The Man Behind EBONY." *Saturday Evening Post* Oct. 1975: 96.
11. "Robert E. Johnson, Editor of JET." *The Mike Douglas Show*. CBS, 8 Jan. 1969.
12. Burns, Ben. *Nitty Gritty: A White Editor in Black Journalism*. Mississippi: University Press of Mississippi, 1996: 50.

13. Johnson, John H. and Lerone Bennett Jr. *Succeeding Against the Odds*. First Printing. Johnson Publishing Company, Inc., 1989: 164.
14. Long, Mia Chandler. Seeking a Place in the Sun: Sepia Magazine's Endeavor for Quality Journalism and Place in the Negro Market 1951-1982.
15. Burns, Ben. *Nitty Gritty: A White Editor in Black Journalism*. Mississippi: University Press of Mississippi, 1996: 130.
16. Ibid., 130.
17. Ibid., 131.
18. Ellison, Richard. *Invisible Man*. Random House, 1952.
19. Woodson, Carter Godwin. *The Mis-Education of the Negro*. Dover Publications, 2005.
20. Johnson, John H. and Lerone Bennett Jr. *Succeeding Against the Odds*. First Printing. Johnson Publishing Company, Inc., 1989: 239.
21. Ibid.
22. Thimmesch, Nick. "John H. Johnson: The Man Behind EBONY." *Saturday Evening Post* Oct. 1975: 96.
23. Hall, Carla. "John H. Johnson: From Office Worker to Millionaire Publishing Mogul." *The Washington Post* 14 Sept. 1980.
24. *EBONY* Jan. 1982: 24.
25. Ellison, Richard. *Invisible Man*. Random House, 1952.
26. Carter, Reon. "EBONY Publisher Still on a Mission: Founder Fights to Keep His Black Magazine Dominant." *Detroit News* 1 Nov. 1990: 2.
27. Marshall, Marilyn. "Publisher Defies Failure." *Houston Defender* 3 June 1990: 2.
28. Johnson, John H. and Lerone Bennett Jr. *Succeeding Against the Odds*. First Printing. Johnson Publishing Company, Inc., 1989: 113-114.
29. Woodson, Carter Godwin. *The Mis-Education of the Negro*. Dover Publications, 2005.
30. Johnson, John H. and Lerone Bennett Jr. *Succeeding Against the Odds*. First Printing. Johnson Publishing Company, Inc., 1989: 158.
31. Ibid., 159.
32. Ibid., 157.

33. Hall, Carla. "John H. Johnson: From Office Worker to Millionaire Publishing Mogul." *The Washington Post* 14 Sept. 1980.
34. Martin, Douglas. "John H. Johnson, 87, Founder of EBONY, Dies." *The New York Times.* 9 Aug. 2005.
35. Bennett Jr., Lerone. "EBONY Interview with John H. Johnson." *EBONY* Nov. 1985: 56.
36. Reader's Digest December 1975.

## Chapter 5. More Than Magazines

1. Johnson, John H. and Lerone Bennett Jr. *Succeeding Against the Odds.* First Printing. Johnson Publishing Company, Inc., 1989: 27.
2. Ibid., 27.
3. Thimmesch, Nick. "John H. Johnson: The Man Behind EBONY." *Saturday Evening Post* Oct. 1975: 95.
4. *The John H. Johnson Interview.* Johnson Publishing Company: 2007.
5. "Harvard University Celebrates 'JHJ Day' With Awards, Tributes." *JET* 27 Nov. 1975: 12-16.
6. Johnson, John H. and Lerone Bennett Jr. *Succeeding Against the Odds.* First Printing. Johnson Publishing Company, Inc., 1989: 287.
7. Johnson, John H. *Acceptance Speech by John H. Johnson After Being Named Publisher of the Year.* 1972. Henry Johnson Fisher Award Luncheon.
8. Johnson, John H. and Lerone Bennett Jr. *Succeeding Against the Odds.* First Printing. Johnson Publishing Company, Inc., 1989: 206.
9. Lowe, Rev. A. Ritchie. "Children's Crusade." Nov. 1945.
10. Johnson, John H. and Lerone Bennett Jr. *Succeeding Against the Odds.* First Printing. Johnson Publishing Company, Inc., 1989: 159-160.
11. Bennett Jr., Lerone. "EBONY Interview with John H. Johnson." *EBONY* Nov. 1985: 50.

12. Johnson, John H. and Lerone Bennett Jr. *Succeeding Against the Odds*. First Printing. Johnson Publishing Company, Inc., 1989: 157.
13. Omar, Nathaniel. "Publishing Giant Tells How." *Bilalian News* 18 Feb. 1977: 30-31.
14. Johnson, John H. and Lerone Bennett Jr. *Succeeding Against the Odds*. First Printing. Johnson Publishing Company, Inc., 1989: 157.
15. "The Bicentennial: 200 Years of Black Trials and Triumphs." *EBONY* Aug. 1975.
16. Ibid.
17. Bennett Jr., Lerone. "The White Problem in America." *EBONY* Aug. 1965: 174-181.
18. Ibid.
19. Ibid.
20. Shipp, E.R. "After 40 Years, EBONY Drawing Praise, Criticism." *The New York Times* 21 Dec. 1985.
21. "Letters and Pictures to the Editor." *EBONY*. July 1946. 50.
22. Berler, Ron. "EBONY Is 40: Publisher John Johnson Tells His Auspicious Story." *The Dallas Morning News* 1985: 2.
23. Ibid.
24. Johnson, Paul Lindsey. "Interview: John H. Johnson." *The Crisis* Jan. 1987: 37.
25. "John H. Johnson Honored as Top All-Time Black Publisher." *JET* 24 Mar. 1977: 15.
26. Bennett Jr., Lerone. "EBONY Interview with John H. Johnson." *EBONY* Nov. 1985: 58.
27. Branch, Taylor. *Parting the Waters: America in the King Years 1954-63*. New York: Simon & Schuster, 1988: 681.
28. Gilfoyle, Timothy J. "Chicago Fortunes: Interviews with Lester Crown and John H. Johnson." *Chicago History* Fall 2000: 68.
29. Bennett Jr., Lerone. "EBONY Interview with John H. Johnson." *EBONY* Nov. 1985: 56.
30. Johnson, John H. and Lerone Bennett Jr. *Succeeding Against the Odds*. First Printing. Johnson Publishing Company, Inc., 1989: 288.
31. Ibid., 241.
32. "A Few Words from the Publisher." Johnson Publishing Company. 1963.

33. Johnson, John H. and Lerone Bennett Jr. *Succeeding Against the Odds*. First Printing. Johnson Publishing Company, Inc., 1989: 159.
34. Sweet, Neesa. "Leadership Profile Series on John H. Johnson: Publisher, Chairman & CEO Johnson Publishing Company." *Sky* 1988: 40.
35. Omar, Nathaniel. "Publishing Giant Tells How." *Bilalian News* 18 Feb. 1977: 30-31.
36. Sweet, Neesa. "Leadership Profile Series on John H. Johnson: Publisher, Chairman & CEO Johnson Publishing Company." *Sky* 1988: 40.
37. "Failure Is a Word I Don't Accept: An Interview With John H. Johnson." *Harvard Business Review* (1976): 79-88.
38. *Salute to Greatness Dinner Speech*. 1988. Unpublished. Atlanta Marriott Marquee Hotel in Atlanta, Ga.
39. Burns, Ben. *Nitty Gritty: A White Editor in Black Journalism*. Mississippi: University Press of Mississippi, 1996: 119.
40. Ibid., 89.
41. Ibid., 88.
42. Hall, Carla. "John H. Johnson: From Office Worker to Millionaire Publishing Mogul." *The Washington Post* 14 Sept. 1980.
43. "Payroll Kickback Charge Hits Rep Charles Diggs." *JET* 6 Apr. 1978: 8.
44. Hall, Carla. "John H. Johnson: From Office Worker to Millionaire Publishing Mogul." *The Washington Post* 14 Sept. 1980.
45. Ibid.
46. Gilfoyle, Timothy J. "Chicago Fortunes: Interviews with Lester Crown and John H. Johnson." *Chicago History* Fall 2000: 66.
47. Ibid.
48. Ibid.
49. "Failure Is a Word I Don't Accept: An Interview With John H. Johnson." *Harvard Business Review* (1976): 79–88.
50. Ibid.
51. Burns, Ben. *Nitty Gritty: A White Editor in Black Journalism*. Mississippi: University Press of Mississippi, 1996: 90.
52. Thimmesch, Nick. "John H. Johnson: The Man Behind EBONY." *Saturday Evening Post* Oct. 1975: 94.

53. Johnson, John H. and Lerone Bennett Jr. *Succeeding Against the Odds*. First Printing. Johnson Publishing Company, Inc., 1989: 213.
54. "Black on Black Crime: The Causes, The Consequences, The Cures." *EBONY* Aug. 1979.
55. Hall, Carla. "John H. Johnson: From Office Worker to Millionaire Publishing Mogul." *The Washington Post* 14 Sept. 1980.
56. Ibid.
57. Ibid.
58. "The 55 Most Intriguing Blacks of 2000." *EBONY* Nov. 2000: 64.
59. "Commencement Address Conferring of Degree: Mr. Bryant C. Gumbel." Education. *Howard University*.
60. People staff. "Gumbel Causes Grumbles." *People.com*. 12 June 2001; Strahler, Steven R. "Valid Reason for EBONY Magazine to Cut One of Its Celebs This Year." *Crain's Chicago Business* 3 June 2001; Rutenberg, Jim. "Media Talk: Gumbel and EBONY Argue Over Recent Remarks." *The New York Times* 11 June 2001.
61. Shipp, E.R. "After 40 Years, EBONY Drawing Praise, Criticism." *The New York Times* 21 Dec. 1985.
62. Ibid.

## Chapter 6. A Decision That Changed History

1. Nelson, Stanley. "The Murder of Emmett Till." *American Experience*. PBS, 2003.
2. Weller, Sheila. "The Missing Woman." *VanityFair.com* 26 Jan. 2017.
3. Michaeli, Ethan. *The Defender: How the Legendary Black Newspaper Changed America*. Boston New York: Houghton Mifflin Harcourt, 2016.
4. Nelson, Stanley. "The Murder of Emmett Till." *American Experience*. PBS, 2003.
5. Johnson, John H. *Succeeding Against the Odds*, 240.
6. *The John H. Johnson Interview*. Johnson Publishing Company: 2007.

7. Ibid.
8. Hampton, Henry. "Eyes on the Prize: America's Civil Rights Years 1954-1964." PBS, 1987.
9. Christian, Margena A. "Emmett Till's Legacy 50 Years Later." *JET 19 Sept. 2005:* 21.
10. Johnson, Paul Lindsey. "Interview: John H. Johnson." *The Crisis* Jan. 1987: 37.
11. Ibid.
12. Dewan, Shaila. "How Photos Became Icon of Civil Rights Movement." *The New York Times* 28 Aug. 2005.
13. "JET Magazine August 29, 2005 John H. Johnson: Founder & Publisher of JET & EBONY Magazines." 2005: 7-8.
14. "John H. Johnson Honored as Top All-Time Black Publisher." *JET* 24 Mar. 1977: 15.
15. Ibid.
16. Prince, Richard. "JET Magazine Could Return to Newsstands." *The Root* 17 Feb. 2017.
17. Weller, Sheila. "The Missing Woman." *VanityFair.com.* 26 Jan. 2017.
18. Ibid.

## Chapter 7. The Gospel Truth

1. Johnson, John H. and Lerone Bennett Jr. *Succeeding Against the Odds.* First Printing. Johnson Publishing Company, Inc., 1989: 207; "Patti LaBelle and Mario Van Peebles Host American Black Achievement Awards 13th Annual TV Show." *JET* 13 Jan. 1992: 54-62.
2. "Meet First White Alpha Dr. Bernard Levin." Black Greek-Lettered Organizations. *Watchtheyard.com.* 10 Nov. 2015.
3. Burns, Ben. *Nitty Gritty: A White Editor in Black Journalism.* Mississippi: University Press of Mississippi, 1996: 159.
4. Ibid., 160.
5. Johnson, John H. and Lerone Bennett Jr. *Succeeding Against the Odds.* First Printing. Johnson Publishing Company, Inc., 1989: 238-239.
6. Robinson, Louie. "Hottest Young Group in History." *EBONY* 11 Sept. 1970: 150-154.

7. Ibid.
8. Robinson, Louie. "Family Life of the Jackson Five." *EBONY* Dec. 1974: 30.
9. "The Jackson Family Has an Artist: Michael." *EBONY Jr.* Sept. 1975: 5-6.
10. Berry, William L. "Michael of the Jackson Five." *EBONY Jr.* July 1973: 52-54.
11. Johnson, John H. and Lerone Bennett Jr. *Succeeding Against the Odds.* First Printing. Johnson Publishing Company, Inc., 1989: 18.
12. Ibid.
13. Ibid., 19.
14. Ibid.
15. Johnson, Robert E. "The Michael Jackson Nobody Knows." *EBONY* Dec. 1984: 156.
16. Collier, Aldore. "Michael Jackson Tries to Keep Career From Crumbling As He Fights Addiction to Painkiller Drugs and Charges of Child Molestation." *JET* 6 Dec. 1993: 54–58.
17. "Michael Jackson's Statement: Full Statement Issued by Jackson." News. *CNN.com.* N.p., 6 Feb. 2003.
18. "Hundreds Pay Respects at Funeral for JET Executive Editor Robert E. Johnson." *JET* 26 Jan. 1996: 12-18, 53-57.
19. "Why It Took MTV So Long to Play Black Music Videos." *JET* 9 Oct. 200AD: 16–18.
20. Kinnon, Joy Bennett. "EBONY October 2005: Celebrating the Life and Legacy of John H. Johnson 1918-2005." Oct. 2005: 62.
21. Robinson, Louie. "Bad Times on the Good Times Set." *EBONY* Sept. 1975: 34.
22. Ibid.
23. "Week's Best Photo (The Cast of Good Times at Esther Rolle's Funeral)." *JET* 21 Dec. 1998: 41.
24. Christian, Margena A. "Where Is the Cast of Good Times." *JET* 28 Jan. 2008: 31-36.
25. Bennett Jr., Lerone. "The Martyrdom of Martin Luther King Jr." *EBONY* May 1968: 174-181.
26. Gilfoyle, Timothy J. "Chicago Fortunes: Interviews with Lester Crown and John H. Johnson." *Chicago History* Fall 2000: 68.
27. Ibid.

28. Bennett Jr., Lerone. "EBONY Interview with John H. Johnson." *EBONY* Nov. 1985: 56.
29. Ibid.
30. Ibid.
31. Johnson, John H. *Succeeding Against the Odds*. First Printing. Johnson Publishing Company, Inc., 1989: 288.
32. Ibid.
33. "The Man Who Lived Thirty Years as A Woman." *EBONY* 12 Oct. 1951: 23-26.
34. "A Golfing Champion at Six: Tiny Tiger Woods." *EBONY* Nov. 1982: 93-98.
35. "Youngest Ever." *JET* 16 Mar. 1992: 47.
36. Kitt, Eartha. "My Baby Travels with Me." *EBONY* Jan. 1963: 93-98.
37. Christian, Margena A. "Sean 'Puffy' Combs Discusses The Love He's Never Been Able to Shake, His Impact as A Performer and Why He's A Role Model." *JET* 13 Sept. 1999: 54-58.
38. Ibid.
39. Chappell, Kevin. "The Puff Daddy Nobody Knows." *EBONY* Jan. 2000: 74-82.
40. Granton, E. Fannie, and Ronald E. Kisner. "Family Talks About Dead Mother Whose Cells Fight Cancer." *JET* 1 Apr. 1976: 16-18.
41. "'I Guess God Was with Me' Says Lone Survivor of Plane Crash." *JET* 28 Dec. 1967: 53.
42. "'I Guess God Was with Me' Says Lone Survivor of Plane Crash." *JET* 28 Dec. 1967: 59.
43. Higgins, Chester. "What Widow Does with Otis Redding Money." *JET* 18 July 1968: 16-23.
44. Booker, Simeon. "King's Widow: Bereavement to Battlefield." *JET* 25 Apr. 1968: 6-16.
45. Christian, Margena A. "Stanley Tookie Williams: Final Words from Executed Death Row Inmate." *JET* 9 Jan. 2006: 46-50.
46. Christian, Margena A. "Lynching Survivor, 91, Reminds Blacks to 'Never Forget.'" *JET* 5 Dec. 2005: 37.
47. Adderton, Donald. "Deformed Mother Resists Agency Assault: Battles to Keep Normal Baby." *JET* 25 Mar. 1976: 12–18.

48. *Celestine Tate*. 1995. Film. Howard Stern Show.
49. "Celestine Tate Harrington Dies in Atlantic City, NJ." *JET* 16 Mar. 1998: 15-16.
50. "Siamese Twins Learning to Talk, Play." *JET* 13 Nov. 1952: 19.
51. "Siamese Twins Buried in Specially-Made Coffin." 22 Feb. 1993: 16–17.
52. Moore, Trudy S. "Aging Disease Makes 6-Year-Old Boy Look 60." *JET* 5 Dec. 1983: 22-26.
53. "Victim of Aging Disease Peedie Snipes Dies at 14." *JET* 22 June 1992: 9.
54. Christian, Margena A. "Tyler Perry: Meet the Man Behind the Urban Theater Character Madea." *JET*: 60-64.

## Chapter 8. Giving Voice to Black Consumers

1. Hall, Carla. "John H. Johnson: From Office Worker to Millionaire Publishing Mogul." *The Washington Post* 14 Sept. 1980.
2. Thimmesch, Nick. "John H. Johnson: The Man Behind EBONY." *Saturday Evening Post* Oct. 1975: 37.
3. Burns, Ben. *Nitty Gritty: A White Editor in Black Journalism.* Mississippi: University Press of Mississippi, 1996: 120.
4. Johnson, John H. *Succeeding Against the Odds.* First Printing. Johnson Publishing Company, Inc., 1989: 184.
5. Burns, Ben. *Nitty Gritty: A White Editor in Black Journalism.* Mississippi: University Press of Mississippi, 1996: 120.
6. Thimmesch, Nick. "John H. Johnson: The Man Behind EBONY." *Saturday Evening Post* Oct. 1975: 37.
7. Ibid.
8. Woodard, Dustin. "1973-1974 Stock Market Crash." *About.com.* 11 Sept. 2007.
9. "Wall Streets Worst Market Crashes." *Worstmarketcrashes.com.* 11 Mar. 2011.
10. Johnson, John H. *Succeeding Against the Odds.* First Printing. Johnson Publishing Company, Inc., 1989: 242.
11. Ibid., 49.

12. Christian, Margena A. "Decades of Fashion: EBONY Fashion Fair Then and Now." *JET* 17 Dec. 2001: 34–39.
13. Johnson, John H. *Succeeding Against the Odds.* First Printing. Johnson Publishing Company, Inc., 1989: 9, 341.
14. Ibid., 229.
15. Ellison, Richard. *Invisible Man.* Random House, 1952.
16. Johnson, John H. *Succeeding Against the Odds.* First Printing. Johnson Publishing Company, Inc., 1989: 179.
17. *The John H. Johnson Interview.* Johnson Publishing Company: 2007.
18. Hall, Carla. "John H. Johnson: From Office Worker to Millionaire Publishing Mogul." *The Washington Post* 14 Sept. 1980.
19. Thimmesch, Nick. "John H. Johnson: The Man Behind EBONY." *Saturday Evening Post* Oct. 1975: 37.
20. "Illinois Business Hall of Fame." American National Business Hall of Fame Video Series Presents John Johnson. 1989.
21. Johnson, John H. *Succeeding Against the Odds.* First Printing. Johnson Publishing Company, Inc., 1989: 186-187.
22. Ibid., 188.
23. Bennett Jr., Lerone. "EBONY Interview with John H. Johnson." *EBONY* Nov. 1985: 52.
24. Johnson, John H. *Succeeding Against the Odds.* First Printing. Johnson Publishing Company, Inc., 1989: 215.
25. Thimmesch, Nick. "John H. Johnson: The Man Behind EBONY." *Saturday Evening Post* Oct. 1975: 37; Zenith press release 14 Feb. 1974.
26. Burns, Ben. *Nitty Gritty: A White Editor in Black Journalism.* Mississippi: University Press of Mississippi, 1996: 125.
27. Ibid., 126.
28. "Failure Is a Word I Don't Accept: An Interview With John H. Johnson." *Harvard Business Review* (1976): 81.
29. "Remembering John H. Johnson (1918-2005)." *JET* 29 Aug. 2005: 42.
30. Hall, Carla. "John H. Johnson: From Office Worker to Millionaire Publishing Mogul." *The Washington Post* 14 Sept. 1980.
31. Bennett Jr., Lerone. "EBONY Interview with John H. Johnson." *EBONY* Nov. 1985: 50.

32. Johnson, John H. *Succeeding Against the Odds*. First Printing. Johnson Publishing Company, Inc., 1989: 289.
33. Bednarski, P.J. "Persistence Pays Off for Johnson." *Chicago Sun Times* 3 Nov. 1985: 2.
34. Johnson, John H. *Succeeding Against the Odds*. First Printing. Johnson Publishing Company, Inc., 1989: 230-231.
35. "The EBONY Story: 10th Anniversary Ten Years That Rocked the World." Nov. 1955.
36. Johnson, John H. *Succeeding Against the Odds*. First Printing. Johnson Publishing Company, Inc., 1989: 230.
37. Burns, Ben. *Nitty Gritty: A White Editor in Black Journalism*. Mississippi: University Press of Mississippi, 1996: 128.
38. Bennett Jr., Lerone. "EBONY Interview with John H. Johnson." *EBONY* Nov. 1985: 50.
39. Johnson, John H. *Succeeding Against the Odds*. First Printing. Johnson Publishing Company, Inc., 1989: 231.
40. "The EBONY Story: 10th Anniversary Ten Years That Rocked the World." Nov. 1955.
41. Ibid.
42. Gilfoyle, Timothy J. "Chicago Fortunes: Interviews with Lester Crown and John H. Johnson." *Chicago History* Fall 2000: 68.
43. Ibid.
44. Ibid.
45. Johnson, Paul Lindsey. "Interview: John H. Johnson." *The Crisis* Jan. 1987: 37.
46. Johnson, John H. *Succeeding Against the Odds*. First Printing. Johnson Publishing Company, Inc., 1989: 289.
47. Johnson, John H. *Acceptance Speech by John H. Johnson After Being Named Publisher of the Year*. 1972. Henry Johnson Fisher Award Luncheon.
48. Ibid.
49. Moore, Richard. *83rd Commencement Personal Commitment Needed, EBONY Publisher Tells A & T*. 1974. Press release. North Carolina A & T State University.
50. Sweet, Neesa. "Leadership Profile Series on John H. Johnson: Publisher, Chairman & CEO Johnson Publishing Company." *Sky* 1988: 45.
51. "Failure Is a Word I Don't Accept: An Interview With John H. Johnson." *Harvard Business Review* (1976): 84-85.

52. Ibid 88.
53. Graves, Earl G. "John H. Johnson: Leader, Legend and Friend." Earl G. Graves Publishing Company. 2005.
54. "Thousands Join in Historic Farewell Celebration of Publisher John H. Johnson in Chicago." *JET* 29 Aug. 2005: 42.
55. Ibid., 40, 42.
56. Hall, Carla. "John H. Johnson: From Office Worker to Millionaire Publishing Mogul." *The Washington Post* 14 Sept. 1980.
57. Rogers, Steven S. *Black Business Leaders Series: The Entrepreneurship Behind EBONY Magazine.* N.p. Audio Recording. Cold Call (February 2, 2017)
58. Ibid.
59. Bennett Jr., Lerone. "EBONY Interview with John H. Johnson." *EBONY* Nov. 1985: 58.
60. Pogrebin, Robin. "Success and the Black Magazine; As Readers Prosper, Advertising Still Eludes Publishers." *The New York Times* 25 Oct. 1997: n. pag.

## Chapter 9. The Rise of the Empire

1. Johnson, John H. *Succeeding Against the Odds.* First Printing. Johnson Publishing Company, Inc., 1989: 7.
2. Ibid., 156.
3. Reichley, A. James. "How Johnson Made It." *Fortune* Jan. 1968: 178.
4. Shaw, O'Wendell. "Magazines Must Pay Their Writers." *Pep* Nov. 1945: 3.
5. "Former Publisher John P Davis Succumbs at Age 68." *JET* 27 Sept. 1973: 17.
6. Thimmesch, Nick. "John H. Johnson: The Man Behind EBONY." *Saturday Evening Post* Oct. 1975: 94.
7. Ibid.
8. Gilfoyle, Timothy J. "Chicago Fortunes: Interviews with Lester Crown and John H. Johnson." *Chicago History* Fall 2000: 65.
9. Johnson, John H. *Succeeding Against the Odds.* First Printing. Johnson Publishing Company, Inc., 1989: 191.

10. Thimmesch, Nick. "John H. Johnson: The Man Behind EBONY." *Saturday Evening Post* Oct. 1975: 94.
11. Ibid 37.
12. "Gardner Cowles Jr. Is Dead at 82: Helped Build Publishing Empire." *The New York Times* 9 July 1985: n. Pag.
13. Thimmesch, Nick. "John H. Johnson: The Man Behind EBONY." *Saturday Evening Post* Oct. 1975: 94.
14. Ibid.
15. Burns, Ben. *Nitty Gritty: A White Editor in Black Journalism.* Mississippi: University Press of Mississippi, 1996: 119.
16. Ibid., 125.
17. "New Hue, New Copper." *Newsweek* 19 Oct. 1953: 93.
18. Johnson, John H. *Succeeding Against the Odds.* First Printing. Johnson Publishing Company, Inc., 1989: 206.
19. "EBONY Publisher Rebuilding Empire." 10 Dec. 1982. Florida Sentinel-Bulletin.
20. Ibid., 288.
21. Ibid., 289.
22. Bennett Jr., Lerone. "EBONY Interview with John H. Johnson." *EBONY* Nov. 1985: 56.
23. Ibid.
24. Johnson, John H. *Succeeding Against the Odds.* First Printing. Johnson Publishing Company, Inc., 1989: 289.
25. "Black History and Afro-American Studies." *EBONY* Apr. 1973: 150.
26. Morrison, Allan. "Selassie's Message to the Negro." *EBONY Africa* Mar. 1964: 47–53.
27. "Backstage." *EBONY* Jan. 1973: 22.
28. "Black History and Afro-American Studies." *EBONY* Apr. 1973: 150.
29. *John H. Johnson Speech.* 1989. Chicago American Business Hall of Fame.
30. Christian, Margena A. "Glam Odyssey: A Fashion Journey into Bliss & Beyond 2007-2008." *JET* 10 Sept. 2007: 34–37.
31. Christian, Margena A. "Decades of Fashion: EBONY Fashion Fair Then and Now." *JET* 17 Dec. 2001: 38.
32. Johnson, John H. *Succeeding Against the Odds.* First Printing. Johnson Publishing Company, Inc., 1989: 341.
33. Ibid., 36.

34. Thimmesch, Nick. "John H. Johnson: The Man Behind EBONY." *Saturday Evening Post* Oct. 1975: 95.
35. Christian, Margena A. "Decades of Fashion: EBONY Fashion Fair Then and Now." *JET* 17 Dec. 2001: 38.
36. Ibid.
37. "Illinois Business Hall of Fame." American National Business Hall of Fame Video Series Presents John Johnson. 1989.
38. Ibid.
39. Ibid., 184.
40. Ibid., 185.
41. "National Report EBONY and Spiegel Join Forces to Launch New Catalog Clothing Line." *JET* 7 Oct. 1991: 4–5.
42. Norment, Lynn. "EBONY Interview with Linda Johnson Rice." Nov. 1992: 210.
43. Thimmesch, Nick. "John H. Johnson: The Man Behind EBONY." *Saturday Evening Post* Oct. 1975: 95.
44. Johnson, John H. *Succeeding Against the Odds*. First Printing. Johnson Publishing Company, Inc., 1989: 311.
45. Ibid., 314.
46. Ibid.
47. "Sphinx: 67th Anniversary Convention Issue." *Sphinx* May-June 1973.
48. "The Jackson Family Has an Artist: Michael." *EBONY Jr.* Sept. 1975: 5-6.
49. Thimmesch, Nick. "John H. Johnson: The Man Behind EBONY." *Saturday Evening Post* Oct. 1975: 95.
50. Johnson, John H. *Succeeding Against the Odds*. First Printing. Johnson Publishing Company, Inc., 1989: 352.
51. Thimmesch, Nick. "John H. Johnson: The Man Behind EBONY." *Saturday Evening Post* Oct. 1975: 95.
52. "Chicago's Top Black-Owned Business." *The Defender* 21 July 1974: 1.
53. "The Forbes Four Hundred." *Forbes* 13 Sept. 1982.
54. Hall, Carla. "John H. Johnson: From Office Worker to Millionaire Publishing Mogul." *The Washington Post* 14 Sept. 1980.
55. Thimmesch, Nick. "John H. Johnson: The Man Behind EBONY." *Saturday Evening Post* Oct. 1975: 96.

56. Hall, Carla. "John H. Johnson: From Office Worker to Millionaire Publishing Mogul." *The Washington Post* 14 Sept. 1980.
57. Johnson, John H. *Succeeding Against the Odds.* First Printing. Johnson Publishing Company, Inc., 1989: 174.
58. Flax, Steven. "The Toughest Bosses in America." *Fortune* 6 Aug. 1984: 18-23.
59. Ibid., 23.
60. Ibid.
61. Ibid.
62. Ibid;
63. "Failure Is a Word I Don't Accept: An Interview with John H. Johnson." Harvard Business Review (1976): 80.
64. Ibid.
65. Ibid.
66. Bennett Jr., Lerone. "EBONY Interview with John H. Johnson." *EBONY* Nov. 1985: 48.
67. Hall, Carla. "John H. Johnson: From Office Worker to Millionaire Publishing Mogul." *The Washington Post* 14 Sept. 1980.
68. Burns, Ben. *Nitty Gritty: A White Editor in Black Journalism.* Mississippi: University Press of Mississippi, 1996: 90.
69. Johnson, John H. *Succeeding Against the Odds.* First Printing. Johnson Publishing Company, Inc., 1989: 236.
70. Burns, Ben. *Nitty Gritty: A White Editor in Black Journalism.* Mississippi: University Press of Mississippi, 1996: 190-191.
71. Ibid 208.
72. Johnson, John H. *Succeeding Against the Odds.* First Printing. Johnson Publishing Company, Inc., 1989: 206.
73. "Backstage." *EBONY* Oct. 1986: 26.
74. Ibid.
75. Johnson, John H. *Succeeding Against the Odds.* First Printing. Johnson Publishing Company, Inc., 1989: 207.
76. Vega, Tanzina. "JET Magazine Stays Compact but with A New Design." *NewYorkTimes.com* 22 July 2013.
77. Johnson, John H. *Succeeding Against the Odds.* First Printing. Johnson Publishing Company, Inc., 1989: 160.
78. "Backstage." *EBONY* Apr. 1983: 28.

79. Johnson, John H. *Succeeding Against the Odds.* First Printing. Johnson Publishing Company, Inc., 1989: 352.
80. "Backstage." *EBONY* Jan. 1982: 24.
81. Hall, Carla. "John H. Johnson: From Office Worker to Millionaire Publishing Mogul." *The Washington Post* 14 Sept. 1980.
82. Johnson, John H. *Succeeding Against the Odds.* First Printing. Johnson Publishing Company, Inc., 1989: 353.
83. Ibid.
84. Donato, Marla. "Party Debuts Magazine for Black Men." *ChicagoTribune.com* 23 Jan. 1985.
85. Hicks, Jonathan. "A Magazine for Black Men On the Way Up." *The New York Times* 7 Nov. 1985: 34.
86. Ibid.
87. Johnson, John H. *Succeeding Against the Odds.* First Printing. Johnson Publishing Company, Inc., 1989: 353.
88. Ibid 249; Hall, Carla. "John H. Johnson: From Office Worker to Millionaire Publishing Mogul." *The Washington Post* 14 Sept. 1980.
89. "EBONY/JET TV Celebrity Showcase Set to Air in Atlanta; Washington, D.C." *JET* 30 Aug. 1982: 58.
90. Joyner, Tom. *I'm Just a DJ But...It Makes Sense to Me.* New York: Grand Central Publishing/Hachette Book Group, 2005.
91. Hicks, Jonathan. "For Black Men on the Way Up." 7 Nov. 1985: 1.
92. Backstage. *EBONY* Dec. 1987: 23.
93. Bennett Jr., Lerone. "EBONY Interview with John H. Johnson." *EBONY* Nov. 1985: 58.
94. "Illinois Business Hall of Fame." American National Business Hall of Fame Video Series Presents John Johnson. 1989.
95. Channick, Robert. "Johnson Publishing Sells EBONY, JET to Texas Firm." *Chicago Tribune* 15 June 2016.
96. Marek, Lynne. "Linda Johnson Rice Retakes EBONY CEO Post." *Crain's Chicago Business* 9 Mar. 2017.
97. "Debut of EBONY South Africa Continues EBONY Magazine's 50th Anniversary Celebration." *JET* 11 Dec. 1995: 36.
98. Cauvin, Henry E. "EBONY Ends Publication in South Africa." 17 July 2000.

99. Streit, Meghan. "Staff Shakeup at EBONY, JET: Report. Crain's Chicago Business 2 Feb. 2009.
100. Ibid.

## Chapter 10. End of A Dynasty

1. Hall, Carla. "John H. Johnson: From Office Worker to Millionaire Publishing Mogul." *The Washington Post* 14 Sept. 1980.
2. "Succeeding Against the Odds." *EBONY* October 2005: 74h.
3. Hall, Carla. "John H. Johnson: From Office Worker to Millionaire Publishing Mogul." *The Washington Post* 14 Sept. 1980.
4. Ibid.
5. "John H. Johnson Avenue." *JET* 28 Nov. 2005: 8.
6. "Friends and Admirers View Body of Pioneer Publisher John H. Johnson at Company Headquarters." *JET* 29 Aug. 2005: 62.
7. "Thousands Join in Historic Farewell Celebration of Publisher John H. Johnson in Chicago." *JET* 29 Aug. 2005: 4-10, 59-61.
8. "John H. Johnson Avenue." *JET* 28 Nov. 2005: 8.
9. "Johnson Publishing Company Names VP & Editorial Director for EBONY & JET." 7 Aug. 2006: 65.
10. "Johnson Center to Offer Scholarships and Support Research on African-American Issues in the Media." 23 Aug. 2007.
11. "Johnson Publishing Co. Pledges $2.5 Mil. to New Communication Center at USC." *JET* 10 Sept. 2007: 32.
12. "Anne Sempowski Ward Named President and Chief Operating Officer of Fashion Fair Cosmetics." *JET* 15 Oct. 2007: 10.
13. "Anne Sempowski Ward Named President and Chief Operating Officer of Johnson Publishing Company, Inc." *JET* 20 Oct. 2008: 24.
14. "Johnson Publishing: Reorg and Re-Up." News. *Minonline.com.* 3 Feb. 2009.
15. Roeder, David. "Columbia College Buys Home of EBONY, JET." *Chicago Sun Times* 2 Dec. 2010.
16. Baeb, Eddie, and Ann Saphir. "Legacy on the Line." *Crain's Chicago Business* 20 June 2009.

17. Kapos, Shia. "Last of the EBONY Fashion Fair Collection to Be Auctioned." *Crain's Chicago Business* 14 May 2015.
18. Walker, Dionne. "Close of EBONY Fashion Fair Means End of an Era." *TheSeattleTimes.com* 4 Mar. 2010.
19. Talbert, Marcia Wade. "Black Enterprise, Magic Johnson in Talks to Buy Johnson Publishing." *Black Enterprise* 16 Feb. 2010.
20. Horowitz, Jason. "White House Announces Resignation of Social Secretary Desiree Rogers." *WashingtonPost.com.* 27 Jan. 2010.
21. "Desiree Rogers Named Obamas' White House Social Secretary." *Los Angeles Times* 24 Nov. 2008.
22. Kapos, Shia. "EBONY Names Amy DuBois Barnett Editor in Chief." *Crain's Chicago Business* 2 June 2010.
23. Smith, Steve. "Johnson Publishing Pres/COO Resigns." *Minonline.com.* 13 July 2010.
24. Rosenthal, Phil. "Johnson Publishing CEO Desiree Rogers Trying to Breathe New Life into EBONY, JET Magazines." *Chicago Tribune* 6 Mar. 2011.
25. "About Johnson College Prep." *Johnson College Prep.* johnsoncollegeprep.noblenetwork.org; West Fresno School District administration office press release.
26. "Johnson Publishing Co. to Sell Its Iconic Headquarters to Columbia College Chicago." *Target Market News* 17 Nov. 2010.
27. Watson, Jamal. "Howard University Attempting to Re-Establish Ties to Late John H. Johnson." Education. *DiverseEducation.com.* 3 Nov. 2013.
28. "Howard University Announces the Cathy Hughes School of Communications." Education. *HowardUniversity.edu.* 6 Oct. 2016.
29. Cohn, Steve. "JET Editor in Chief Mira Lowe Resigns." *Minonline.com.* 16 Dec. 2010.
30. "Mitzi Miller Named Editor in Chief of JET Magazine." *Atlanta Daily World* 2 May 2011.
31. Rosenthal, Phil. "Johnson Publishing CEO Desiree Rogers Trying to Breathe New Life into EBONY, JET Magazines." *Chicago Tribune* 6 Mar. 2011.

32. Behme, Todd J., and Lynne Marek. "JP Morgan Unit Buys Stake in EBONY Owner Johnson Publishing." Advertising. *AdvertisingAge.com.* 6 July 2011.
33. "Legendary Publisher Honored: U.S. Postal Service's Black Heritage Forever Stamp Salutes John H. Johnson." United States Postal Service. *USPS.Com.* 31 Jan. 2012.
34. Marek, Lynne. "Johnson Publishing Adjusts Strategy on JET Magazine." *Crain's Chicago Business* 9 Aug. 2012.
35. "Cheryl Mayberry McKissack Named Chief Operating Officer of Johnson Publishing." *Target Market News* 10 Jan. 2013.
36. Marek, Lynne. "Johnson Publishing Lands New Financing." *Crain's Chicago Business* 16 Sept. 2013.
37. Marek, Lynne. "EBONY Taps JET Editor to Take Top Slot." *Crain's Chicago Business* 23 Apr. 2014.
38. Sebastian, Michael. "JET Magazine Dumps Print, Goes Digital." *Crain's Chicago Business* 7 May 2014.
39. Ibid.
40. Prince, Richard. "Final Print Issue of JET Never Reached Some Magazine Stands." News. *TheRoot.com.* 7 June 2014.
41. Channick, Robert. "Johnson Publishing to Sell Historic Photo Archive." *Chicago Tribune* 23 Jan. 2015.
42. Kapos, Shia. "Editor-in-Chief of EBONY Magazine Resigns." *Crain's Chicago Business* 20 Feb. 2015.
43. Marek, Lynne. "New Editorial Chief at EBONY's Johnson Publishing." *Crain's Chicago Business* 15 June 2015.
44. Channick, Robert. "Johnson Publishing Sells EBONY, JET to Texas Firm." *Chicago Tribune* 15 June 2016.
45. O'Shea, Chris. "Former EBONY Editor Kierna Mayo Joins Interactive One." Advertising. *Adweek.com.* 22 June 2016.
46. Gallun, Alby. "Columbia College to Sell Johnson Publishing Building." *Crain's Chicago Business* 14 June 2016.
47. Wright, Sarafina. "John H. Johnson Legacy Continued at Howard U." *Washington Informer* 3 Nov. 2016.
48. "Johnson Publishing Building to Be Considered for Landmark Status." *Cityofchicago.org.* 2 Feb. 2017.
49. Prince, Richard. "JET Magazine Could Return to Newsstands." *The Root* 17 Feb. 2017.
50. Marek, Lynne. "Linda Johnson Rice Retakes EBONY CEO Post." *Crain's Chicago Business* 9 Mar. 2017.

51. Lewis, Andy. "WME Signs JET, EBONY Magazines (Exclusive)." *TheHollywoodReporter.com*. 4 May 2017.
52. "Linda Johnson Rice Takes Back Control of JPC, Denies Company Has Plans to Leave Chicago." *Target Market News* 7 May 2017.
53. Channick, Robert. "EBONY Cuts a Third of Its Staff, Moving Editorial Operations to LA." *Chicago Tribune* 5 May 2017.
54. "Linda Johnson Rice Takes Back Control of JPC, Denies Company Has Plans to Leave Chicago." *Target Market News* 7 May 2017.
55. Marek, Lynne. "Desiree Rogers Leaving Johnson Publishing." *Crain's Chicago Business* 6 May 2017.
56. Umoh, Ruth. "Tesla Just Welcomed This CEO to Its Board. Here's Why It's a Big Thing for Silicon Valley." *CNBC.com* 21 July 2017.
57. The Tesla Team. "Tesla Welcomes Linda Johnson Rice and James Murdoch As New Independent Directors to Its Board." *Tesla.com* 17 July 2017.
58. Prince, Richard. "EBONY Editor Confirms She's Left the Company." *Journal-isms.com*. 12 Oct. 2017.
59. Prince, Richard. "Johnson Rice Steps Down at EBONY's New Company." News. *Journal-isms.com.* 13 July 2018.

## Epilogue

1. "Thousands Join in Historic Farewell Celebration of Publisher John H. Johnson in Chicago." *JET* 29 Aug. 2005: 10.
2. Ibid., 4-10, 59.
3. Bennett Jr., Lerone. "EBONY Interview with John H. Johnson." *EBONY* Nov. 1985: 58

## Bibliography

"A $500 Loan Fueled EBONY's 30-Year Rise." Detroit Free Press 21 Nov. 1975: 2.

"A Golfing Champion at Six: Tiny Tiger Woods." EBONY Nov. 1982: 93-98.

"About Johnson College Prep." Johnson College Prep. johnsoncollegeprep.noblenetwork.org

"About Us." Official company site. Chicago Defender.

Adderton, Donald. "Deformed Mother Resists Agency Assault: Battles to Keep Normal Baby." JET 25 Mar. 1976: 12-18.

"African-American Newspapers and Periodicals." Wisconsin Historical Society. Freedom's Journal.

Alpha Kappa Alpha Sorority.

Alpha Phi Alpha Fraternity.

"Anne Sempowski Ward Named President and Chief Operating Officer of Fashion Fair Cosmetics." JET 15 Oct. 2007: 10.

"Anne Sempowski Ward Named President and Chief Operating Officer of Johnson Publishing Company, Inc." JET 20 Oct. 2008: 24.

"Backstage." EBONY Jan. 1973: 22.

—. EBONY Jan. 1982: 24.

—. EBONY March 1982: 18.

—. EBONY Apr. 1983: 28.

—. EBONY Oct. 1986: 26.

—. EBONY Dec. 1987: 23.

Baeb, Eddie, and Ann Saphir. "Legacy on the Line." Crain's Chicago Business 20 June 2009.

Bednarski, P.J. "Persistence Pays Off for Johnson." Chicago Sun Times 3 Nov. 1985: 2.

Behme, Todd J., and Lynne Marek. "JP Morgan Unit Buys Stake in EBONY Owner Johnson Publishing." Advertising. AdvertisingAge.com. 6 July 2011.

Bennett Jr., Lerone. "EBONY Interview with John H. Johnson." EBONY Nov. 1985: 44-58.

—. "Homage to 'The Beginner.'" EBONY Oct. 2005: 81-94.

—. "In Memoriam: Mrs. Gertrude Johnson Williams (1891-1977)." EBONY July 1977: 124.

—. "The Martyrdom of Martin Luther King Jr." EBONY May 1968: 174-181.

—. "The White Problem in America." EBONY Aug. 1965: 174-181.

Berler, Ron. "EBONY Is 40: Publisher John Johnson Tells His Auspicious Story." The Dallas Morning News 1985: 2.

Berry, William L. "Michael of the Jackson Five." EBONY Jr. July 1973: 52-54.

"Black History and Afro-American Studies." EBONY Apr. 1973: 150.

"Black on Black Crime: The Causes, The Consequences, The Cures." EBONY Aug. 1979.

Blackwell, Victor. "Family Files $5 Million Lawsuit Over EBONY Stories on Kendrick Johnson Case." News. CNN.com. 29 Aug. 2014.

Booker, Simeon. "King's Widow: Bereavement to Battlefield." JET 25 Apr. 1968: 6-16.

—. "My JET Years 1953-2006: Simeon Booker, Washington, D.C., Bureau Chief." JET 13 Nov. 2006: 32-36.

Boone, Dorothy Deloris. "A Historical Review and A Bibliography of Selected Negro Magazines 1910-1969." University of Michigan, 1970.

Boyd, Herb. "Has BET's Emerge Submerged?" New York Amsterdam News 14 June 2000.

Branch, Taylor. Parting the Waters: America in the King Years 1954-63. New York: Simon & Schuster, 1988.

Brown, Dorothy Deloris. Personal interview. August 25, 1969. Chicago, Illinois.

Buck, Genevieve. "Publisher Johnson Reads 'Disadvantage' As 'Advantage.'" Chicago Tribune 18 June 1998: 1.

Burns, Ben. Nitty Gritty: A White Editor in Black Journalism. Mississippi: University Press of Mississippi, 1996.

Caliver, Ambrose. "Certain Significant Developments in the Education of Negroes during the Past Generation." Journal of Negro History 35.2 (1950): 111-134.

Carter, Reon. "EBONY Publisher Still on a Mission: Founder Fights to Keep His Black Magazine Dominant." Detroit News 1 Nov. 1990: 2.

Cauvin, Henry E. "EBONY Ends Publication in South Africa." 17 July 2000.

"Celebrating the Life and Legacy of John H. Johnson." EBONY Oct.

2005: 53-71.

"Celebrities Pay Tribute to Publishing Titan John H. Johnson." JET 29 Aug. 2005: 44-54.

Celestine Tate. 1995. Film. Howard Stern Show.

"Celestine Tate Harrington Dies in Atlantic City, NJ." JET 16 Mar. 1998: 15-16.

Channick, Robert. "EBONY Cuts a Third of Its Staff, Moving Editorial Operations to LA." Chicago Tribune 5 May 2017.

—. "Johnson Publishing Sells EBONY, JET to Texas Firm." Chicago Tribune 15 June 2016.

—. "Johnson Publishing to Sell Historic Photo Archive." Chicago Tribune 23 Jan. 2015.

Chappell, Kevin. "The Puff Daddy Nobody Knows." EBONY Jan. 2000: 74-82.

Cheek, James E. John H. Johnson Agrees to Participate in 14th Annual Communications Conference As Key Speaker to Opening Session at Howard University. 24 Jan. 1985. Letter.

"Cheryl Mayberry McKissack Named Chief Operating Officer of Johnson Publishing." Target Market News 10 Jan. 2013.

"Chicago Gambler Buried in Cadillac-Style Coffin." JET 19 March 1984: 22-24.

"Chicago's Top Black-Owned Business." The Defender 21 July 1974: 1.

Christian, Margena A. "Decades of Fashion: EBONY Fashion Fair Then and Now." JET 17 Dec. 2001: 34-39.

—. "Emmett Till's Legacy 50 Years Later." JET 19 Sept. 2005: 20-25.

—. "Glam Odyssey: A Fashion Journey into Bliss & Beyond 2007-2008." JET 10 Sept. 2007: 34-37.

—. "Lynching Survivor, 91, Reminds Blacks to 'Never Forget.'" JET 5 Dec. 2005: 36-40.

—. "The 51st Annual EBONY Fashion Fair Presents: The Runway Report." JET 15 Sept. 2008: 38-41.

—. "Sean 'Puffy' Combs Discusses The Love He's Never Been Able to Shake, His Impact as A Performer and Why He's A Role Model." JET 13 Sept. 1999: 54-58.

—. "Sean 'Puffy' Combs Tells How He Got His Nickname, How He Is Handling Fame and How James Brown Influenced Him." JET 12 Jan. 1998: 32-36.

—. "Stanley Tookie Williams: Final Words from Executed Death Row

Inmate." JET 9 Jan. 2006: 46-50.
—. "Tyler Perry: Meet the Man Behind the Urban Theater Character Madea." JET: 60-64.
—. "Where Is the Cast of Good Times." JET 28 Jan. 2008: 31-36.
—. "Why It Took MTV So Long to Play Black Music Videos." JET 9 Oct. 200AD: 16-18.
Christian, Margena A., and Jesse Jackson Sr. "He Chronicled Our Struggles but Found the Good and Praised It." EBONY Nov. 2010: 104–107.
Cohn, Steve. "JET Editor in Chief Mira Lowe Resigns." Minonline.com. 16 Dec. 2010.
Colin III, Scipio A. J., and Talmadge Guy. "An Africentric Interpretive Model of Curriculum Orientations for Course Development in Graduate Programs in Adult Education." PAACE Journal of Lifelong Learning 7 (1998): 43-55.
Collier, Aldore. "Michael Jackson Tries to Keep Career From Crumbling As He Fights Addiction to Painkiller Drugs and Charges of Child Molestation." JET 6 Dec. 1993: 54-58.
"Color Success Black." Time 2 Aug. 1968: 32.
"Commencement Address Conferring of Degree: Mr. Bryant C. Gumbel." Education. Howard University.
"Comment." Negro Digest Jan. 1942.
—. Negro Digest Feb. 1942.
"Confederate Mound." National Cemetery Administration. U.S. Department of Veterans Affairs.
Deardorff, Julie. "EBONY's Johnson: 'You Can't Dream Too Big'." Chicago Tribune Magazine 5 Jan. 1997: 13.
"Debut of 'EBONY South Africa' Continues EBONY Magazine's 50th Anniversary Celebration." JET 11 Dec. 1995: 36.
"Debut of EBONY South Africa Continues EBONY Magazine's 50th Anniversary Celebration." JET 11 Dec. 1995: 36.
Delta Sigma Theta Sorority.
"Desiree Rogers Named Obamas' White House Social Secretary." Los Angeles Times 24 Nov. 2008.
"Desiree Rogers Was Named the First African-American White House Social Secretary This Week." Publication. Essence.com. 16 Dec. 2009.
"Died: James Williams." JET 23 Nov. 1961: 23.
Dewan, Shaila. "How Photos Became Icon of Civil Rights

Movement." The New York Times 28 Aug. 2005.
"Doctoral Duo." JET 6 July 1972: 17.
Donato, Marla. "Party Debuts Magazine for Black Men." ChicagoTribune.com 23 Jan. 1985.
Dougherty, Philip H. "EBONY's Search for Attention." The New York Times.
DuBois, W.E.B. The Souls of Black Folk. New York: Signet Classic, 1969.
—. The Souls of Black Folk. New York: Signet, 1969.
Kinnon, Joy Bennett. "EBONY October 2005: Celebrating the Life and Legacy of John H. Johnson 1918-2005." Oct. 2005: 53-71.
"EBONY/JET TV Celebrity Showcase Set to Air in Atlanta; Washington, D.C." JET 30 Aug. 1982: 58.
"EBONY-JETours." EBONY Apr. 1973.
"EBONY's African World." Nov. 1995: 88-95.
"EBONY Publisher Rebuilding Empire." Florida Sentinel-Bulletin 10 Dec. 1982.
Ellison, Richard. Invisible Man. Random House, 1952.
"Failure Is a Word I Don't Accept: An Interview With John H. Johnson." Harvard Business Review (1976): 79–88.
Melton, John Gordon. "Father Divine: American Religious Leader." Encyclopedia Brittanica.
"A Few Words from the Publisher." Johnson Publishing Company. 1963.
Fitzgerald, Mark. "Oprah 'Furious' at 'Chicago Defender' Editor." Editor & Publisher 26 Aug. 2005.
Flax, Steven. "The Toughest Bosses in America." Fortune 6 Aug. 1984: 18-23.
"The Forbes Four Hundred." Forbes 13 Sept. 1982.
"Former Publisher John P Davis Succumbs at Age 68." JET 27 Sept. 1973: 17.
"Former Teacher Mary Herrick Feted By Her Well Known Students." JET 14 May 1984: 8.
"Founder and Publisher of EBONY and JET Magazines Dies at 87." The Associated Press 11 Aug. 2005.
Franklin, John Hope, and Alfred A. Moss Jr. From Slavery to Freedom: A History of African Americans. 7th ed. McGraw-Hill Companies, 1994.
"Friends and Admirers View Body of Pioneer Publisher John H.

Johnson at Company Headquarters." JET 29 Aug. 2005: 62.
Fuller, Hoyt W. "Editor's Notes." Black World May 1970.
Gallun, Alby. "Columbia College to Sell Johnson Publishing Building." Crain's Chicago Business 14 June 2016.
"Gardner Cowles Jr. Is Dead at 82: Helped Build Publishing Empire." The New York Times 9 July 1985:
Gilfoyle, Timothy J. "Chicago Fortunes: Interviews with Lester Crown and John H. Johnson." Chicago History Fall 2000: 58-72.
Gite, Lloyd. "Marathon Men Revisited: The Veterans. The Godfathers. The Cornerstones of the BE 100s." Publication. Black Enterprise. 1 June 2002.
Goodman, Amy. "Media Giant John H. Johnson Paved the Way for Black-Owned Press." Democracy Now. 16 Aug. 205AD.
Granger, Bill, and Lori Granger. Lords of the Last Machine: The Story of Politics in Chicago. Random House, 1987.
Granton, E. Fannie, and Ronald E. Kisner. "Family Talks About Dead Mother Whose Cells Fight Cancer." JET 1 Apr. 1976: 16-18.
Graves, Earl G. "John H. Johnson: Leader, Legend and Friend." Earl G. Graves Publishing Company. 2005.
Graveyards of Illinois Oak Woods Cemetery.
"Great Black Men in History: John H. Johnson/My Childhood." ProjectBlackMan.com: 2007.
Greenberg, Jonathan. "It's A Miracle." Forbes 20 Dec. 1982: 104, 106, 110.
Grossman, James R. Land of Hope: Chicago, Black Southerners, and the Great Migration. University of Chicago Press, 1991.
Haber, Matt. "EBONY Looks to Its Past as It Moves Forward." The New York Times 7 Dec. 2012.
Hall, Carla. "John H. Johnson: From Office Worker to Millionaire Publishing Mogul." The Washington Post 14 Sept. 1980.
"Halle Berry, Denzel Washington Get Historic Wins at Oscars." JET 8 Apr. 2002: 14-18, 51-59.
Hampton, Henry. "Eyes on the Prize: America's Civil Rights Years 1954-1964." PBS, 1987. Documentary.
Harvard Business School Global Alumni Conference. Unpublished speech. 1998.
"Harvard Law Review Gets First Black President." JET 26 Feb. 1990.
"Harvard University Celebrates 'JHJ Day' With Awards, Tributes." JET 27 Nov. 1975: 12-16.

Hicks, Jonathan. "A Magazine for Black Men On the Way Up." The New York Times 7 Nov. 1985: 34.

—. "For Black Men on the Way Up." 7 Nov. 1985: 1.

Higgins, Chester. "What Widow Does with Otis Redding Money." JET 18 July 1968: 16-23.

Hobbs, Allison. "Guide to the Ben Burns Collection, 1939-1999." Uncovering Chicago Archives Project. Uncovering Chicago Archives Project. 2006.

Horowitz, Jason. "White House Announces Resignation of Social Secretary Desiree Rogers." WashingtonPost.com. 27 Jan. 2010.

"Howard University Announces the Cathy Hughes School of Communications." Education. HowardUniversity.edu. 6 Oct. 2016.

"Hundreds Pay Respects at Funeral for JET Executive Editor Robert E. Johnson." JET 26 Jan. 1996: 12-18, 53-57.

"'I Guess God Was with Me' Says Lone Survivor of Plane Crash." JET 28 Dec. 1967: 52-63.

"Illinois Business Hall of Fame." American National Business Hall of Fame Video Series Presents John Johnson. 1989.

Jackson Sr., Jesse. "The TV Networks Owe Us an Apology For Ignoring John H. Johnson." Target Market News 18 Aug. 2005.

"JET Celebrates 45 Years of the Hottest Black Music, TV and Movie Stars." JET 3 Nov. 1997: 58-64.

"John H. Johnson: Founder & Publisher of JET & EBONY Magazines." JET 29 Aug. 2005.

John H. Johnson. Chicago, Illinois: 1989. Film. American Illinois Business Award.

"John H. Johnson Avenue." JET 28 Nov. 2005: 8.

"John H. Johnson Honored as Top All-Time Black Publisher." JET 24 Mar. 1977: 15.

"John H. Johnson School of Communications; Mr. Johnson Contributes $4 Million to Howard University Capital Campaign." JET 17 Feb. 2003: 6-10.

John H. Johnson Speech. 1989. Chicago American Business Hall of Fame.

"Johnson Center to Offer Scholarships and Support Research on African-American Issues in the Media." 23 Aug. 2007.

Johnson, Erick. "End of an Era: How EBONY and JET Fell into the Hands of a Little Known Firm in a Deal Shrouded in Mystery."

Chicago Crusader 16 June 2016.
Johnson, John. "Publisher's Statement." Black Stars Nov. 1971: 6.
Johnson, John H. Acceptance Speech by John H. Johnson After Being Named Publisher of the Year. 1972. Henry Johnson Fisher Award Luncheon.
—."Blacks Must Abandon Politics of Poverty, Philosophy of Despair." Sphinx May-June 1973: 29-34.
—. "Publisher's Statement." Tan Confessions Nov. 1950.
—. "Publisher's Statement." EM Nov. 1985: 3.
—. "Publisher's Statement." EBONY Aug. 1994: 25.
—. "Remarks by John H. Johnson on the Occasion of the Dedication of the New Johnson Publishing Company Building." Johnson Publishing Company. 1972. Dedication of Johnson Publishing Company.
—.Salute to Greatness Dinner Speech. 1988. Unpublished. Atlanta Marriott Marquee Hotel in Atlanta, Ga.
—.Succeeding Against the Odds. First Printing. Johnson Publishing Company, Inc., 1989.
—. "Why EBONY Jr?" EBONY Jr. May 1973: 4.
Johnson, Kevin. "Interview: As His EBONY Magazine Turns 40, The Founder of the USA's Top Black Business Talks About Riches, Responsibilities, Reagan and Race Relations in the '80s." Chicago Tribune 1 Nov. 1985: 8-10.
Johnson, Paul Lindsey. "Interview: John H. Johnson." The Crisis Jan. 1987: 32-48.
"Johnson Publishing Building to Be Considered for Landmark Status." Cityofchicago.org. 2 Feb. 2017.
"Johnson Publishing Co. Names Bryan Monroe EBONY/JET VP, Editorial Director." Target Market News 7 July 2006.
"Johnson Publishing Co. Pledges $2.5 Mil. to New Communication Center at USC." JET 10 Sept. 2007: 32.
"Johnson Publishing Co. to Sell Its Iconic Headquarters to Columbia College Chicago." Target Market News 17 Nov. 2010.
"EBONY Magazine's January 2009 Barack Obama Collector's Issue Breaks Sales Records." EBONY, John H. Johnson.
"Johnson Publishing Company Names VP & Editorial Director for EBONY & JET." 7 Aug. 2006: 65.
"Johnson Publishing Moving Its Chicago Offices to New Michigan Ave. Address." 8 Jan. 2012.

"Johnson Publishing: Reorg and Re-Up." News. Minonline.com. 3 Feb. 2009.

Johnson, Robert E. "The Michael Jackson Nobody Knows." EBONY Dec. 1984: 155-162.

Joyner, Tom. I'm Just a DJ But...It Makes Sense to Me. New York: Grand Central Publishing/Hachette Book Group, 2005.

"JPC Publisher Succeeds Against Odds and Daughter Prepares for Next 50 Years." JET 9 Nov. 1992: 6.

Kapos, Shia. "EBONY Names Amy DuBois Barnett Editor in Chief." Crain's Chicago Business 2 June 2010.

—. "Editor-in-Chief of EBONY Magazine Resigns." Crain's Chicago Business 20 Feb. 2015.

—. "Last of the EBONY Fashion Fair Collection to Be Auctioned." Crain's Chicago Business 14 May 2015.

Kitt, Eartha. "My Baby Travels with Me." EBONY Jan. 1963: 93-98.

Kornegay, Sharon. "Johnson Says Blacks Must Start Own Firms." Chicago Sun Times 1 Nov. 1976: 83.

Martin, Douglas. "John H. Johnson, 87, Founder of EBONY, Dies." The New York Times. 9 Aug. 2005.

Laramie, Eddie. "Black Publisher Advises Young People to Learn." People 26 May, 1974.

"Legendary Publisher Honored: U.S. Postal Service's Black Heritage Forever Stamp Salutes John H. Johnson." United States Postal Service. USPS.Com. 31 Jan. 2012.

Leonard, Walter J. "A Tribute to John H. Johnson." 7 Nov. 1975.

"Lerone Bennett Jr. Cuts Ties with Johnson Publishing." News. PostNewsGroup.com. 16 Oct. 2009.

"Letters and Pictures to the Editor." EBONY. April 1946: 51.

"Letters and Pictures to the Editor." EBONY. July 1946. 50.

"Letters and Pictures to the Editor." EBONY. Dec. 1945. 51.

"Letters to the Editor." Tan Confessions Dec. 1950: 6.

Levine, Joe. "Jack Mezirow, Who Transformed the Field of Adult Learning, Dies at 91." Columbia University. In Memoriam. 11 Oct. 2014.

Lewis, Andy. "WME Signs JET, EBONY Magazines (Exclusive)." TheHollywoodReporter.com. 4 May 2017.

"Linda Johnson Rice Gets MBA, Named President of Johnson Publishing Co." JET 6 July 1987: 6-8.

"Linda Johnson Rice Takes Back Control of JJPC, Denies Company

Has Plans to Leave Chicago." Target Market News 7 May 2017.
Long, Mia Chandler. Seeking a Place in the Sun: Sepia Magazine's Endeavor for Quality Journalism and Place in the Negro Market 1951-1982.
Lord, Deane W. John H. Johnson to Speak At Harvard University. 1975. Press release. Cambridge, MA.
Lowe, Rev. A. Ritchie. "Children's Crusade." Nov. 1945.
Marek, Lynne. "Desiree Rogers Is New CEO of Johnson Publishing." Crain's Chicago Business 10 Aug. 2010.
—. "Desiree Rogers Leaving Johnson Publishing." Crain's Chicago Business 6 May 2017.
—. "EBONY Taps JET Editor to Take Top Slot." Crain's Chicago Business 23 Apr. 2014.
—. "Johnson Publishing Adjusts Strategy on JET Magazine." Crain's Chicago Business 9 Aug. 2012.
—. "Johnson Publishing Lands New Financing." Crain's Chicago Business 16 Sept. 2013.
—. "Linda Johnson Rice Retakes EBONY CEO Post." Crain's Chicago Business 9 Mar. 2017.
—. "New Editorial Chief at EBONY's Johnson Publishing." Crain's Chicago Business 15 June 2015.
"Mary J. Herrick Collection." 1970.
"Mary Herrick, 89, Retired Chicago Teacher Succumbs." JET 5 Nov. 1984: 18.
Marshall, Marilyn. "Publisher Defies Failure." Houston Defender 3 June 1990: 2.
Mayor Richard J. Daley Honors Johnson with Commendation On 10th Anniversary of EBONY. 1955. Press release. City Hall in Chicago.
McCalope, Michelle. "Blacks Furious Over Exclusion from New Great Books of the Western World." JET 19 Nov. 1990: 14-18.
McDowell, W. H. Historical Research: A Guide for Writers of Dissertations, Theses, Articles and Books. 1st ed. Longman, 2002.
"Meet First White Alpha Dr. Bernard Levin." Black Greek-Lettered Organizations. Watchtheyard.com. 10 Nov. 2015.
"Michael Jackson Calls Child Molestation Charges Lies." JET 8 Dec. 2003: 16.
"Michael Jackson's Statement: Full Statement Issued by Jackson." News. CNN.com. 6 Feb. 2003.

Michaeli, Ethan. The Defender: How the Legendary Black Newspaper Changed America. Boston New York: Houghton Mifflin Harcourt, 2016.

"Mitzi Miller Named Editor in Chief of JET Magazine." Atlanta Daily World 2 May 2011.

Moore, Richard. 83rd Commencement Personal Commitment Needed, EBONY Publisher Tells A & T. 1974. Press release. North Carolina A & T State University.

Moore, Trudy S. "Aging Disease Makes 6-Year-Old Boy Look 60." JET 5 Dec. 1983: 22-26.

Morrison, Allan. "Selassie's Message to the Negro." EBONY Africa Mar. 1964: 47-53.

"National Report EBONY and Spiegel Join Forces to Launch New Catalog Clothing Line." JET 7 Oct. 1991: 4-5.

Nelson, Stanley. "The Murder of Emmett Till." American Experience. PBS, 2003. Television.

"New Hue, New Copper." Newsweek 19 Oct. 1953: 93.

Nitkin, Alex. "3L Approved For Conversion of Johnson Publishing Building." *TheRealDeal.com.* 29 May 2018.

"Ninety-Second Annual Communication Proceedings: Most Worshipful Prince Hall Grand Lodge F. and A.M." 14 Oct. 1958.

Norment, Lynn. "EBONY Interview with Linda Johnson Rice." Nov. 1992: 208–215.

"Oak Woods Cemetery." https://www.graveyards.com/IL/Cook/oakwoods/

Omar, Nathaniel. "Publishing Giant Tells How." Bilalian News 18 Feb. 1977: 30-31.

O'Shea, Chris. "Former EBONY Editor Kierna Mayo Joins Interactive One." Advertising. Adweek.com. 22 June 2016.

Palmer, Mercedes. "Johnson Speaks." Bay State Banner 17 Mar. 1977: 11.

Parish, Norman. "Basil Phillips: Longtime Photo Editor for EBONY, JET Dies." Chicago Sun Times 30 Aug. 2007.

"Patti LaBelle and Mario Van Peebles Host American Black Achievement Awards 13th Annual TV Show." JET 13 Jan. 1992: 54-62.

"Payroll Kickback Charge Hits Rep Charles Diggs." JET 6 Apr. 1978: 8.

Penn, I. Garland. The Afro-American Press and Its Editors.

Springfield, Massachusetts: Wiley & Co., 1891.
People staff. "Gumbel Causes Grumbles." People.com. 12 June 2001.
Peters, Jeremy W. "Desiree Rogers, Post Crash." The New York Times 1 Oct. 2010.
Peterson, Elizabeth A., ed. Freedom Road: Adult Education of African Americans. Revised. Krieger Pub Co, 2002.
"Photog Griff Davis Dies in Atlanta at 70." JET 16 Aug. 1993: 15.
Pogrebin, Robin. "Success and the Black Magazine; As Readers Prosper, Advertising Still Eludes Publishers." The New York Times 25 Oct. 1997.
"Powerful Positive Thinker: The Life of John H. Johnson, Chicago's Self-Made Millionaire." Chicago Tribune 30 Apr. 1989: 1.
"Preliminary Summary of Information (Submitted to the Commission on Chicago Landmarks in February 2017. Johnson Publishing Company Building." Cityofchicago.org. Feb. 2017.
Presidential Medal of Freedom Awarded by the President of the United States of America, William J. Clinton, at the White House. 1996. Unpublished.
Prince, Richard. "Final Print Issue of JET Never Reached Some Magazine Stands." News. TheRoot.com. 7 June 2014.
—. "Johnson Rice Steps Down at EBONY's New Company." News. Journal-isms.com. 13 July 2018.
—. "JET Magazine Could Return to Newsstands." The Root 17 Feb. 2017.
"Publisher's Statement: Four Decades of the Most Important Events and the Most Important People." 18 Nov. 1991: 4-6.
Raffin, Deborah. Sharing Christmas. Grand Central Publishing 1990: 89-90.
Reader's Digest December 1975.
Reardon, Patrick T. "Not Much on Their Plates: When It Comes to Influence, Owners of Low License Numbers Take a Back Seat to No One." Chicago Tribune 17 Jan. 1999.
Reichley, A. James. "How Johnson Made It." Fortune Jan. 1968: 178.
"Remembering John H. Johnson (1918-2005)." JET 29 Aug. 2005: 12-43.
"Robert E. Johnson, Editor of JET." The Mike Douglas Show. CBS, 8 Jan. 1969. Television.
Robinson, Louie. "Bad Times on the Good Times Set." EBONY Sept. 1975: 33-42.

—. "Family Life of the Jackson Five." EBONY Dec. 1974: 33-42.

—. "Hottest Young Group in History." EBONY 11 Sept. 1970: 150-154.

—. "The Black Press: Voice of Freedom." EBONY Aug. 1975: 52-58.

Roeder, David. "Columbia College Buys Home of EBONY, JET." Chicago Sun Times 2 Dec. 2010.

Rogers, Steven S. Black Business Leaders Series: The Entrepreneurship Behind EBONY Magazine. Audio Recording. Cold Call (February 2, 2017).

Rosenthal, Phil. "Johnson Publishing CEO Desiree Rogers Trying to Breathe New Life into EBONY, JET Magazines." Chicago Tribune 6 Mar. 2011.

—. "Johnson Publishing CEO Desiree Rogers Trying to Breathe New Life into EBONY, JET Magazines." Chicago Tribune 6 Mar. 2011.

Ross, Austyn. "Fox News and EBONY Magazine Receive 'Thumbs Down' Award from NABJ." NABJ.com. 13 July 2017.

Rowan, Carl T. "Words That Give Us Strength." Reader's Digest Apr. 1987: 49-58.

Rutenberg, Jim. "Media Talk: Gumbel and EBONY Argue Over Recent Remarks." The New York Times 11 June 2001.

"School of Communications Named to Honor Cathy Hughes." Howard Magazine Oct. 2016.

Sebastian, Michael. "JET Magazine Dumps Print, Goes Digital." Crain's Chicago Business 7 May 2014.

"Selassie's Message to the Negro." EBONY Africa 1964: 47-53.

Shaw, O'Wendell. "Magazines Must Pay Their Writers." Pep Nov. 1945: 3.

Shipp, E.R. "After 40 Years, EBONY Drawing Praise, Criticism." The New York Times 21 Dec. 1985.

—. "EBONY, Marking 40th Anniversary, Considered More Than A Magazine." The New York Times 6 Dec. 1985: 1.

"Siamese Twins Buried in Specially-Made Coffin." 22 Feb. 1993: 16-17.

"Siamese Twins Learning to Talk, Play." JET 13 Nov. 1952: 19.

Sikes, Alfred C. "Honoring John H. Johnson: Center for Communication Annual Award Luncheon." 6 Mar. 1995: n. pag.

Smith, Steve. "Johnson Publishing Pres/COO Resigns." Minonline.com. 13 July 2010.

— "Update: Johnson Publishing Reorg and Re-Up" Minonline.com. 2 Feb. 2009.
Sowell, Thomas. Black Education: Myths and Tragedies. David McKay Company, 1974.
"Sphinx: 67th Anniversary Convention Issue." Sphinx May-June 1973.
Starling, Kelly. "EBONY Contest Winner Scores in Education and Art." EBONY May 1998: 126-130.
Strahler, Steven R. "Valid Reason for EBONY Magazine to Cut One of Its Celebs This Year." Crain's Chicago Business 3 June 2001.
Streit, Meghan. "Staff Shakeup at EBONY, JET: Report. Crain's Chicago Business 2 Feb. 2009.
"Succeeding Against the Odds." EBONY October 2005: 74-78.
Sweet, Neesa. "Leadership Profile Series on John H. Johnson: Publisher, Chairman & CEO Johnson Publishing Company." Sky 1988: 39-45.
Talbert, Marcia Wade. "Black Enterprise, Magic Johnson in Talks to Buy Johnson Publishing." Black Enterprise 16 Feb. 2010.
Terry, Don. "An Icon Fades: EBONY Shaped the Black Middle Class, Then Misread Its Digital Moment." Columbia Journalism Review. Apr. 2010.
"The $5,000 Gertrude Johnson Williams Literary Award.'" EBONY March 1988: 96.
"The 55 Most Intriguing Blacks of 2000." EBONY Nov. 2000: 45-98.
"The Bicentennial: 200 Years of Black Trials and Triumphs." EBONY Aug. 1975.
The Cultural Landscape Foundation Oak Woods Cemetery. https://tclf.org/landscapes/oak-woods-cemetery
"The EBONY Family: Employee Excellence and Loyalty Help Make EBONY a 35-Year Success." EBONY Nov. 1980: 35-41.
"The EBONY Story: 10th Anniversary Ten Years That Rocked the World." Nov. 1955.
"The Jackson Family Has an Artist: Michael." EBONY Jr. Sept. 1975: 5-6.
The John H. Johnson Interview. Johnson Publishing Company: 2007. DVD.
"The Man Who Lived Thirty Years as A Woman." EBONY 12 Oct. 1951: 23-26.
"The Medal of Freedom Awards: Publisher John H. Johnson and 10 Others Receive Nation's Highest Civilian Honor." EBONY Nov.

1996: 34.
"The Press. Quick End." Time.com. 27 April 1953.
"The Secret of Selling the Negro." May 1954.
The Tesla Team. "Tesla Welcomes Linda Johnson Rice and James Murdoch As New Independent Directors to Its Board." Tesla.com 17 July 2017.
The University of Chicago press release. Founders of Johnson Publishing Co. Inc., establish fellowship to study black diseases. Sept. 13, 1983.
Thimmesch, Nick. "John H. Johnson: The Man Behind EBONY." Saturday Evening Post Oct. 1975: 36-37, 94-96.
"Thousands Gather to Remember John H. Johnson." Press Release. The University of Chicago News Office. 15 Aug. 2005.
"Thousands Join in Historic Farewell Celebration of Publisher John H. Johnson in Chicago." JET 29 Aug. 2005: 4-10, 59-61.
Treadway, Tyler. "Johnson Turns $500 Loan Into Publishing Powerhouse." Arkansas Business 13 Feb. 1995.
Tutu, Archbishop Desmond. "My First EBONY." Nov. 1995: 35.
"TV's Greatest Black Moms." JET 15 May 2006: 15-18.
Umoh, Ruth. "Tesla Just Welcomed This CEO to Its Board. Here's Why It's a Big Thing for Silicon Valley." CNBC.com 21 July 2017.
U.S. Department of Veteran Affairs. https://www.cem.va.gov/cems/lots/confederate_mound.asp
U.S. History.org. The Red Scare.
Vega, Tanzina. "JET Magazine Stays Compact but with A New Design." NewYorkTimes.com 22 July 2013.
"Victim of Aging Disease Peedie Snipes Dies at 14." JET 22 June 1992: 9.
Walker, Dionne. "Close of EBONY Fashion Fair Means End of an Era." TheSeattleTimes.com 4 Mar. 2010.
"Wall Streets Worst Market Crashes." Worstmarketcrashes.com. 11 Mar. 2011.
Watson, Jamal. "Howard University Attempting to Re-Establish Ties to Late John H. Johnson." Education. DiverseEducation.com. 3 Nov. 2013.
"Week's Best Photo (The Cast of Good Times at Esther Rolle's Funeral)." JET 21 Dec. 1998: 41.
Weller, Sheila. "The Missing Woman." VanityFair.com. 26 Jan. 2017.
West, Cassiette Angela. "Blacks Urged to Start Their Own

Businesses." Detroit News 16 July 1986: 1.977.
West Fresno School District administration office press release. 2 Nov. 1977.
"What's Online in September: New Voices and Culture."' EBONY Sept. 2008: 20.
White, George. "The Potential of Black Buying Power." Detroit Free Press 16 July 1986: 1.
White, Jack E. "A Militant Voice Silenced." Time 12 June 2000.
"William J. Clinton XLII President of the United States 1993-2001: Remarks on Presenting the Presidential Medal of Freedom." The American Presidency Project. 9 Sept. 1996.
Woodard, Dustin. "1973-1974 Stock Market Crash." About.com. 11 Sept. 2007.
Woodson, Carter Godwin. The Mis-Education of the Negro. Dover Publications, 2005.
Wright, Sarafina. "John H. Johnson Legacy Continued at Howard U." Washington Informer 3 Nov. 2016.
"Youngest Ever." JET 16 Mar. 1992: 47.
Zenith press release. 14 Feb. 1974.
Official site. The Crisis.
Official site. NAACP.
Official site. American Treasures of the Library of Congress.
Oak Woods Cemetery. Oak Woods Cemetery.

# INDEX

**Margena A. Christian, Ed.D.** is a distinguished lecturer in the English department at the University of Illinois at Chicago where she helped to develop and to design the public research institution's professional writing concentration in 2016. Christian is a former senior editor and senior writer with *EBONY* magazine. Also a former *JET* magazine features editor, the St. Louis native is the only person in the history of Johnson Publishing Company editorial to have written for *EBONY, JET, EBONY Man, EBONY South Africa, EBONY Fashion Fair,* and EBONY.com.

For more information, visit: www.margenachristian.com

Make-up by George Robert Fuller

The author and the Reverend Jesse L. Jackson, Sr. at his Rainbow PUSH's Community House in Chicago on October 6, 2018.

www.ingramcontent.com/pod-product-compliance
Lightning Source LLC
Chambersburg PA
CBHW071844090426
42811CB00035B/2317/J